Carpetbagger of Conscience

John Emory Bryant

Carpetbagger of Conscience

A Biography of John Emory Bryant

Ruth Currie-McDaniel

Fordham University Press

New York • 1999

Copyright © 1999 by Ruth Currie-McDaniel
All rights reserved
LC 99-18335
ISBN 0-8232-1937-2 (hardcover)
ISBN 0-8232-1938-0 (paperback)
ISSN 1523-4606
Reconstructing America, no. 3

Library of Congress Cataloging-in-Publication Data

Currie-McDaniel, Ruth.
    Carpetbagger of conscience : a biography of John Emory Bryant / Ruth Currie-McDaniel.
       p. cm.—(Reconstructing America ; no. 3)
    Originally published: Athens : University of Georgia Press, 1987.
    Includes bibliographical references and index.
    ISBN 0-8232-1937-2 (hc).—ISBN 0-8232-1938-0 (pbk.)
    1. Bryant, John Emory. 2. Politicians—Georgia Biography.
3. Reconstruction—Georgia. I. Title. II. Series: Reconstructing America (Series) ; no. 3.
F291.B9C87 1999
975.8′041′092—dc21
[B]
                                                            99-18335
                                                                 CIP

The photograph of John Emory Bryant is reproduced courtesy of the Maine State Archives.

Contents

Introduction to the 1999 Edition vii
Acknowledgments xvii
Introduction 1
One *Maine Background* 4
Two *Bryant in the Civil War* 19
Three *Presidential Reconstruction* 42
Four *Congressional Reconstruction* 77
Five *Bryant and the Strategic Shift of Republicans in the 1870s* 118
Six *The Closing Decades* 155
Conclusion: John Emory Bryant in Retrospect 180
Notes 185
Selected Bibliography 221
Index 233

Introduction to the 1999 Edition

Carpetbagger of Conscience: A Biography of John Emory Bryant was first published in 1987. Since that time, various reviews of the book, plus monographs concerning Reconstruction history, have continued to assess the career of John Emory Bryant. This reissue of *Carpetbagger of Conscience* offers the opportunity to respond to recent publications and to take another look at this man who generated so much conflict during his lifetime and who still requires careful scrutiny to evaluate properly.

Reviewers continued the book's dialogue regarding Bryant's "conscience." The title of the book could well have displayed a question mark after it. Was Bryant, after all, a carpetbagger of conscience, or was he "just another corrupt politician"? The ambiguity emerged at every stage of his career, and reviewers rightly sensed the difficulty of a definitive answer. One pundit thought that in *Carpetbagger of Conscience* John Emory Bryant received "less than his due as a courageous champion of justice and equality."[1] But another wrote that the biographer "largely exonerates . . . [him] from the taint of political opportunism."[2] One rightly noted that the book gathered "too much damaging evidence to proclaim him virtuous."[3] Actually, the biography never claimed that JEB was "a paragon of consistency and virtue," as another reviewer charged.[4] Rather, it showed him egotistical and abrasive, openly devoted to "'look[ing] out for No. 1'" (p23), and "'determined to go forward . . . regardless of the consequences'" (p18). At the same time, clearly, Bryant came out of the evangelical reform movement of the nineteenth century. He was self-righteous and given to seeing the evils of society as his own personal crusade, as a matter of conscience. That same devotion to his causes made him the controversial politician that he was and a formidable enemy to those who opposed him. This does not make him a virtuous man. But neither does it diminish the validity of his causes of equal political rights for African American men in Georgia: suffrage, the right to sit on juries, the opportunity for free labor, and social justice. Throughout his study on Reconstruction, Eric Foner frequently quotes from John Emory Bryant to illustrate the centrality of this Republican agenda and the strong allegiance of Northern reformers to "self-directed labor," educated workers as part of the Republican economic ideology: "The more intelligent men are the more wants they have, hence it is for the interest of all that the laborers shall be educated." Labor relations were central to Republican politics, and justice for workers was primary, both for the party and for Bryant.[5]

Unfortunately, Foner's book also contains an error that, if it had been factual, could have raised questions about Bryant's ethical judgment. As he struggled with the twin goals of furthering education for blacks in Georgia as well as putting the Augusta *Loyal Georgian* on sound footing, JEB negotiated a $3,000 loan from Harper & Brothers, with the newspaper's stock as collateral and the promise that he would attempt to influence the sale of Harper textbooks in the state. One reviewer of *Carpetbagger of Conscience,* picking up Foner's error, called the loan $30,000 and charged that "curiously" (and ominously, no doubt) Bryant's biographer "makes no mention of this episode."[16] On reflection, other than the fact that Bryant as editor probably overestimated his paper's value, the incident reeks less of a corrupt intention than of a creditable attempt to seek financial backing for two valid and worthy goals. Bryant also invited Harper to send its own representative to market its books, an offer the company declined.[7] At the time of the loan, Bryant and Rufus Bullock, Republican candidate for governor, still planned together to give official state printing to the *Loyal Georgian*. JEB expected this state business not only to keep the newspaper afloat but also to enable him to repay the loan to Harper.

Paul Cimbala's excellent study and examination of the Freedmen's Bureau in Georgia further underlines the significant role Bryant played in the early days of the Bureau and the problems he faced. Cimbala rightly notes that Bureau head Davis Tillson and Bryant were not far apart in their understanding of the important labor contracts between freedpeople and planters. He also notes that Tillson's handling of the feud with Bryant made it grow unnecessarily personal and vindictive on both sides. That grudge made it unlikely that Bryant would defend Tillson against the charges that he sided with the Georgian planters. Cimbala's research makes it possible to see the motivation for Tillson's controversial policies in the best light, in the context of his goals for the Bureau. But it is easy to see how a firebrand like Bryant would find Tillson's conservatism against the best interests of the freedpeople in the short run. In seeking to rehabilitate Tillson, Cimbala makes the same point that Bryant's career so well illustrates: these men were as complex as any modern-day reformer/politician. As noted in *Carpetbagger of Conscience,* both Tillson and Bryant were partly right (p68), and neither can be fairly judged by a single event or action. Cimbala claims that "bad judgment and pettiness in this particular instance did not define Tillson's Reconstruction ideology."[8] Bryant may be granted the same dispensation.

Reviewers found it easy to conclude that Bryant's treatment of his wife, Emma Spaulding Bryant, proved he was far from a man of conscience. While his behavior toward her was deplorable, it is at least fair to note that the dichotomy between public aspirations/service and private morals is a longstanding and continuing dilemma in the assessment of public figures. Bryant may be condemned for neglect of his wife and family because their correspondence reveals that he did put his career first. Among the idealistic and ambitious carpetbaggers, however, it was not unusual for wives to be left alone for long periods and to suffer great hardships. While there are few extant sources for knowing this group of women, those available reveal remarkable unanimity of experience.[9] In one example, the biographer of carpetbagger Albion Tourgée gives a rather grand assessment of his political crusade in North Carolina. But a different view of the hero may be noted in reading his wife's correspondence.[10] The biographer of Rufus Bullock claims no evidence for information on Bullock's home life but acknowledges that Bullock was a workaholic, a characteristic not unlike that which led to the loneliness of many wives of carpetbaggers. The record also reveals that Bullock died from syphilis, a disease rarely reflective of family values.[11]

One must remember, of course, that the women were also actors in this drama. As noted in *Carpetbagger of Conscience,* to the extent that John allowed her participation, Emma Bryant was ready to sacrifice for his cause (p182). Again, because some of the letters survived, her own words show that she materially, as well as emotionally, supported his career and his best dreams. As she became more independent, she also came to have reforms of her own. While it is difficult to assess his allegiance to such, it also must be noted that Bryant did attend with his wife at least one suffragist rally, date unknown (p218–19). Another reviewer wished for some indication of JEB's aspirations for black women, perhaps missing the note that Bryant apparently paid for the college education of at least one young African American (p201)—until she chose marriage over a career.[12]

In recent examinations of the Georgia Equal Rights Association, some historians highlighting the actions of African Americans have downplayed or made conspicuous their omission of John Emory Bryant's role in the formation of that body. While the significance of the Freedmen's Convention may be debated, as well as the way in which "who used whom," denying Bryant's central involvement is both disingenuous and puzzling. Bryant clearly enjoyed the confidence of the freedmen who elected him president of the association, and his leadership is indisputable, well documented in speeches and resolutions and reflected in his editorials in the *Loyal Georgian,* the official organ of the organization.[13]

More elusive to document is the shifting allegiance of blacks during Bullock's dubious leadership of the state of Georgia into the third reconstruction. While the majority of African American leaders stuck with him after Bullock's demise as governor, many saw the wisdom of Bryant's consistent advice and the validity of JEB's goal for their political and economic empowerment. Also, Bryant's record in granting patronage jobs to blacks when he had the power to do so far outweighed Bullock's record in the same category (p106). In 1874 Henry Turner claimed that he " 'had never seen Bryant turn his back on the negro since I was born. I have never known him to desert our rights' " (p129). The only chink in that claim was the fact that in 1872 Bryant actively sought the patronage position of Edwin Belcher, who was serving as assessor of internal revenue for Georgia's third district. No doubt, Bryant's action was an example of political ambition, but as noted in *Carpetbagger of Conscience,* one must remember that Belcher was a former Freedmen's Bureau officer and legislator so light-skinned that he was not expelled from the Georgia lower house with other African Americans (p122–23). Henry Turner denounced Belcher at that time for denying his African heritage; Belcher himself struggled with acknowledging this part of his bloodline. On these grounds, Bryant probably felt justified in his action in seeking Belcher's post, especially since Belcher had failed to support him in an earlier controversy. In any case, Belcher later supported Bryant's candidacy for office, indicating that they had mended the coalition.[14]

Russell Duncan, biographer of John Emory Bryant's nemesis, Governor Rufus Bullock, dismisses Bryant as a "failed officeholder." Certainly, Bryant was disillusioned and even vindictive after being excluded from Bullock's administration, but it is unfortunate that Duncan fails to analyze the factions of the Georgia Republican Party more closely. He sweeps aside the criticisms of Bullock's administration as merely caused by his inattention to detail or "carelessness in bookkeeping," or calls what he did justfiable because of assumed good motives and cause, as in exorbitant printing costs, in one case rising to the dimension of a bribe.[15] Also exonerated in Duncan's broad brush stroke is the nefarious career of Foster Blodgett. It will be remembered that both Methodist minister John Caldwell and Bryant named Bullock's allegiance to Blodgett as a matter of grave concern and a major reason for their opposition to the governor. Blodgett's career cries out for a biographer's closer scrutiny and objective evaluation.

Each reader may evaluate Duncan's tortured logic by which Bullock's strategy was to further African American interests by voting against their office-holding rights in the constitutional convention in the first place (against Bryant's advice); by manipulating the vote against the Fifteenth Amendment in the second place (when Bryant's was one of the courageous votes for it); and by remanding Georgia to a second military rule in the face of strong party opposition (in addition to Bryant's), all for the sake of Bullock's tenure. At the least, Bryant's own radical philosophy, by which he backed black suffrage and officeholding rights from the outset, and sought to purge the Republican Party of those elements he called corrupt, must at least be given some credibility.

In *The Road to Redemption: Southern Politics, 1869–1879*, Michael Perman offers an insightful analysis of Reconstruction strategy. But Duncan's facile and dismissive use of Perman's "centrist" label does not do justice to the complexity of Georgia politics. Bryant did not vote to expel African Americans from the legislature; in fact, he railed against it. Bryant's action may be called "centrist" in his short-lived, ill-conceived allegiance with former governor Joseph Brown et al., but he himself failed to defend this strategy later, and the mistake haunted the remainder of his career. Richard Abbott's research on the radical press in Georgia shows Bryant's key role in shifting Republican alliances with editor Samuel Bard as well as Brown; Abbott also points out Bullock's questionable commitment to black rights. To call Bryant "centrist" beyond the legislative effort to unseat Bullock, and to claim that Bryant opposed the governor *because* Bullock espoused equality for blacks, is simply not accurate.[16]

The irony of the charge is that Bryant was the outsider in this game, while Bullock was well aware of Joe Brown's central role in the survival of the Republican Party, and he continually sought Brown's accommodation. Bullock's later acquittal and the revamping of his image and stature among New South Redeemers restored him to the circle of insiders where Bullock felt he belonged, as Duncan clearly shows. As C. Vann Woodward has noted, by the 1880s, for the Redeemers, "economic carpetbaggers were a different kettle of fish, and had become acceptable because of new priorities."[17] Born to wealth and privilege and even owning slaves for a time, Bullock ensured that his business interests always came ahead of his concern for black suffrage and other rights for African Americans, as Duncan admits. Bryant's background, on the other hand, was that of the evangelical reformer, the abolitionist tradition linking change to politics, a much different motivation for seeking office. The unanswerable question is this: Why *did* Bullock turn aside John Caldwell and John Emory Bryant, who had been so instrumental in electing him? Perhaps the answer lies in subtle class differences among the Republicans.

It is perhaps instructive, and at the least interesting, that at the end of the nineteenth century old colleagues O. O. Howard and John Emory Bryant swapped stories and versions of the Reconstruction years as they worked together on various mission projects for the poor in New York. Albion Tourgée and Bryant shared the last impossible crusade in the lyceum circuit and the Union League, where, with other of the idealistic, erstwhile carpetbaggers, they expounded the theory of two competing civilizations of North and South. Bryant's political involvement continued, but he died with no estate. Rufus Bullock, on the other hand, hobnobbed with the Atlanta elite, enjoying his business fortune; Tillson lost money as a planter in Georgia but made a fortune in granite back in Maine.

One reviewer raised the intriguing question of why Bryant stayed in the South and persevered for so long.[18] The answer to JEB's longevity is perhaps further evidence of the conscience that drew him in the first place, the struggle to redefine his career in the light of shifting political strategies in the 1870s, and then his determination to leave an unblemished reputation in his office as U.S. marshal, with recognition at last at the Georgia bar. Using the language of religious purpose, as he frequently did, he continued to seek the link between education, social reform, and politics as the avenue for change.

As noted in *Carpetbagger of Conscience*'s retrospective on JEB, the best measure of the man was in his friends and enemies. And the list of Bryant's supporters remains formidable. Mansfield French, Rufus Saxton, Charles Stearns, John Caldwell, Henry Turner, Amos Akerman, Erasmus Q. Fuller, Volney Spalding, and William Pledger all witness to the credentials of the carpetbagger from Maine.

Upholding Bryant's credentials, however, does not mean he was the only Republican who espoused the radical agenda, nor that there was unanimity among the reformers. That Republican politicians disagreed on how to achieve their goals is not a revelation; nor is the fact that personal ambition played a role in the decisions they made. The factionalism of the Republicans in Georgia, so well illustrated in the career of Bryant, has long been identified as the party's debilitating flaw.

To debate the comparative "radical" credentials of the carpetbaggers, therefore, is ill advised. They faced not only rivalries among themselves but different viewpoints on strategy even when their goals and principles coincided. Behind the prior query about JEB's longevity is the question of how the Republican Party survived at all in light of the massive campaign against it. Party members faced overwhelming odds in the battlefield of racism and violence that characterized the years of Reconstruction. Their intraparty squabbles must be seen in the light of the insurmountable obstacles to reform. Even as more evidence is gleaned on the careers of individual politicians, recent historians of Reconstruction are unanimous in noting, as *Carpetbagger of Conscience* did (p183), the impossibility of the task.[19]

The thesis offered in 1987 still stands: John Emory Bryant was probably close to the "typical" carpetbagger, with high aspirations for changing the South and limited success in office holding. The reform agenda of the Radical Republicans, so well illustrated by the career of JEB, and the mixed motives among individuals, also seen in Bryant, allow the claim that "this man embodies the Reconstruction era with all its ambiguities and makes a particularly intriguing mirror through which to view the elusive carpetbagger."

Ruth Douglas Currie
Appalachian State University
August 1998

NOTES

1   Otto H. Olsen, *Journal of Southern History* LIV, 2 (May 1988).
2   Michael Fitzgerald, *Journal of Southwest Georgia History* V (Fall 1987).
3   William Harris Bragg, *Civil War Times* (Oct. 1988).
4   Thomas C. Holt, "Georgia Carpetbaggers: Politicians Without Politics," *The Georgia Historical Quarterly* 72, 1 (Spring 1988).
5   John Emory Bryant, Address to Georgia Equal Rights Association, 13 Jan. 1866, quoted in Eric Foner, *Reconstruction: America's Unfinished Revolution, 1863–1877* (New York: Harper & Row, 1988), 147. See also 156–57, 350, 525.
6   Holt, "Georgia Carpetbaggers."
7   Richard Abbott correctly identifies both the amount of loan and Bryant's attempt to keep the radical press afloat in Georgia. See his "The Republican Party Press in Reconstruction Georgia, 1877–1874," *The Journal of Southern History* LXI, 4 (Nov. 1995):725–60. For the correspondence between Bryant and Harper, see JEB to Harper & Brothers, 1 Apr. 1867 and 15 June 1867, and Harper & Brothers to JEB, 14 May 1868, John Emory Bryant Papers. I found no evidence regarding whether the loan was made or when/if it was repaid.
8   Paul A. Cimbala, *Under the Guardianship of the Nation: The Freedmen's Bureau and the Reconstruction of Georgia* (Athens: University of Georgia Press, 1997), 20.
9   Ruth Currie-McDaniel, "The Wives of the Carpetbaggers," in *Race, Class, and Politics in Southern History: Essays in Honor of Robert F. Durden,* ed. Jeffery J. Crow, Paul D. Escott, and Charles L. Flynn Jr. (Baton Rouge: Louisiana State University Press, 1989), 35–78.
10   Otto H. Olsen, *Carpetbagger's Crusade: The Life of Albion Winegar Tourgée* (Baltimore: Johns Hopkins University Press, 1965); Ruth Currie-McDaniel, "Courtship and Marriage in the Nineteenth Century: Albion and Emma Tourgée, A Case Study," *North Carolina Historical Review* 61 (July 1984):285–310. In reviewing *Carpetbagger of Conscience,* reviewer Richard Current discounts the claim that "historians have tended to make either heroes or villains" of carpetbaggers (p183). Current states, "It seems extremely difficult, though, to name many, if any, historians who have made heroes of them ... individually...." But I would submit that Olsen himself presented Tourgée as a hero against all odds in North Carolina. See Richard Current, review of *Carpetbagger of Conscience, Alabama Review* (July 1988).

11 Russell Duncan, *Entrepreneur for Equality: Governor Rufus Bullock, Commerce, and Race in Post-Civil War Georgia* (Athens: University of Georgia Press, 1994).

12 Jonathan W. McLeod, *Civil War History* 35, 1 (1989). McLeod questioned Bryant's response to Elizabeth Cady Stanton and Susan B. Anthony, but by the 1880s these reformers had silenced their support for black male enfranchisement because of the abolitionists' failure to support women's suffrage. There is one letter from Virginia L. Minor (6 June 1882) in JEB's correspondence, in which she solicits his support for women's rights, but no record exists of his response. The project now under way to edit the Bryant correspondence will highlight Emma Spaulding Bryant's evolution into an independent woman.

13 Jonathan M. Bryant, " 'We Have No Chance of Justice before the Courts,' The Freedmen's Struggle for Power in Greene County, Georgia, 1865–1874," in *Georgia in Black and White: Explorations in the Race Relations of a Southern State, 1865–1950*, ed. John C. Inscoe (Athens: University of Georgia Press, 1994), 13–37. In discussing the Georgia Equal Rights Association, Jonathan Bryant does not even mention John Emory Bryant's role or the fact that the freedmen elected him president of the association. In his later monograph, after describing the Freedmen's Convention and highlighting Davis Tillson's speech, Jonathan Bryant notes in one sentence that delegates elected JEB president of the association. He then fails to identify the quotes from the association "purpose" as John Emory Bryant's. See Jonathan M. Bryant, *How Curious a Land: Conflict and Change in Greene County, Georgia, 1850–1885* (Chapel Hill: University of North Carolina Press, 1996), 102–5. Edmund L. Drago, in *Black Politicians and Reconstruction in Georgia* (Baton Rouge: Louisiana State University Press, 1982), recognizes the carpetbagger's role but implies that the freedmen used Bryant for their own purposes (p28). As noted in *Carpetbagger of Conscience*, this is "a neat—though not necessarily accurate—twist to the traditional treatment of such coalitions between blacks and radical Republicans" (p196). Mildred Thompson, a student of W. A. Dunning, had said Bryant was a "skillful manipulator of the negro vote." See her *Reconstruction in Georgia: Economic, Social, Political, 1865–1872* (New York: Columbia University Press, 1915), 190.

14 On the struggle of Republicans for patronage positions, see Lawrence N. Powell's article "Politics of Livelihood: Carpetbaggers in the Deep South," in *Race, Region, and Reconstruction: Essays in Honor of C. Vann Woodward*, ed. J. Morgan Kousser and James M. McPherson (New York: Oxford University Press, 1982), 315–47; and Foner, *Recon-*

struction, 349–50. Thomas Holt, in his review of *Carpetbagger of Conscience*, harshly judges Bryant for this transgression and refuses to believe any decent motive on his part. Holt's interpretation goes beyond the existing evidence, though it is not difficult to believe that JEB would have harbored ill feeling against Belcher because of his earlier actions.

15   See Abbott, "The Republican Party Press," 754–55, for his assessment of Bullock's printing costs.

16   Michael Perman, *The Road to Redemption: Southern Politics, 1869–1879* (Chapel Hill: University of North Carolina Press, 1984), 4–21; Abbott, "The Republican Party Press," 754; Duncan, *Entrepreneur for Equality*, 80, 123.

17   C. Vann Woodward, *Reunion and Reaction: The Compromise of 1877 and the End of Reconstruction* (Boston: Little, Brown, 1966), 64.

18   Richard H. Abbott, *American Historical Review* (June 1988).

19   See Joseph P. Reidy, *From Slavery to Agrarian Capitalism in the Cotton Plantation South: Central Georgia, 1800–1880* (Chapel Hill: University of North Carolina Press, 1992), for an impressive display of the overwhelming evidence for this conclusion.

Acknowledgments

Acknowledgments for assistance in producing this book begin with my advisor at Duke University, Dr. Robert F. Durden, who first directed me to the John Emory Bryant collection and guided me through the first drafts. Dr. Richard L. Watson also made a significant contribution. I remain grateful to Dr. Mattie Russell for initially allowing me exclusive use of the Bryant papers and for the assistance that she and the staff of the Manuscript Department have given me, including in the most recent stage of the project. The staffs of other libraries who deserve my appreciation include those of the University of Georgia, the Georgia Department of Archives and History, the Rutherford B. Hayes Presidential Center, the Maine State Archives, the Amistad Research Center, and Bowdoin College, where Susan Ravdin was especially helpful.

My thanks go to Helen McDaniel, who typed the first draft of the study, and to Marie D. Moore, who read the penultimate version and made editorial and substantive suggestions. I am indebted to Anne Kinnaird, who not only graciously allowed me the use of her word processor for typing the revised draft of the manuscript, but more than once saved me from BDOS errors. Bill and Betty Foreman's generous gift of a Kaypro made it possible for me to complete the project.

I am grateful to the readers for the University of Georgia Press who saw potential in the manuscript and made specific suggestions for improving it. Their interest in Emma Spaulding Bryant's contribution was particularly gratifying.

My thanks to all who encouraged me to persevere until JEB and Emma's story was in print.

John Emory Bryant, c. 1860.

Emma Frances Spaulding (Bryant), c.1863.

Bryant family, c.1896. From left: John Emory Bryant, daughter Emma Alice Bryant Zeller, granddaughter Miriam Irene Zeller, wife Emma Spaulding Bryant. All photos on this page courtesy of Josephine Zeller Megehee.

Introduction

Many concerns of nineteenth-century Americans centered on the forces of nationalism and reform. With the vigor and enthusiasm of youth, Americans after the War of 1812 set out to control their continent, to win their fortunes, and to improve their good society, bringing it closer to the nation's best ideals. These goals were valued for a number of sometimes contradictory reasons, and the variety produced results that could not have been anticipated. By the end of the century, the continent was secure, and the nation was industrialized and territorially united. But the Civil War and the failures of Reconstruction had led many Americans to turn their backs on reformist ideals.

John Emory Bryant, or JEB, as I will often call him, was one participant in the central drama of the nineteenth century as the United States struggled with national priorities and goals. Accepting the evaluation of Bryant made by his Southern contemporaries, historians have tended to view him as just another dishonest carpetbagger. The notion that the carpetbaggers were uniformly corrupt dies hard. It has been too easy to accept the majority Southern opinion regarding them and too difficult to disprove long-held distortions of Reconstruction historiography. In Bryant's case, his own self-defense for the most part fell on deaf ears. Nevertheless, he doggedly struggled on, trying to achieve his goals of change for the South. Fortunately, he left a voluminous collection of letters, speeches, and personal records, which prove again that one-dimensional caricatures are rarely fair.

The "carpetbagger," as the designation is understood in this volume, was not one of the myriad Northerners who came South to engage in farming or business. Rather, he was one of those who came for whatever reason but eventually landed in Republican politics, simultaneously entering the public spotlight and attracting the likely hostility of Southerners.

While this book does not offer massive statistics or a computer profile of carpetbaggers and then claim that John Emory Bryant fits the composite portrait, one suspects that the typical carpetbagger was neither hero nor villain, neither governor nor senator, but a state or local office seeker and holder—a person with both sociopolitical and personal goals.

This study claims that John Emory Bryant was a typical carpetbagger because he tried in the political arena to win office and to make changes; he often failed but displayed remarkable tenacity and garnered little love for himself by his efforts. Some people believed in him, supported him, and thought he was to be trusted to effect Republican principles. Others mistrusted him, believed him corrupt, and despised his aggressive style.

One purpose of this book is to analyze Bryant's career from the inside. The carpetbaggers, an enigmatic group, remain shadowy. But understanding of a man such as Bryant, who became a significant state political figure, can provide enormous insight into the expectations and accomplishments of local Republicans. His own vicissitudes as well as those of his wife are evident; one sees not just a political adventurer but a real person with a family, someone who must cope with rent, babies, and a marriage that suffers from absences. In examining the life of any official, it is impossible to remain oblivious to the interplay between the private and public existence; between "social" and "political" history.

The book has a second purpose. Bryant was a Radical Republican who participated in and was influenced by the reform movements of the 1840s and 1850s and made his home in the South after the Civil War. He was, as his papers indicate, an eyewitness to crucial years of the nineteenth century. His career was so intricately bound up with the shifts in Republican policy during the years of Reconstruction that it is possible through him to see something of the strengths and weaknesses of the Republican aspirations in the South. His story highlights the politics of education for blacks and whites, the debilitating factionalism of Southern Republicans, the love/hate relationship of black versus white and of Northern versus Southern Republicans, all against a backdrop of changing party goals and instructions from Washington.

It is a great temptation for biographers to love their subjects too much or to despise them greatly. Bryant defies such neat extremes. As one of his contemporaries remarked with ambivalence: "We admire his pluck and not the man." One wonders how tainted Bryant really was and what contradictions remain submerged in the rhetoric of equalitarianism coupled with the arrogance of chauvinism. Such lingering questions further demonstrate that this man embodies the Reconstruction era with all its ambiguities and makes a particularly intriguing mirror through which to view the elusive carpetbagger.

One

Maine Background

I am glad to feel that I am worthy of one so good.

The cataclysmic events that colored the lives of all Americans in the middle of the nineteenth century were already prefigured in the decade into which John Emory Bryant was born. Even before the 1830s, people in all parts of the United States were alert to the effect that slavery in the Southern states could exert upon both the South and the free North. The nation's increasing preoccupation with the issue of slavery brought recalcitrance on both sides and a growing unwillingness to compromise. Bryant grew up in a time of perplexing decisions as the country plunged toward civil war. His youthful activities and experiences in Maine were influenced by the forces that were molding men and women into reformers in the North and were impelling them to counter the expanding defense of slavery in the South. The twin energies of religion and education, the heritage of the Puritans in New England, combined to inspire some few individuals to attempt to change the entire nation.

As a seventeen-year-old student, John Emory Bryant wrote of Daniel Webster: "His father was poor and worked a small farm—When Dan'l was young he worked on the farm but that didn't suit his inclination, and if left alone to work he was sure to have a book—At Exeter Academy when he first [went] here his manners were very poor—The teacher told him he must not pay attention to the jokes of others but study hard and try to excel them in knowledge."[1] Perhaps a clue to the way in which Bryant viewed himself was his absorption with the climb to prestige from poverty and obscurity. In the journal he kept as a young man, he repeatedly revealed his admiration for men of determination and ambition in American history.

Bryant's family was poor and hardworking. According to the 1850 census, Benjamin Bryant, forty-five, a Methodist minister, and his wife, Betsey, forty-three, had six children and lived in Union, in Lincoln County, Maine. The children at that time were Benjamin, sixteen; John, fourteen; Lucy, ten; Lewella, eight; Thomas, six; Maria, four; and Mary, one. Mary Bryant, twenty-five, presumably Benjamin's sister, lived with them.[2] John was born on October 13, 1836, and was probably named for the beloved Methodist bishop John Emory. The death of Bishop John Emory after an accident in the winter of 1835 produced a rash of namesakes across America.

Whether because of the Methodist itinerancy or because of restlessness, a trait that Benjamin passed on to his son John, the Bryant family moved often during JEB's youth. While relatives remained rooted in Union and in Fayette, Maine, the Benjamin Bryants' places of residence included not only Union but other towns in southern Maine, such as Bristol, Rockport, and Wayne, John's birthplace. In later years John was identified with Skowhegan, Maine. There is no evidence that the relatively migratory existence in any way marred the family's cohesiveness, but the Bryants never seemed to have sufficient funds. When John was a teenager, his chores included chopping wood and odd jobs of carpentry, such as shingling the roof and repairing steps. He earned money by helping neighbors and relatives with haying and barn building. The hard times stayed in his memory; even when he no longer lived at home, he sent money to his mother.[3] Financial security remained one of his key goals as an adult, but wealth forever eluded him.

Books and reading became Bryant's ticket out of the poverty of his childhood. Like Daniel Webster, he always had a book nearby, and he became an avid reader. He showed an obvious proclivity for history and biography, reading Macaulay's *History of England,* the *History of the French Revolution,* and biographies of Napoleon, Washington, John Adams, James Monroe, Henry Clay, Thomas Jefferson, Andrew Jackson, Martin Van Buren, and, of course, Daniel Webster. Before he went to boarding school for his formal education, Bryant was apparently taught by his father and wrote of having recited Latin to him.[4] His journal suggests that Bryant was a determined and zealous young man, reading between chores in snowbound Maine and gathering knowledge with which to excel as Daniel Webster had done.

When Bryant left home, he managed to stay financially self-sufficient by alternating work with study; work paid for study at the Maine Wesleyan Seminary at Kent's Hill in Readfield. In the summer he toiled on his uncle's farm, and he taught school in fall and winter when he did not have enough money for a full term. He changed schools and communities often but always returned to Kent's Hill term after term until he received his college certificate in November 1858, at the age of twenty-two. The classes that he taught during these years were supported by subscription. Bryant obtained permission from the local or district school committee to set up a school, advertised for scholars, and sometimes enrolled as many as thirty-five for a session. Parents of the students usually supplied most of the teacher's salary and provided free room and board in this "rate school" system. John earned between twenty and thirty dollars for a one- to three-month term.[5]

Bryant taught in the first such school at the youthful age of fifteen and from the outset exhibited the strict discipline that was to be his hallmark as a teacher. In one incident the irate parent of a student charged Bryant with "cruelty." An intermediary between parent and teacher wrote Bryant that he had "violated not only the rules of propriety & the dictates of prudence, but . . . had laid himself grossly liable to the law." "There is not a shadow of doubt in my mind," the writer charged, "that you have . . . abused that position of parental authority temporarily delegated to you." Chastised but still adamant in his belief in corporal punishment, Bryant later wrote in his journal, "Schoolmasters have the same right to punish scholars that parents have children."[6] This logic might lead one to conclude that Bryant had himself been physically punished by his own strict and perhaps rigid father.

After the first early try, Bryant did not teach again for three years, when he was a seasoned eighteen-year-old. His chronicle of an event in the meantime, however, reveals that he had not lost his tendency to seek swift physical retribution when he perceived that a wrong had been done. The incident that aroused his wrath was the prank of a boy, "shooting at our cat," a transgression for which young Bryant "flogged" the offender. The boy's father was furious and struck John a blow of his own, claiming that if possible he would "have taken [Bryant's] heart out." Benjamin Bryant was forced to pay a five-dollar fine for John's action and an additional one dollar for the assistance of John's brother Benjamin.[7] One wonders whether Benjamin Bryant, in turn, flogged John.

It would be unjust to note only the trouble spots of Bryant's teaching career. He conducted numerous schools between 1854 and 1860 without recording any incident of difficulty or discord. There were, however, enough serious conflicts to create an observable pattern. One episode in North Wayne, Maine, led the community to coin the phrase "a Bryant scrape" and made it clear that the earlier incidents were not aberrations but symptoms of a developing character. In North Wayne, Bryant's belief in strict discipline was dramatized in his handling of a problem child who happened to be the son of Mr. Taylor, the school superintendent. Because the boy had been "sassy" to him after repeated warnings, Bryant "cuffed" him with a book while holding him by the hair. The boy then grabbed Bryant, and the schoolmaster, by his own admission, struck the pupil "with my right fist and made his left eye as black as my boot before he would let go. When he let me alone I stopped pounding him."[8]

The first ruling of the school committee, which hastily visited Bryant's class, was that he should apologize to both the boy and the school. Bryant, however, refused to accept this verdict, pleading the need for time to consider. The next day he requested a public hearing, which the committee granted him. The forum drew the entire community into a discussion of the merits of firm discipline, while Bryant proved through witnesses that he had given the difficult child every chance to behave. JEB was well aware that no one in the past had possessed the fortitude to deal with this son of the school's highest official. "Most of the inhabitants of this school district are under his employment and as he has been in the habit of turning off his men as soon as they displease him they look out pretty sharp to do as he wishes them to do." Until Bryant, "no person has ever in this place . . . successfully crossed him."[9]

Bryant thrived on such a challenge. In this case he successfully focused on a community problem and helped minimize the autocratic control of Taylor. A friend later informed Bryant that Taylor had been proven dishonest and was on the way out. Many members of the community were grateful. The youthful teacher gleefully accepted congratulations when the committee "reported that they thought I had done right." He termed it "the most important day of my life." The official ruling of the committee nevertheless did not neglect the schoolmaster. Its statement included the recommendation that he was "not to request of a scholar, or scholars, by a show of hands or otherwise, an answer as to whether he *had,* or *had not* whispered, unless [Bryant] had reason to suppose he had whispered."[10] The comment indicates that Bryant's classroom was rigid indeed.

In any case, Bryant had been vindicated in his own eyes. He returned to North Wayne in the spring, found a measure of support among "Bryant scholars," and held a successful school in the face of opposition from Taylor, who sponsored a rival school. At the close of the term, in which Bryant claimed he had "no trouble," he wrote in his journal, "I have *conquered* in spite of all opposition that could be brought against me." In 1853 Bryant had written in a composition about his hero George Washington: "Washington when he was convinced that he was in the wrong, gave up his opinions and took the right; but when he was convinced he was right, he went forward with his design regardless of the consequences." JEB seemed determined that his own character would embody that same resolution. The question of what was *right* permeated his thought and actions. Once convinced that right was on his side, he remained immovable. In North Wayne, people remembered the incident long after Bryant had departed. One year after he had moved he learned from a friend that "the same spirit prevails as when you left; it is talked about with as much feeling as ever."[11] The iron will and singlemindedness of such a personality are traits to be admired, but they can also be the undoing of someone who must have public support, such as a politician. Bryant was becoming a man who would elicit passionate responses both for and against him.

It is important to consider the few events in his youth that are recorded and to seek a balanced view of this complex future reformer. His personality included sensitivity to beauty in the world around him. He chose to note, for example, the first robin of spring and "the plum trees in bloom." He enjoyed "strawberrying" and on at least one occasion "went into the woods and got some May flowers." He seemed a typical adventuresome youth in 1858 when he signed on as a "green" hand for a fishing vessel. But seasickness and conflict with the crew convinced him that his calling was not the sea.[12]

Afterward, his itinerary unplanned, Bryant made his way through western Maine. He commented in his journal on the historic aspects of each small town he visited. This interest seems more consistent with the teacher that was glimpsed before, but again a blemish of character emerged. Chronically short of cash, JEB devised a scheme to accommodate his small budget: he offered as payment for lodging a five-dollar bill, claiming that he had no other money. As few innkeepers could make change for so large a sum, he rarely paid a penny! His conscience apparently untroubled, Bryant traveled by this ingenious, if questionable, method to New Hampshire, where a hike to the "tip top" of Mount Washington was the highlight of his trip. Though the ascent was steep, the view was magnificent; "in every direction could be seen a vast sea of mountains and hills."[13]

The picture of a serious young scholar determined to do right must now be reconciled with that of a budding shylock. As a well-meaning elder advised Bryant after one of his teaching posts, "Your courage and perseverence [sic] will win you success. But be sure, my dear friend, that your *ambition* is noble. Remember man's best inducements lie in another world."[14] Bryant struggled all his life with this hard saying.

John's journal suggests that he had few vacations or extended moments for the contemplation of nature and the inducements of another world. More frequently he engaged in politics and social reform when he was free from teaching duties. In 1846 Maine had passed a law prohibiting the manufacture or sale of intoxicating beverages. In 1853, at the age of seventeen, Bryant supported the temperance candidate for governor. Later he was active in regional and state temperance organizations. In addition to temperance, the subjects of slavery, natural rights, and duty seemed to fascinate JEB. He read *Uncle Tom's Cabin* and then *The Key to Uncle Tom's Cabin,* reading in the book almost every day for a month. The impact on his thinking must have been enormous. Another unidentified volume he found to be "a capital story against slavery." In Pope's *Essay on Man,* he found a creed that was in keeping with his own:

> God loves from whole to parts: but human soul
> Must rise from individual to the whole.
> . . . .
>
> Self-love but serves the virtuous mind to wake,
> As the small pebble stirs the peaceful lake;
> . . . .

> Friend, parent, neighbor, first it will embrace;
> His country next; and next all human race;
>
> . . . .
>
> That reason, passion, answer one great aim;
> That true self-love and social are the same.[15]

Bryant clearly illustrates the well-known traits of the nineteenth-century reformer: "the compulsion to probe, to question, and to agitate." Measured against accepted categories and origins of the reformer's values, JEB's experience is typical. The first and perhaps most obvious source of definitions for virtue and evil was religion. There can be little doubt that for Bryant, as a "preacher's kid," religion was an important part of his formative years. The Methodist church in general was waging a rigorous campaign against the problem of drunkenness and had restored Wesley's original rule of abstinence in the years that Bryant was under the influence of his father. Benjamin Bryant apparently instilled in John from a very early age a hatred of drinking, for John was ever convinced of the importance of temperance and proud that he himself had confirmed the vow of abstinence his father made for him when he was baptized. In 1864 he wrote to his future wife, Emma Spaulding, "I have not broken my pledge since I was first pledged—at six months of age."[16] John's father influenced the direction of his son's life with that vow, and in addition he had given him the name of a Methodist bishop. It is impossible to measure the effect of these factors on Bryant's psyche, but they must have had some impact, for he was clearly a person searching for purpose. Bryant later labeled Republicanism "God's cause" and regularly cast his work in the language of mission.

Bryant's journal reveals that as a teenager, he faithfully attended services on Sundays and participated in the Methodist community of faith. He attended at least one large camp meeting, and he accompanied his father on visits to parishioners. His mind ever active, John used the early years to explore variations of Christianity as well. He seemed curious about such sects as the Millerites, a group of dedicated millennialists, and attended several of their prayer meetings. He noted dryly in his journal on May 26, 1854, "This was the day set by the Millerites for the end of the world, but it has not ended and there seems to be no sign of it."[17]

It is not clear at what age Bryant rejected the faith of his youth, but for a period in his early twenties, he claimed, "I do not profess religion."

Notwithstanding this repudiation, however, Bryant retained his appreciation for right and for "righteousness," as he defined it. He prided himself on being free from the evils of drunkenness and gambling and, with little modesty, bragged in speaking to and of his future wife, "I am glad to feel that I am worthy of one so good."[18] Nevertheless, he continued to manifest ambiguities of judgment and of conscience.

Bryant later confessed to Emma Spaulding that his rejection of religion was tentative and that he continued to pray, though only in secret. He wrote, "I do not know that I have ever told anyone but you that I pray[,] because I do not profess religion and if I told others that I prayed they might think I was a hypocrite and I would much rather be thought irreligious." (To what extent this confession was a play for the pious young lady's sympathies is unknown.) Bryant's daughter, Alice, recounted in her autobiography that her father was reconverted to Christianity in the hazardous years of Reconstruction and then became "a most devout lay member" of the Methodist church. She attributed his temporary rejection of the organized church to his struggle against a call to be a minister. "He felt that if he became a Christian he would have to become a minister and he did not want to as he wished to become a lawyer." She surmised that "had he become a minister in his early life he would have been a great preacher. Persuasive as a speaker, of great personal magnetism, men followed him and believed in him."[19] This comment may elicit some skepticism, but it does lend some insight into Bryant's powers of rationalization and perhaps his effectiveness as a speaker.

In any case, the foundations of a Christian faith had been laid early in Bryant's life, and it permeated his definition of good and evil. As an adult, he eventually returned to the Methodist faith he had known best as a child. Bryant's experience followed the pattern of the reform movement in general: "The churches gave the reformers attitudes and ideas.... The sons and daughters of Puritans and of other religious strains ... felt a need to remodel the world they inhabited." Many also felt "a need for a more vigorous and enveloping faith."[20]

A second fountainhead of the reformer's values was education. In the optimism regarding the potential for individuals and for the American society in the nineteenth century, education represented the great hope; it was "the key to unlock all doors."[21] The factor of education worked in two directions: the stimulation of learning produced reformers, and the reformers in turn advocated a program of education for all. The first facet was operative in Bryant's formative years; the latter influenced his methods of reform during his career in Georgia.

Bryant's curriculum as a young scholar followed the pattern of a standard classical education, with studies in Latin, Greek, mathematics, literature, and history. The first motivation for his education was his own intellectual curiosity; the second was the encouragement of his father. He noted with pride that the first book he purchased for his own personal library was *The Life of Benjamin Franklin*.[22]

In the realm of education outside his home and the formal requirements of Maine Wesleyan, the most important formative influence for Bryant seems to have been the lyceum, a community organization for cultural improvement. An important aspect of the efforts to "educate America," the lyceum movement was specifically nonreligious and concentrated primarily on debates and lectures in local communities. A supplement to formal education, it stimulated interest in libraries and encouraged awareness of social and political issues. The Calliopen Society, which Bryant joined in 1853 at Kent's Hill, was the school's debate club, but most likely it had a very close kinship with the lyceum movement, as was often the case in a college town. When he was away from the school, one of the first things Bryant did in communities where he taught was to initiate lyceum groups, often serving as an officer. An obviously enthusiastic report of his activities led a friend to respond in the winter of 1855, "I think your Lyceum and Temperance Division must be very amusing & instructive. I suppose when they address The President you feel quite dignified."[23]

Bryant found the intellectual forensics of the lyceum tremendously exciting, and he spent days preparing for his part in them. The topics of the numerous debates exhibit an impressive range and vitality (although there are curious omissions, such as women's rights). Sample brainteasers included "Has ambition caused more evil than superstition?" "Does the farmer lead a happier life than the professional man?" "Who contributes more to the community, the man of action or the man of thought?" and "*Resolved,* That all men are not created with equal faculties or amount of mind."[24]

The question of slavery found a prominent spot on the agenda of the lyceum with such topics as "*Resolved,* That the slave in the South is more deserving of our sympathy than the aborigines of this country" and "*Resolved,* That the Indian in Maine deepens our sympathy toward the slave in the South." Bryant's own affinity for the slave in the South was evidently growing, deepened already by his reading on the subject. He proposed a scheme for compensated emancipation in a composition in 1858, and as early as 1855 a friend wrote, "From your writing I should infer that you was [sic] an abolitionist, I think you always have been one."[25]

Few reliable indexes remain to the emotion involved in Bryant's antislavery sentiments. How deep were his feelings? How personal were they? To what extent did he expect blacks to prove inferior? The fact that he was suspected of being an abolitionist implies a certain revulsion for the institution of slavery, but recent scholarship has shown that even ardent abolitionists did not escape the racist attitudes that characterized white Americans in the nineteenth century. Also, his scheme for compensated emancipation suggests that aspects of the slavery dilemma other than the need for black freedom troubled him. Bryant's firsthand knowledge of blacks was presumably quite limited. He did record hearing a "colored man" speak on one occasion and claimed that the man "did quite well."[26]

In the main, however, Bryant likely embodied the prevailing liberal position and relied on abolitionist literature for his evidence. His strong preoccupation with *Uncle Tom's Cabin* and *The Key to Uncle Tom's Cabin* suggests that his perception was at least influenced by the school of "romantic radicalism." George Frederickson has convincingly shown that Harriet Beecher Stowe's antislavery circle treated an "idealized Negro" as the convenient symbol of docility and trust and thereby contrasted strongly with the Caucasians who enslaved blacks. Later novels by Mrs. Stowe identified blacks with the "feminine" virtues of longsuffering and forgiveness.[27]

Bryant's experience with black troops during the Civil War would bring a measure of realism to his view. Nevertheless, the chauvinism of the dominant white male society was nearly impossible to overcome. As late as the 1880s, Bryant described a toy that he gave his daughter as "dancing darkeys," apparently oblivious to any contradiction a twentieth-century mind might note in his attitudes. As David Potter has stated, the nineteenth-century mind was able to compartmentalize the issues of slavery and race neatly.[28] Bryant's antislavery sentiments were most probably the expression of an abstract principle of moral rebellion against human servitude, combined with a fear for the future of American society if slavery were perpetuated.

Another topic of interest in Bryant's Calliopen Society was that of nativism. Debate subjects included the following: "*Resolved,* That Catholics ought not to hold offices of trust in this country"; "*Resolved,* That none but a native American should be able to hold office in the United States Senate"; and "*Resolved,* That all religious belief ought to be tolerated." Nativism was a revival of the anti-Catholic, anti-immigration sentiment of the 1840s, and it culminated in the American party, better known as the Know-Nothings because of the evasion used by members of its secret lodges. The ethnocultural issues raised by the presence of large numbers of Catholic immigrants, many of them Irish, were emotional and strongly held. A staunch, American-born Protestant like John Emory Bryant represented the type of person most easily persuaded by such a movement. America was "too much under foreign influence," he believed, "for the good and well being of her free institutions and her moral and intellectual welfare, and wise legislation [was] required to check this influence."[29]

Bryant was engrossed with the subject and prepared a composition on nativism that he delivered on occasion at Kent's Hill, in the Calliopen Society, and at the school's exposition. He attended lectures on the Know-Nothing philosophy and applauded speakers biased against Catholics. Besides his fear of popery, which he shared with other Protestants, John was suspicious of the Catholic immigrant's disregard for temperance. "German and Irish immigrants were known to enjoy a good drink, and regularly voted against prohibition legislation."[30]

Despite the impact of these visceral issues, for Bryant the slavery question was crucial. Ultimately, he came "down on the Know-Nothings on account of their position in regard to Slavery," and he was not alone in his disaffection with the American party over this point. Refusing to take an unequivocal stand against slavery, "almost immediately, the party began to break up under the impact of the slavery issue, and as antislavery men abandoned it, political nativism increasingly was confined to [those] who were much more concerned with nationalism than Know-Nothingism."[31]

Yet his intense interest in social issues and moral questions, as well as his predeliction for action, drew Bryant inexorably into politics. Unable to find a home with the Know-Nothings, he moved on, drifting as many people did during the political upheaval and realignment of the 1850s. As late as 1853 he participated in the election of delegates to a Democratic caucus in Bangor, Maine. Finally, however, he embraced the Republican party with a radical fervor, finding there an avenue for action and change.

John Bryant illustrates Eric Foner's point in describing the birth of the Republican party: "There is no question that Republicanism was in part an expression of the hopes and fears of northern native-born Protestants. . . . Reform movements such as temperance and antislavery, which proposed to use state power to attack moral evils, appealed to New England Protestants because of their tradition of 'moral stewardship,' . . . their 'zeal for making others act correctly.' "[32]

The reform movements of temperance and antislavery could both find an advocate in such a man as John Emory Bryant, for these causes were compatible. The entire reform movement of the nineteenth century had been ignited by the shift from a rationalistic concept of gradual progress to a theology of immediate perfectibility. If humans were perfectible, then they had to choose the moral path and end the evils in society while they could—at once. Temperance thus became abstinence; colonization became abolition. The antislavery cause could profit from association with reforms that had already gained respect, such as temperance. Temperance "served the cause of abolition" by helping to give "respectability to its agitators, who might have been called fanatical, but not corrupt. The demand for 'immediate' temperance added an argument to abolitionist appeals for 'immediate abolition.' "[33]

It was not, however, expedient for a national political party to combine the twin concerns. The Republicans were forced to abandon the prohibition issue both because of its narrow appeal and because of the party's hope for capturing the immigrant vote. Just as nativism represented a narrow viewpoint in contradiction to the cornerstones of free labor and economic expansion, so temperance posed a threat to the constituency of an already sectional party.[34] Slavery—more specifically, the extension of slavery—was the issue that touched all the business, political, and reform bases and provided the glue for the new Republican party. In the summer of 1854, the Kansas-Nebraska bill, in nullifying part of the Missouri Compromise, made the extension of slavery again an issue, and the clamor for a new political party became impossible to overlook.

The reasons for the uproar over the bill were complex and involved the spectrum of Northern attitudes regarding the Negro as well as slavery itself. The entire "free soil" ideology had complicated national politics since the 1840s, when the issues involved with western expansion raised the specter of *black* expansion. George Frederickson has linked a fervent desire for racial homogeneity with radical nationalism, hence the impetus for excluding blacks from newly won American land. In addition, white labor had a deep aversion to the idea that blacks might compete for jobs. Perhaps more virulent than either of these motives, though endemic to them both, was the deep-seated belief that association with any black person at all would bring contamination. This attitude, combined with the economic motive, produced a hybrid excuse for excluding blacks from the western territories. Association with blacks would, in the words of Free-Soiler David Wilmot, "bring disgrace upon free labor."[35]

Many settlers in the West, then, were Negrophobic and embodied the simple desire to keep the West for whites only. Formative Republican ideology saw the extension of slavery as a threat to the free-labor ideal of a capitalistic America, but the new party also had a pragmatic need for the western vote. The "antislavery myth," which identified all Northern and western attitudes against extension as morally based, was discredited long ago. As Foner has shown relatively recently, the issue of nonextension enabled the Republican party to join together the evangelical antislavery of the early abolitionists with the racially motivated exclusion issue. Not since the termination of the slave trade had the politics of slavery produced such unlikely bed partners. One of Bryant's friends candidly identified the point of seeming contradiction: "I see no reason for the North to oppose slavery. The North is no more concerned for the African than the South."[36]

Like other observers, Bryant was apprehensive about the Kansas-Nebraska bill and slavery during the crucial year of 1854. He heard the "liberty candidate" for Congress speak, and he lauded the report of those who aided runaway slaves. Although he was still only eighteen years of age, Bryant pored over the speeches against the Kansas-Nebraska bill by Senators Salmon P. Chase (Free-Soil, Ohio) and Benjamin F. Wade (Whig, Ohio). He observed in September that the issue that defeated the Democratic candidate in one congressional race in Maine was the Kansas-Nebraska bill. John kept abreast of the debate over the extension of slavery through the newspapers and journals that he apparently read regularly. The *Chicago Tribune* and the *Washington National Era* were his favorites. He urged that the library at Maine Wesleyan subscribe to them as well as to the *New York Tribune*.[37]

While his journal ends in 1855 and there is no complete record of Bryant's activities between 1856 and 1857, several letters mention that he was involved in Republican politics on the local level. By 1858 the public had identified him with the Republican cause and with his "black Republican friends." It is impossible to know the extent of Bryant's political activity, but the letters he received show that he was an early organizer for the Republican party. Between the defeat of John C. Frémont in 1856 and the success of Abraham Lincoln in 1860, many men like Bryant organized Republican clubs and attempted to "effect change" in local, state, and national politics.[38] Applying the valuable lessons that he had learned in the process, Bryant would later try to duplicate the formation of Republican strength in Georgia after the war.

In addition Bryant continued his efforts in support of temperance. Though official Republican doctrine did not identify alcohol as an issue, Bryant did, and he was active in temperance leagues in every community in which he lived. In towns like North Wayne, where he had not been accepted for membership in the existing temperance club, Bryant simply inaugurated a new group.[39] One may speculate as to why Bryant was denied membership in a temperance club, but it was probably no more than lingering animosity from his career as a teacher there. Bryant was always to provoke strong reactions to his beliefs, and he usually found both the adherents and the energy to sustain a separate, "purer" faction within any organization of which he was a part. This pattern also would be repeated with schismatic effect on Republican politics in Georgia.

The crucial election year of 1860 found Bryant engaged as a teacher in Buckfield, Maine. There he enjoyed the luxury of having been employed for a full year, or three terms, in advance. He conducted his school successfully and taught "all subjects," including Latin, astronomy, and mathematics.[40] In Buckfield, in the family with whom he boarded, he met his future wife—Emma Spaulding, one of the students in his school and the daughter of one of his strongest supporters. His association with the Spaulding family, which included several children, allowed John to become Emma's "brother," while she was called his little "sister." Their relationship was to develop mostly by letter. Emma Spaulding was an intelligent, diligent, and sensitive student. The hardship and loneliness that she would encounter as John Bryant's wife would make her strong, self-assured, and independent as well.

Bryant and others anticipated the Republican victory in the presidential election of 1860, and he undoubtedly supported Abraham Lincoln as the party's nominee. Lincoln exemplified the hard worker who rises from poverty to prominence, an image that Bryant had long admired. On the other hand, Lincoln represented the moderate Republican view, which condemned only the expansion of slavery.[41] Bryant would probably have preferred a strong attack on the institution itself. But in the South, Lincoln's "moderate" views seemed radical enough, and his election signaled the imminent failure of attempts to compromise sectional differences. By the spring of 1861, only an incendiary incident was needed to start a civil war. The firing on Fort Sumter provided it.

In the North, the news of Sumter consolidated many factions behind President Lincoln. Men rushed to enlist in the Union army. John Emory Bryant also volunteered in the summer of 1861. He joined Northern troops armed with the Republican ideology that sought to save the Union, to which he added the more radical desire to destroy slavery. Several years passed before Lincoln publicly acknowledged this as one of his administration's goals. Perhaps no one could anticipate the ordeal that lay ahead for the nation and its people. Least of all could young Bryant, egotistical, ambitious, and determined to go "forward with his design regardless of the consequences."

Two

Bryant in the Civil War

I think I shall be successful this time as usual.

The direction of Bryant's future was determined by the orders that the War Department gave to the Eighth Maine Infantry Regiment. This regiment joined other troops transported by the massive armada that sailed from Annapolis, Maryland, in November 1861 to establish a Federal beachhead on the eastern coast of the Confederacy. Those who participated in the securing and holding of this "Department of the South" gathered some of the first empirical evidence for the federal government concerning the potential and future of the freed slaves. The events that occurred in this arena, removed as it was from most of the actual fighting of the war, have been called by historian Willie Lee Rose the "rehearsal for Reconstruction," so important a proving ground did the "Port Royal Experiment" become.[1] Bryant shared in the events that helped to change public sentiment regarding the black man as soldier and, indeed, regarding the goals of the entire war. Because of his abolitionist sentiments, Bryant was actively involved; because of his abrasive personality, he was once again embroiled in controversy.

The Eighth Maine Infantry gathered at Augusta, Maine, in August of 1861 under the command of Colonel Augustus H. (Lee) Strictland. John E. Bryant, an acquaintance of the colonel, aided both in the recruitment of the enlisted men and in securing Strictland's commission. Bryant, determined that he would enter the regiment as an officer or not at all, considered the operation both a patriotic venture and an avenue for personal advancement. "I am full of business," he wrote, "and all [that I do] is for aiding me in the future. . . . I think I shall be successful this time as usual." Probably because of his education and connections, Bryant was commissioned a captain and was made the first officer of the Eighth Maine's Company C.[2]

The regiment joined General E. L. Viele's command in Long Island, New York, in September 1861 and from there deployed to Annapolis, Maryland, where it gathered with units under the direction of General Thomas W. Sherman. During the troop movements, John, as an officer, was "well taken care of" and did not seem to find life in the army unpleasant. For example, he had a bed while his men slept on the ground. As the company readied itself for shipping out, Bryant felt himself caught up in the historical sense of the moment. He exulted in the glories of the American past as he retraced the steps of his hero, George Washington. "I stood today in the place where [George Washington] is said to have stood when he resigned [his commission]," he wrote. Bryant himself was ready to "do his duty."[3]

An impressive army force of thirteen thousand men and a battalion of marines sailed from Annapolis in three flotillas on October 18, 1861. Sherman's troops were joined by Commodore (later Rear Admiral) Samuel Francis DuPont and his naval fleet. The men of the company, uninformed of their destination until they sailed, learned that they were headed for the Sea Islands, on the coast of South Carolina. Determined to take the war to the South, the War Department wanted to establish a base for a thrust from the underside of the Confederacy. Hilton Head was an excellent beachhead because it had one of the best harbors on the southeast coast, it was a vital link in the Confederate supply line via the Atlantic Ocean, and it would serve as a base for a future blockade. Moreover, the port was only thirty miles from Savannah, Georgia, and fifty miles from Charleston, South Carolina, and was guarded by Fort Pulaski, twenty miles to the south. It was a strategic choice.[4]

The people of the coastal islands afterward remembered the day the ships arrived, November 7, 1861, as the "day of the gun-shoot at Bay Point." The contest was "short but brilliant"; victory for the Northern fleet came quickly as the ill-prepared Southerners scattered under the onslaught of Federal ships and guns. The Eighth Maine Infantry, with an excellent view of the battle, had only to watch and cheer the triumph as they prepared to land.[5]

Even after the residents of the islands had fled, confusion reigned for a

Battle flag of Company C, Eighth Maine Volunteers. (Courtesy of the Maine State Museum.)

time before order was restored. Slaves who had balked at the command to leave with their masters vented their stored-up anger by plundering the deserted mansions of the whites. Uninstructed in the beginning, Union soldiers joined in a measure of looting, some merely looking for "Rebel souvenirs." John managed to secure for Emma Spaulding a "toilet basket" from the plantation of one Judge Pope, a man of "great wealth and influence." He reported that, when they first landed, "all the men rushed out to get cotten [sic]" (and presumably other items), actions Bryant deemed acceptable, since the objects had belonged to "these South Carolina traitors." General Sherman, however, "for political effect stopped [the plunder] and ordered us to give up what we had got so I lost everything except the basket." Bryant later paid $1.50 to the provost marshal for the basket, which could not be returned, since it had been mailed to Maine.[6]

The gathering of rebel war mementos led to more serious escapades. Bryant soon found that a black man had been robbed by "a captain and men" of $101.50 and that he himself had been accused of the crime. After twenty days under restriction, he was "relieved of arrest" and returned to duty. John made light of the incident, claiming that "putting an officer in arrest in the army amounts to nothing unless they are punished." He attributed the false charge to resentment some of the men felt against him as an officer. In his customary pattern, Bryant claimed that from the beginning he had demanded strict discipline from his company and had tried to impose on the men his own standards of conduct. He seemed to excuse the looting, since it had been directed against Southerners, but he strongly opposed the use of alcohol and cards. As early as September 1861, he had held a temperance meeting in the camp and had spoken to the gathering on the values of morality and abstinence from liquor.[7]

Bryant was identified by at least two soldiers as the officer who had robbed the Negro. Bryant had earlier ordered one of the two soldiers demoted, and the other had previously been reprimanded by the captain for "gambling and drinking" and was in danger of demotion, a penalty that he incurred anyway after Bryant was cleared. John was convinced, or so he claimed, that the entire incident had made him stronger. "I know," he wrote, "that I am regarded by Gen'ls—Viele and Sherman—as one of the best if not the best officer in the Reg't. My company has been highly complimented by Gen. Viele. . . . You know I never failed yet of coming out ahead and I shant fail here *be assured of that*. . . . When I started all were friendly but my discipline was so strict that nearly all at one time disliked me. I kept a steady hand, kept my discipline strict and now they all like me again. Such is life! Do not give yourself any uneasiness about me for I always look out for No. 1." Bryant fully expected to gain a major's commission after the matter of the stolen money was concluded. For "some unaccountable reason," however, his letters of recommendation "were not received [in Maine] until some two or three weeks after they were sent." In fact, the so-called recommendation was a noncommittal letter to the governor of Maine stating that Bryant was a man of "capacity and energy." The writer stated, "It is not my purpose to advocate or oppose his appointment, but to bring his name before you to comply with his wishes."[8] Not surprisingly, another officer got the available promotion.

Emma Spaulding proved to be a faithful correspondent throughout the war. To her the young captain recounted his exploits, his difficulties, and the justifications for his actions. John was not the only soldier in the Eighth Maine who corresponded with the folks back home, and he used Emma to keep him abreast of what his "friends or enemies" were saying about him. Usually she wrote all the latest gossip, but in early 1862 she apparently became unhappy with his priorities. He had seemed more concerned that his letters arrive on schedule than about expressing his sympathies when she wrote of her sister's death.

Bryant hastened to set things right. He had only wished not to add to her burden, he wrote. "Remember, I am your brother and hope to be true to my sister. Pour out all your troubles into my ears and I will sympathize." He was hurt that she had not trusted his motives. "Please banish such thoughts in the future." He signed the letter, "A kiss from your John."[9]

Captivated by the April weather, John began to write about the advantages of living in the South in winter and in Maine for the summer months. He was clearly planning his future around Emma Spaulding. He gave his "sister" advice that would only further his intentions. She should beware of "flirting," of becoming entangled with "little beaux," and should set her sights on a "smart man," which he presumably thought he was. He wrote that he wanted "to say more" to her and that he "expected her company" during his upcoming leave.[10]

Oddly, the leave, granted for sixty days beginning June 21, seems to have provided little opportunity for John and Emma to be together, though they stayed in touch by mail. Bryant had suffered from some unspecified illness from mid-May to late June that made a lengthy leave desirable. Recuperating in Buckfield, Maine, he asked Emma to come home while he was there. After a visit with her that received little comment in the letters, he traveled around the state, seeing other friends. John attended a county Republican convention and supposedly saw Emma again in Buckfield before returning to South Carolina in late August 1862.[11]

By this time, Bryant was resigned to the fact that, although he would probably be physically safe in his wartime assignment, he would not have the opportunity for very much "honor." The future would include more hazardous escapades than he then anticipated, but for the time being he was relatively secure. He nevertheless participated in one of the more significant aspects of the Port Royal experience, namely, the deployment of blacks as soldiers. Bryant had been designated provost marshal on February 22, 1862; on March 5, 1862, General Viele had ordered "all contrabands arriving on this island" to be placed in the custody of the provost marshal.[12]

The term "contraband" had become important in the spring of 1861 after General Benjamin Butler at Fortress Monroe, Virginia, designated runaway slaves the "contraband of war." Blacks themselves thrust the slavery issue into the war by deserting their masters and converging on Union army camps. Unadvised of an administration policy on the matter, individual officers made ad hoc decisions for their own commands. Butler's solution was to give Negroes servile tasks such as cooking, chopping wood, and drawing water. Such an unoffensive place for the runaways within the Union lines was publicly acceptable. The designation of them as contraband represented a painless first step toward training blacks for military purposes.[13]

Although abolitionists and others criticized Lincoln for his silence on the matter of the contrabands, a minority president had good reasons to treat the sensitive issue of slavery with caution. Lincoln had repeatedly maintained that his primary aim in the war was "to save the Union"; slavery could stay or go, depending on whether it served that cause. Many Northerners, including some Republicans and probably most Democrats, had no desire to destroy slavery. Furthermore, the North's hold on the border states that still maintained slavery within the Union was tenuous and Lincoln was unwilling to force the issue. The president, as one critic noted, was "backing slowly into God's faith with his face always turned to Kentucky."[14] While the abolitionists argued and pleaded that the second war aim should be to emancipate the slaves, throughout the winter of 1861–1862 Lincoln remained publicly silent.

The Negro's decisive role both in the coming of the war and as participant in the hostilities continually came to public attention thanks to the efforts of individuals who saw the war's far-reaching implications for the future of slavery. The visionaries included generals such as Butler who were forced to cope with the blacks who came to the Union army camps seeking protection and work. General John C. Frémont, head of the Department of the West, went further than Butler and in Missouri proclaimed that all the slaves of rebels in the state were free. President Lincoln reacted by swiftly modifying that order and establishing, for Frémont and all other zealots, that the administration alone had the power to make such policy decisions.[15]

People who considered slavery a crucial matter continued to focus on the role of blacks in the war, however, and Northern newspapers in 1862 indicated a shift in attitude.[16] The Port Royal locale captured the imagination of the nation and helped draw attention to the question, primarily because of General David M. Hunter. In the spring of 1862 Hunter sought to make black troops a fait accompli, even without the approval of the administration. This time Lincoln withheld comment, waiting to see how the nation would view Hunter's action.

In his zeal, Hunter made numerous mistakes. First, he proclaimed the slaves in the states of South Carolina, Georgia, and Florida "forever free" in an order that Lincoln quickly rescinded. Second, unwilling to settle for recruits from Bryant's camp of contrabands and other enlistees that stepped forward for the Negro regiment, the general gathered "volunteers" from the areas of the islands where the former slaves were now farming. This initiative did nothing to win him the respect and confidence of the terrified blacks, who in some cases fled from this Yankee "liberator."[17]

Hunter's policies also created dissension among the white troops and exposed the extreme hostility to blacks of some Union soldiers. The black troops concentrated on drill and parade technique but were exempt from fatigue detail, a policy that thoroughly demoralized the camp. The white men resented the fact that Hunter allegedly played favorites; they claimed that he was "arbitrary and wholly taken up with his negro question."[18]

Hunter made his final and fatal mistake when the House of Representatives asked for a report on operations at Port Royal. Seeing a chance to make his project and his views on the subject of black troops better known, on June 23, 1862, the general wrote a clever, sarcastic letter to Secretary of War Edwin Stanton that was destined to stir controversy. Radicals in the House thoroughly enjoyed the caustic, flippant tone that Hunter employed as he maintained that there were no "fugitive slaves" at Port Royal, only "a fine regiment of persons whose late masters are 'fugitive rebels.'" More conservative congressmen found the tone of the letter insulting. While Hunter did succeed in drawing the nation's attention to the question of black troops, he had undermined his own effort. Lincoln declined to use immediately even the power available to him, and Hunter, defeated by insufficient support and lack of funds to pay the men, disbanded his black regiment.[19]

Nevertheless, the matter was not closed. Two significant actions by Congress kept the issue alive. One was the Second Confiscation Act, which empowered the president "to employ as many persons of African descent as he may deem necessary and proper for the suppression of this rebellion." Second, Congress repealed a section of the Militia Act of 1792 that barred blacks from service in the army of the United States.[20]

Still the president waited. Things were not going well for the Union's war effort, and morale in the North was at its nadir in the summer of 1862. The president had the option of raising the conflict to a new plane by attacking slavery; in addition, the North's need for manpower was constantly increasing. Policy that took a new direction would provide a much needed psychological boost at home, his advisers argued, and would perhaps aid in securing greater material support from nations abroad. In addition, the issue of black participation would be resolved. Persuaded at last, Lincoln, in the late summer of 1862, prepared to issue the preliminary Emancipation Proclamation and waited only for a Northern military victory to provide the proper moment.

While administration officials debated and observed the direction of the war and the potential role of black troops, in the Department of the South a second general was charting new plans for a black regiment. Two weeks after Hunter's letter informed Secretary of War Edwin Stanton of the disbanding of the First South Carolina Volunteers, another letter reached Stanton's desk asking permission to raise a black regiment. General Rufus Saxton had been in Port Royal since the landing in November 1861, serving as chief quartermaster. On April 29, 1862, he became military governor of the Sea Islands, under the direct command of the War

Department. When Saxton asked permission to rejuvenate the First South Carolina Volunteers, Stanton consented, commenting that "the instructions given at the time of your appointment were sufficient to enable you to do what you have now requested authority for doing."[21]

Saxton had considerable support in his project to employ black soldiers, including that of John Emory Bryant. During the crucial year 1862, as sentiment in the North was shifting with regard to the use of black troops, Bryant's own attitudes were becoming clearer as he saw the situation of the freed slaves at first hand and learned of their true potential. Bryant had rather quickly identified himself with the educational aspect of the Port Royal Experiment, the effort that was staffed by missionaries representing the Port Royal Relief Committee in the North. One of his closest associates was the Reverend Mansfield French, a controversial Methodist minister who led the first band of Northern teachers to Port Royal and was later chaplain in the army. Because of his friendship with two officers of the American Missionary Association, Lewis Tappan and George R. Whipple, French had been able to go to Port Royal and to become an influential part of the project. French had been a college president in Ohio before the war, and the causes of education and emancipation were close to his heart. Except for a few men such as Saxton and Bryant, he did not fully trust the agents of the Treasury and War departments.[22] Furthermore, there were various conflicts of interest, not to mention differences of approach and attitude, between the missionaries and the army. Part of John's troubles may have arisen because of his friendly associations with the missionaries and teachers.

Bryant increasingly preferred the companionship of the missionary band to that of his comrades in arms. The drunkenness and gambling of the men, which were perhaps encouraged by the minimum-security regimen, repelled him. Possibly it was JEB who organized the intellectual and literary discussions of the camp, which were similar to those of the lyceum in Maine, in an effort to upgrade the activities of the men. Dissatisfied with the results, he became "more and more disgusted" with the army and by September 1862 "had determined to resign in the spring." In the meantime, the cause of the blacks enabled him to identify with the war, which sometimes seemed far away.[23] He even found time to assist one of the missionary teachers in her classroom.

In telling Emma Spaulding about his teaching assignment, John maximized his own gallantry and minimized his contact with the schoolmarm. He wrote that, on visiting the schoolroom of one of the women missionaries whom he had met previously, he discovered "140 black brats who had come to learn," but the young woman had no help with the children, "because of course she was not handsome." In order to prove to "the [missionary] agents" that "the plain should have attention also," Bryant agreed to return and assist in the teaching. He did not record whether he modified his old strict standards or how successful any disciplinary attempts proved.[24]

He did, however, tell Emma that, if she herself were the teacher, he would "steal a kiss." His letters were now more forthright. As usual he advised Emma to be a "lady," and he showed a streak of possessiveness (later to be more fully revealed) when she mentioned having a new pen pal from the South. She must "not even regard him as a friend" and must cease corresponding with him. For the first time, JEB revealed that he had already spoken to Emma of marriage. Under such circumstances, he said, it was "best to avoid temptation."[25] In his own case, on the other hand, he apparently trusted his ability to resist it.

The children in school did not provide John's only contact with black people. One evening in the fall of 1862, and on other occasions, he participated actively in one of the religious "negro meeting[s]" that were held two or three times weekly on the islands. "Nearly all negros in this part of the South are religiously inclined," he noted, although prayer services in the camp for the soldiers were actually just as frequent. A black prayer meeting, Bryant wrote, "can beat a Methodist meeting out and out."[26]

Attracted on this particular night by the sounds of singing, Bryant found a group of blacks seated on wooden benches in one of the crude slave cabins, shouting and singing with great enthusiasm, using a singing method common in the nineteenth century that was known as "lining out." "The leader would repeat a few lines then all would sing—for negroes are natural singers. They were just beginning to get up steam—some of the old covies [sic] kept a constant swinging of their bodies and clapping of hands. I could see that they were warming up and by the time that the singing closed there was considerable excitement." The leader, in his remarks, "made up for sense with sound," calling out, "God loves we," and "God died for we"; the preacher "ranted to his heart[']s content." The leader's prayer was in "good part . . . for the soldiers," not surprising, since Bryant sat in the congregation. The observer was amused when three men and three women came forward during the singing of the hymn "Come Ye Sinners Poor and Needy." He wrote, "They were, I suppose, 'sinners poor and needy.'" Inspired with a sense of mission, Bryant "'stood up in the midst' of these people" and read a psalm when he was asked to do so. He interpreted the scripture to the congregation and explained to his correspondent, "So, you see I was a teacher of the people." The blacks all said "Thank you 'massa,'" and Bryant could hear their singing as he walked away.[27]

In another foray into the black community, Bryant dined with Christiana, a very light-skinned mulatto woman who was known as the "Queen of Little Island." The soldiers informed Bryant that it was "the fashion" for the officers on picket duty on the island to dine with Christiana, who was consulted for advice by former slaves on the island and generally had her wishes carried out. When he was on picket duty nearby, Bryant did not pass up his opportunity to sup with her. He reported to Emma Spaulding that the "queen" had been a favorite of her master's and still, at forty-five, showed her youthful beauty. Her husband, who had been black and the driver of their owner's plantation, was now dead. Christiana, Bryant observed, was "as neat as the neatest white woman. She has no education but remarkably good sense." The house in which she lived was clean, and Bryant was served "chicken and drop cakes, very good and peculiar to the negroes. All for fifty cents. Don't think I should eat many such dinners at that price but then I have eaten dinner with the queen and that is worth something you know." Bryant asked Christiana why she did not remarry. Her revealing answer was, "S'pos I would have a black niggar—No! and I won't have a white man until the war is over 'cause he may be killed."[28]

The significance of this episode need not be exaggerated. It does show, nevertheless, a young man gathering empirical evidence about a people whom before the war he had known only in sentimental literature. Although his description of the prayer meeting, quoted above, reinforces certain stereotypes, to Bryant Christiana seemed to show that the black race was somewhat malleable. Bryant considered her home clean and her character shrewd. But he also belittled the vanity of this former "pet of her master." The evening's potential for moral compromise and the possibility that the other soldiers had sent the straitlaced captain to Christiana as a joke were apparently lost on Bryant, or so he wished it to appear.

While Bryant's relationships with the black community flourished, he was having greater difficulty relating to his military colleagues. After December 1861 he expressed growing disappointment with Colonel John D. Rust, commander of the Eighth Maine, whom he found to be a "different man from what I supposed him to be." As late as July 1862, Rust had written a warm letter to "my dear captain and friend," inviting Bryant to visit Rockport while he was on leave. Now the relationship had soured, and John chafed under the obligation to obey men whom he regarded as his "inferiors and yet superior in command, men corrupt as they can be and I do not think it my duty to stay under such men."[29]

The conflict with Rust reached its climax at the end of 1862, when Bryant found himself again under arrest and faced this time with a court-martial. Shortly before his trial Bryant spent Christmas at the home of Mansfield French, "the headquarters of the antislavery people of Beaufort," engaging in prayers with those ladies and gentlemen present. He scorned the pastimes of the military personnel, most of whom spent the day drinking and racing horses. "I am more and more disgusted with the army," he again wrote. "Down here gamblers and drunkards rule. I am thankful that I did not form such habits when I was a boy for now instead of desiring to join with those who 'indulge' I loathe it." He made light of his own situation and claimed that the word around camp was "They are afraid either to try Bryant or release him—he will whip the whole gang yet."[30]

The court-martial actually began two days later. There were five charges against him, with seven additional specifications. John agonized through proceedings that lasted for the better part of a month, serving mostly as his own counsel. While the charges ranged from failure to obey orders on the drill field to insubordination, the more substantial ones involved an alleged lack of respect for Rust's authority. In a conflict between Bryant and another officer, Rust had refused to support Bryant's position. When the angered captain complained to the colonel, Rust insisted that Bryant was speaking in a "boisterous and threatening manner, . . . [and] a contemptuous and disrespectful . . . tone of voice" when he informed Rust, "I will not have my manhood trampled upon," and when he explained what "he [Bryant] would or would not stand." Rust discounted the letter of apology Bryant wrote after the incident and was instrumental in gathering the charges that Bryant finally confronted.[31]

The army's counsel was able to prove eight of the twelve counts to the satisfaction of the judges, but Bryant's sentence was not severe because of the often confusing and contradictory evidence given by witnesses and because of "the mistakes made by his superior officers and other mitigating circumstances." The captain was "suspended from rank and pay for one month," and he received an official reprimand from the commanding general, which reminded Bryant "that the spirit of an officer's duty is a respectful subordination." He was "released from arrest, and ... return[ed] to duty" on January 23, 1863. Apparently dissatisfied with this sentence, Rust initiated an appeal "to inquire into and report upon the Military Capacity and Conduct of said Captain John E. Bryant while serving this Department."[32]

While Bryant languished in military limbo under Rust's control, General Rufus Saxton had been working to fulfill his dream of making black troops into a viable fighting unit on the seaboard. He was convinced "that the services of 50,000 effective men can do more here to break down this rebellion than twice that number in any other field. It would take a large portion of the rebel army to keep the slaves in check. A vast amount of cotton and rice could be obtained, and such a fire in their rear would be started as to call off all the southern portion of the rebel army in Virginia. Possessing as we do the power on the ocean, all these southern posts would form secure bases of operations, which could be protected entirely by the navy, leaving the whole army force available for the interior service."[33]

Armed with the official approval of the administration, and with the psychological boost of the preliminary Emancipation Proclamation, which had been issued on September 22, 1862, Saxton moved to make his plan a reality. His first task was to overcome the negative attitude toward the project that his predecessor had engendered. Apart from the prejudice among the white men and officers against blacks, the former slaves showed no great rush to join the ranks. Hunter's men had been unpaid to the last, and the Negroes on the islands did not forget his highhanded induction methods. In addition, the number of potential recruits was limited after laborers had been secured for farming and for the needs of the military personnel in Port Royal. Still, Saxton was a popular general and was able to muster in a new First South Carolina Volunteers, one company of which had remained in continuous service from Hunter's regiment.[34] Determined to avoid previous mistakes, Saxton did not confine the activities of the blacks to drill and parade but compelled them to share equally in the picket and detail duties of the camp. Also, by November 1862 the general was sending the men on patrols, raw as they were.

At first, white volunteers served as officers in the black regiment. John

Bryant was embroiled with his own troubles at the time and was not among these officers initially, but a significant number from the Eighth Maine did opt to work with the black recruits. The most important contribution to leadership, however, came from the man Saxton tapped to command the First South Carolina, Colonel Thomas Wentworth Higginson. Higginson joined the Department of the South in December 1862, bringing with him an impressive reputation as an abolitionist. He had recently joined the war effort and had trained with the Fifty-first Massachusetts Regiment in Worcester. Higginson's own contact with blacks, perhaps more extensive than Bryant's because of his involvement with the personal liberty laws of Massachusetts following the Compromise of 1850, had nevertheless been limited. He described his black recruits as "simple" and "docile" and tended to emphasize public drill and discipline, as Hunter had. He eventually became concerned because the "childlike" former slaves seemed hardly to resemble the heroic revolutionaries he had glorified in his published articles on Denmark Vesey and Nat Turner. But whatever his private assessments, morale began to rise as Higginson's charisma took effect. As the fortune of the black troops in South Carolina changed, Negroes serving in other experimental units in Mississippi and Louisiana at the same time began to receive a good press.[35]

At this point General Saxton rescued John Emory Bryant from Rust's jurisdiction and chose him to execute a special assignment. With Saxton's evident interest in his case, in the appeal hearing, Bryant was acquitted of the charges against him. JEB remained convinced that "had it not been for villainy I should have been acquitted the first time. As it is I have lost more than a hundred dollars [in pay] and at length have been acquitted of all. But that does not annul the previous sentence." Despite that minor inconvenience, the captain felt that he had "completely triumphed. . . . I am congratulated on all sides. . . . Gen'l Saxton made me the superintendant [sic] of the draft of colored men in the Department and gave me the command of the camp in which they were placed." The "greater compliment" for Bryant was that the general "gives me credit for considerable ability." Saxton had indirectly rebuked Rust by placing "perfect confidence" in Bryant. The pugnacious captain was certain that he was "all through with my difficulty and it has pushed me *up* a considerable distance. . . . Fortune smiles now." The burden that Rust had placed upon him was removed at last when the official Board of Examination found

Bryant to be a "capable and efficient officer fully qualified to hold his present position in the Service."[36]

JEB was soon to be vindicated in another way. In March 1863, the Eighth Maine had shipped out to Florida, though Bryant was not with the regiment. When the men returned to camp, Bryant found that his opinion of Colonel John Rust was no longer a minority view; twenty-seven of Rust's junior officers filed an official complaint against their colonel, questioning his "military capacity and conduct." The company had just returned from an expedition to Jacksonville, Florida, during which some of the Eighth Maine served among the companies reinforcing Higginson's First South Carolina Regiment, which had preceded them there. Higginson had welcomed the chance to prove his black troops under battle conditions, and their first days in the Jacksonville campaign had shown them capable. After ten days, however, as the Southerners mounted a siege of the captured city, Higginson needed assistance. He knew it would come in the form of white troops, and he feared the consequences of having black and white units serve together. In one mission he commanded a party composed of four black and six white companies, one of the first such integrated units to see action in the Civil War.[37]

The unfortunate conclusion of the attempt to take Jacksonville at this time was the ordered evacuation and the wanton burning of portions of the city. Many people, even in the North, were disturbed by this "lamentable" method of warfare, while Higginson, other officers, and reporters were swift to lay the blame for the devastation on white soldiers and to forestall any anger that might be directed against the black troops present. Among the white companies, the Eighth Maine and the Sixth Connecticut accused each other of responsibility for the deed. In his official report, Rust concluded, "A portion [of the fires] undoubted [were lighted] by secessionists; these fires were not confined to the lines of any regiment."[38]

By forcing black troops and white troops to cooperate in the expedition, the army command had created the potential for conflict, even as Higginson had feared. Indeed, a reporter from the *New York Tribune* cited racial overtones as the key to the entire round of charges between Rust and his officers. The reporter's original story held that Rust had successfully put down a mutiny among his officers who resented the administration's policy of mustering black troops. According to his account, two officers in Rust's company were forced to resign. The reporter possibly misconstrued anger toward Rust as antagonism toward the blacks. As Higginson put it, the "eager" Maine troops were disappointed that Rust allowed the black soldiers to take the major portion of the action to the exclusion of the Down-easterners. He also reported that Rust himself had remained on shipboard through most of the engagement, which the men had apparently noted with chagrin.[39]

John Emory Bryant and others wrote letters to the editor protesting the *Tribune*'s initial account of the Rust affair. Bryant's version was that the Eighth Maine Regiment as a whole held strong antislavery views and that none had given more hearty support to Saxton's effort to raise black troops than the Eighth, which "warmly advocat[ed] this policy." None of the officers had opposed Rust because of "his support of the Administration's policy" of raising black troops, as the reporter had stated. On the other hand, "Col. Rust was [the person] at first opposed to arming colored men."[40] From his secure position on General Saxton's staff, Captain Bryant could afford publicly to join the other officers of his Maine regiment in criticizing Colonel Rust.

The association with Saxton transformed Bryant's war record into one of distinction. Indeed, it appeared that his troubles lay behind him as he accepted top responsibility for recruiting blacks into the Army of the South. The Union's need for black manpower made necessary this special office, which permitted innovative means to be used in attracting new recruits. Though Colonel James Montgomery had joined Saxton in January 1863 and was attempting to organize the Second South Carolina Volunteer Regiment, another black unit, the pace was slow.[41]

Bryant plunged with enthusiasm into his new role. Soon after assuming his post with Saxton, he planned a raid into the mainland of South Carolina to "bring off many slaves." Such a raid, as he saw it, would not only liberate "so many human beings" but would also gain soldiers "to assist in crushing this Rebellion." The raid was approved by his superiors and was highly successful. Eight hundred slaves were brought out, according to Bryant, "among them men to fill two companies." JEB seemed touched at the sight of reunions between blacks who had previously been separated from their families because of some members' earlier escape. "This is a holy cause Emma," he wrote. "God smiles upon those who bless the families of these poor degraded blacks by revisiting them. I care not what may be said, from this time forward while I remain in the Army I will assist this degraded race."[42]

Public opinion in the North increasingly supported a cause that had been unpopular in the beginning. Good publicity in the first months of 1863 was giving the black soldier the reputation of being an excellent and obedient fighter, both in South Carolina and in other parts of the country, such as Mississippi, Louisiana, and Kansas. After the raid that he commanded, Bryant reported, "I had a chance to see how black soldiers will fight and I can assure you that no men could do better." A comment by a white soldier from Pennsylvania reflected the changing attitude of the Northern soldier: "They've as much right to fight for themselves as I have to fight for them."[43]

That the Civil War might end slavery was made clear by the Emancipation Proclamation, which took effect on January 1, 1863. Although the proclamation had little actual impact in the border states where slavery still existed, and the Confederate states did not recognize Lincoln's authority, the proclamation had enormous psychological significance.

In Port Royal, South Carolina, every participant in the New Year's celebration of 1863 was touched when Dr. William Henry Brisbane, "a native Sea Island planter turned abolitionist" who had freed his slaves before the war, read the Emancipation Proclamation aloud. Colonel Higginson, newly arrived commander of the First South Carolina Volunteers, accepted a flag for his regiment, prompting blacks present at the festivities spontaneously to sing "My Country, 'Tis of Thee." Though Bryant later contended, perhaps prejudicially, that "but few [of the freed people] understood the importance of the change," initially he maintained that the former slaves "have more reason to celebrate than we do on July 4." They were raised from the lowest condition in creation "and now have the rights which God desires for all of his people."[44]

The record of blacks in the Federal army strengthened the conviction that was growing in various Northern quarters that the newly freed men and women in America's society deserved a better lot. A black soldier at Port Royal expressed this hope in the poem "Coosaw Island":

> Have I been tried with the good sword of Steel
> Yet I deny that ever a man did made me y[i]eld
> For in my body there is strength,
> As by my manhood may be seen
> and I with that good sword of length.[45]

John Bryant's fortunes had languished and then risen with those of his black troops. By early 1863 he had evidently become impatient to put his relationship with Emma Spaulding to the test. He was at the time under court-martial and therefore not in the strongest position to press his suit, but John could always argue convincingly that he was on the side of right. In any case he was "truly sick," he said, of Emma's "non-committal letters." They could continue with the "farce" of being brother and sister, but if so, he must seek another, "dearer friend." For him their platonic relationship had clearly served its purpose; he was now ready for a serious commitment. Was she willing to be his lover? He wanted her to "be free" and to "love him freely," he said, probably meaning the latter more than the former. Alarmed and perhaps frightened by his bluntness, Emma drew back and asked that he send "no more love letters." JEB, turning sarcastic, then revealed the other side of his persuasive powers. Had she tired of love letters "in flashy love stories?"[46]

Emma Spaulding seemed to be struggling with her captain's reputation as she examined her feelings for him. She frequently asked about the progress of his trial and apparently tried to retain John's goodwill while resisting his charms. But he was characteristically relentless. He sometimes wished he were with "a darling friend" there in the Sea Islands while she was so far away, but he would "try to practice [faithfulness] as well as preach." That he thought he could find such a "friend" was perhaps presumptuous; "you know I am egotistic," he apologized in an understatement of some proportion. John's new status under Saxton afforded him another twenty-day leave on June 14, 1863. This time he concentrated on his mission and returned to camp with Emma's commitment to marry him. The salutations that had begun as "dear little sister" and later became "my darling sister" now read "my darling."[47]

By July 1863, Bryant had the authority to recruit his own unit of black troops and was promised the rank of lieutenant colonel when the regiment was complete. Throughout the summer and fall of 1863, as he continued to work toward his goal, he enjoyed the special favor of Saxton, who by November allowed the captain from Maine to pass through Union lines whenever he wished, "a privilege he grants to no other person under his command," Bryant reported. By November also, JEB had been nicknamed "The Scout," and Higginson called him "the most experienced scout in that region."[48] Saxton allowed him to "cross into enemy country with as many men" as he desired and gave him authority that was unique among officers under the general's command.

One expedition that earned him prestige was the attempt to tap Confederate telegraph lines on the mainland of South Carolina. Although

Bryant claimed in his letters that he had suggested the mission, the history of the Eighth Maine Regiment (perhaps written by Bryant) actually attributes the failed scheme to General Gillmore, who then commanded the Department of the South. In any case, JEB directed the mission, which succeeded only temporarily. Bryant, a former officer from the Eighth Maine, and his black company in the First South Carolina Volunteers went "far up the Combahee River to cut the telegraphic wires and intercept dispatches. . . . They ascended the river, cut the wires, and read the dispatches for an hour or two. Unfortunately, the attached wire was too conspicuously hung and was seen by a passenger on the railway train in passing."49

Bryant's account of the foray emphasized the "safe route through the enemy's country" that he had selected, which enabled the party "to move undiscovered between [Confederate] picket posts." They chose "a secluded spot in the woods near a road for the receiving station," and by daylight they were ready. Messages were received until 10:00 A.M., "some of which were of great importance to General Gillmore," but "owing to the unskil[l]ful manner in which the connection had been made by the operator, their operations were discovered about 10 A.M." Though the rebels discovered the attempt and took several of the men prisoners, the Northern press praised the raid for its daring and, because of it, had occasion to emphasize the courage of black soldiers under pressure.50

Bryant returned from a similar exploit in mid-November 1863 to learn that he had been reported "dead or captured." When he arrived for Sunday dinner at the home of Mansfield French, where "teachers and friends of the freedmen" lived, he "found them just mourning my loss." Happy that his "Christian family and friends" had thought so well of him, John was "flattered." French had written to Bryant earlier, "I think you have a mission to perform for the country and for humanity."51

Bryant maintained his friendship with the missionary band at Port Royal, and his relations with military personnel apparently improved as well. Certainly JEB's witness to the performance of black soldiers under fire found its way into the reports that Higginson and Saxton returned to Washington. The most complete account in Bryant's records relates an expedition in late November 1863, when Bryant led Companies E and K of the First South Carolina. The raid was successful, and Bryant was particularly pleased to report the bravery of the black troops while being chased by "mounted riflemen with half a dozen trained bloodhounds. . . . Near the landing on the Rebel shore the last of the Blood Hounds was killed," he reported to Higginson. "I send it to you as a trophy because when alive it is one of the worst enemies to the colored man." In speaking of the courage of the men, Bryant went on to exclaim, "Are they not Veterans? Yet all were a few months ago Slaves, Cattle, Mules, Horses with no rights which white men were bound to respect. . . . I can truly say that it was the proudest day of my life . . . witnessing the bravery of these black men." In his official report, Saxton commended Bryant's "skillful guidance" of the mission. He was obviously proud that the black troops conducted themselves "as cooly as if they had been on dress parade." He concluded, "I regard the expedition of Captain Bryant as a most daring one, and its whole conduct reflects great credit upon his bravery and skill."[52]

Newspapers, meanwhile, were also enthusiastic. One applauded the "gallantry of [this] Maine officer," who "for some time past has been a thorn in the side of our 'secesh' neighbors." Another declared that "Captain Bryant has gained quite a reputation among the rebels by his visits of late." JEB himself, content at last that "fickle fates now smile," claimed to Emma Spaulding that "perservance [sic] conquers!" Bryant was especially gratified when one Adjutant Raynolds, whom Bryant described as "the direct cause of my trouble" and the one "who did all in his power to have me dismissed," came to the captain and admitted that he "had done wrong and congratulated me on my success." John felt that he was "never higher" in the regard of the officers of his own company, the Eighth Maine.[53]

Basking in the warmth of this success, Bryant contemplated the end of his army term in September 1864 and the law partnership that awaited him as a civilian. The military had afforded him new legal experience. After his successful trial, other officers had requested that he defend a comrade.[54] Friends in the army urged him to request a promotion, which, they said, surely would be his for the asking, since they expected him to go on to further glory in the military.

The attempt to raise a black regiment, however, was proving to be a struggle, and Bryant was "succeeding slowly." He claimed that "Gen. Gil[l]more will offer me a position of Colonel of a colored regiment. The offer," he said, "I shall not accept." The reason for this decision became apparent later in the month when a slot for lieutenant colonel in the Eighth Maine became available and Bryant chose to try for this instead, confident as he was that "all my friends will try to have me promoted."

Yet, despite several letters to the governor, including the commendation of General Saxton, who called JEB "a brave, intelligent, and efficient officer," and the praise of Mansfield French, who described him as an "honest and honorable man"—one whose "manly and soldierly bearing reflect honor on his regiment, as his *name* strikes terror to the hearts of the rebels, wherever they believe him near"—Bryant failed to receive the promotion in March of 1864. He reported that "a letter from the North" arrived, "and I learn that I am not promoted."[55]

It was not surprising, perhaps, that Bryant was passed over, for he was still identified with the anti-Rust faction that had attempted to discredit the colonel of the Eighth Maine, and an informant was reporting to Rust on Bryant's activities. The attempt had failed, for though a military court had ruled to dismiss Rust, "he was restored by the President through the influence as we suppose of Vice-President Hamlin, Ex-Governor Washburn and others." Though Bryant claimed that he "stayed out of the effort to punish [Rust]" (and credited Emma with the decision that he would do so), it was unlikely that the colonel would forget Bryant's former hostilities. Keenly disappointed, Bryant reacted to the news of his denial first by planning to resign from the army before the summer of 1864. A reappraisal of the situation, however, and the support of General Saxton convinced him that waiting to leave when his term expired in September 1864 would be better.[56]

A third leave, beginning on May 29, 1864, allowed him time to think of other things. Throughout the winter of 1863–1864, Emma Spaulding's parents considered moving west, apparently for financial reasons. John worried that Emma might go with them. He urged her to stay in school and sent money several times to help with her college expenses. He was proud of her academic record which included at least one term when she led her class. In June 1864, he attended her exposition, and they were married before he returned to the coast. The captain, over six feet tall, with dark eyes and hair, was now a handsome young man of twenty-seven. He had convinced Emma, presumably nine or ten years younger, that her future with him would be secure and happy.[57]

Reflecting the nineteenth-century belief that females were morally superior to males, John called Emma "my little angel" and even anticipated that she might bring him back to the church. "I need someone to make me good," he had written her in the fall, but he then added characteristically, "though I am not remarkably bad now." In a revealing exchange, alluded to above, Emma had urged John not to seek revenge against Rust. "I will acknowledge, Emma," he wrote, "that the love of revenge is as strongly implanted in my nature as a love of flirting is in yours. You have broken yourself of that and I will break myself of this." Once again he described her as his "angel."[58]

The decision to remain in the service through the summer of 1864 afforded Bryant the participation in frontline action that he had coveted and that, until then, the war had denied him. He served with General Saxton as provost marshal in Beaufort from February 15 until July 12, 1864, but then his orders compelled him, at last, to rejoin his regiment, which was a part of the Union forces facing a desperate but determined Southern army outside Petersburg, Virginia. As he reluctantly permitted JEB to leave the Department of the South, General Saxton wrote, "In parting with Captain Bryant the Brig. Genl. Commdg. [Saxton] desires to express his high appreciation of the soldierly qualities, the energy, and efficiency which Captain Bryant had ever manifested in the performance of his duty in this command."[59]

In Virginia, Colonel Rust's desertion ironically left Bryant in command of the Eighth Maine just at the outset of the historic Battle of the Crater on July 30. Desertion was, at least, the official charge when Rust failed to assume his responsibilities at the appointed place. Though he claimed illness, he later "failed to file . . . the necessary surgeon's certificate of disability." Faced with actual battle and unable to remain on shipboard as he had in Florida, Rust confirmed the suspicions regarding his character. "In this regiment," Bryant wrote, "where I was in arrest four months and from which I came near being discharged . . . , I am the commanding officer. And if nothing unforeseen prevents, I will cause Rust to be discharged."[60] He would have his revenge after all.

Bryant had found his welcome among the men "cordial," but the morale of the soldiers was low. Especially after the confusion and loss in the battle following the great explosion and creation of the crater, Federal troops were reluctant to face Confederate fire again. Many were "playing sick." Bryant remarked, "Can you wonder when they have a man like Rust to set the example?" News from the North did not cheer the captain. He read of the widespread war weariness, an attitude matching that of the military, and was horrified that some Northerners desired "peace at any price": "If so I do not wish to be a northerner. I would a hundred times rather be a Southerner. Oh! for a nation of brave men! . . . A Southern faction have rebelled and fight—we are ten to one: they are brave and make up for a bad cause by valor and shall we like great cowes [sic] bellow and give up! God forbid! . . . Are we after all a cowardly nation. I have my fears."[61]

Amid all the gloom, as the soldiers endured weeks of trench warfare, Bryant thought it unnatural that the outside world could be brought so close to the place of death on the battlefield. "The news-boy brought the daily papers, and the postmaster the mail, and the men read letters from dear ones at home while the enemy's shells burst, and their bullets fell around them." The Eighth Maine never did, however, become a part of the actual first line of fire. When the fighting did begin, it became their task to be the second line, "to prevent stragglers from passing to the rear." Panicky soldiers pressed against them "to break through, but the men from Maine held firm, and the rout was staid, the troops were rallied and the enemy repulsed."[62]

Bryant resumed command of his old Company C in mid-August and was grateful to relinquish responsibility for the entire regiment to a newly arrived major. Late in August, on the eve of his retirement from the service, Bryant was finally offered the promotion that he considered so long overdue. "The governor has sent to me a majors commission. Shall I accept it?" he asked. But the honor was too late in arriving, for Bryant by this time was determined to leave the army. On September 4, 1864, he and sixty other veterans of the Eighth Maine whose term of service had expired left the regiment and traveled to Maine. There they were mustered out of service on September 15. On that day, the regiment's battle flag, "torn by bullets," was presented to the governor "by Capt. Bryant to be preserved by the State as evidence of the dangers through which the regiment had passed."[63]

It appeared for a time that the turmoil of the war years was over, but Bryant's work in the South and his concern for blacks had not ended. Neither was the future to be secure for John and Emma, no matter how happy. In the fall of 1864, JEB studied law and prepared to take the Maine bar examination. Not many months later, however, General Rufus Saxton, his former commander and supporter, asked Bryant to join him in the new work of the Union among the former slaves in the South, the Freedmen's Bureau. Bryant was not reluctant to accept this new challenge.

Three

Presidential Reconstruction

I am a true friend of theirs.

The Civil War essentially ended at Appomattox in April 1865. Long before that date, however, federal officials were considering the proper policy for Reconstruction, and long after that date they continued to debate it. The transition of administrations following the death of Abraham Lincoln did nothing to answer the crucial questions of who would determine policy and how the Southern states would be returned to full political participation in government.

In the months of so-called presidential Reconstruction, April 1865–March 1867, President Andrew Johnson's rather generous policy of amnesty allowed the South to operate under the illusion that its old life had not been totally destroyed. Since he continually allowed Southern leaders the choice of whether to accept or reject federal proposals, "the legitimacy of their resistance was established." Southern political life went on, though in the stunned atmosphere of defeat. Perhaps a ceremony allowing Southerners to "act out" defeat would have been cathartic and would have encouraged acceptance of Reconstruction. Or perhaps the assumptions of reconciliation were so flawed that Johnson's policy was doomed to fail. In any case, old-style politicians were left to think that their accommodation to the policy was necessary. Their first effort to pick up the political threads, however, resulted in such recessive measures as the state Black Codes, which severely restricted blacks' freedom and represented solutions that the North would clearly find unacceptable. The attempt at "self-reconstruction" was a failure.[1] Meanwhile, men such as Bryant, who soon felt vitally concerned with the political process, were for the present wholly taken up with the immediate needs of the people who had experienced the effects of war most keenly.

Bryant returned to the South, assigned to the Freedmen's Bureau in Georgia. As a Northerner with radical views on slavery, he was viewed with suspicion by Southerners—as were most Yankees. Northerners had started to go south by the end of the first year of the war, and by 1866 the stream had become a flood. Some of the newcomers had served in the Union army during the Civil War, had fallen in love with the South's warmer climate, and now were returning to settle there. Bryant himself had complained about the sand flies and heat during the summers at Port Royal but had appreciated the abundance of fruits, vegetables, and flowers in the Sea Islands. He had written in 1864 to his future bride, "I have learned to love the climate in Georgia and would like to live here if 'twas for the best."[2]

The Yankees headed south because of the weather and for other reasons. Many settlers were idealistic teachers and clergymen, as the missionaries at Port Royal had been, eager to help former slaves achieve their full potential. Some, like Bryant, were assigned to government agencies. Others had hopes for legitimate business ventures, lured perhaps by speculators who saw the need and opportunity for capitalists and entrepreneurs to rebuild the South.[3]

Whatever their original motives for going, the Yankees' involvement with Southern politics led to the coining of a new epithet, "carpetbagger," which gained wide currency after Republican political activity increased in 1867. Richard Current's definition is more or less standard: "The men called carpetbaggers were white northerners who went south after the beginning of the Civil War and, sooner or later, became active in politics as Republicans."[4] It is frequently overlooked that these carpetbaggers brought wives and families as well as their political views into the South.

Not all the carpetbaggers were opportunistic or corrupt, as the term once implied. As business efforts failed or appointments ended, the transplanted Northerners sometimes turned to politics for their livelihood.[5] Often circumstance or the desire to work for change drew them into public life. Race relations in the South particularly attracted Northern Republicans. After all, the reform wing of the Republican coalition party of

1854 had been an important element, comprising those with abolitionist sentiments who believed that the evils of slavery could be dealt with most effectively in the political arena. Some of the carpetbaggers after the war were the political heirs of this group, honestly concerned to see blacks attain their civil rights. Despite ambiguous evidence, it appears that Bryant belonged to this group. His natural inclinations and convictions led to his work among the freed men and women at Port Royal. Then, too, in returning to the South after the war, Bryant was responding to the call of the person he had respected most during the conflict, one who had championed black rights—General Rufus Saxton.

Like others who agreed to work in the South, Bryant was accused by his opponents of trying to "make a living out of the blacks," of "shameless frauds," and of "stirring up jealousy of races."[6] This estimation of him differed greatly from that of Mansfield French, who had called him a "true and reliable friend of the freedmen" at Port Royal and one who had a mission to them and to the nation. In order to reconcile these conflicting views of Bryant, two of his problems should be remembered. Not only was he one of the victorious enemy, but he was viewed as an abrasive extremist. A primary cause of the Northerners' failure in the South was their inability to win the confidence and support of the majority of the white population, although, ironically, they shared many of the South's inherent ideas and racist attitudes. Bryant's enemies would include Southerners as well as Northerners who thought he went too far or who questioned his motives. But Southerners frequently did not distinguish the opposing viewpoints of the Yankees. And among the conquerors, although they had anticipated some resistance, few expected the social ostracism that confronted even those with genuine concern for the future of the region and its people, both white and black. Bryant himself claimed that, when he arrived in the South, he "knew nothing of the prejudice against Northern men."[7]

The extent to which Bryant and the other so-called carpetbaggers should, as a general lot, be considered corrupt and wholly taken up with their own political futures depends upon the background against which they are viewed. Former abolitionists as well as Republican politicians saw politics as the most promising avenue for reform in the South. The matter of Bryant's contribution to the freed slaves must be evaluated both from the viewpoint of his political critics and also from that of the individuals who stood to benefit from his ideas. From the beginning of his stay in Georgia, Bryant identified himself with the needs of blacks and sought to aid them in the transition from bondage to citizenship. Whether or not his motives were purely humanitarian is not altogether clear. It seems unlikely that Bryant or any other white politician of his time was able to separate the cause of the former slaves from personal ambition, but complexity of motive in itself does not invalidate his contribution. For Bryant to take up the cause of blacks when even Republicans were divided on the issue called for a certain amount of courage (though he probably underestimated the amount required). Bryant himself expounded on mixed motives in defending himself against charges that he was a "schemer for [his] own ends." "Two motives governed me [in deciding to stay in Georgia]; one selfish; one philanthropic," he wrote. "One was to provide for myself and family, one was to do good to others. . . . Most of the time since then, my labors have been more for others than for myself. I have made as great sacrifices for others as I was able to make. . . . I have felt that I had a work to do here. I have done that work to the best of my ability."[8]

Just as pertinent to evaluating carpetbaggers' success or failure as their motives and integrity was their attitude of superiority. These men were ambitious, usually young, with an enormous ego and confidence that they could not only succeed in making a living in the South but could also straighten out the errant ways of the rebels. The question of the carpetbaggers' honesty has often obscured their fault of arrogance toward Southern whites, an attitude very close to the racism that clouded relations with Southern blacks. The carpetbaggers, in many cases, seem to have been intent on "northernizing" the South.[9] Bryant certainly was, as will be seen.

Parts of Georgia were ravaged by war, as were other Southern states that felt the wrath of the Union army. General Sherman's famous "march to the sea" had left a swath of desolation sixty miles wide between Atlanta and Savannah, while marauding bands had effected similar destruction in other scattered areas. Some counties were untouched by the soldiers, but the entire state felt the devastating results of an economy that had collapsed, its labor system destroyed. Poverty clutched at blacks and whites alike.

Saxton had summoned Bryant to Georgia to become an agent of the Bureau of Refugees, Freedmen, and Abandoned Lands, better known as the Freedmen's Bureau. The agency had been conceived during the war, when slaves began deserting their masters and fleeing to the Union lines; the country needed ways of feeding, clothing, and employing these runaways. By the time the war ended, there was drastic need for a unified governmental plan for resettling the former slaves. The official title of the bureau indicates that confiscated Confederate lands were expected to play an important role in such a settlement. The land proviso of the bill stated that every male refugee or freedman "shall be assigned not more than forty acres" of abandoned or confiscated land as rental for three years and an option to purchase at the end of that time with "such title thereto as the United States can convey."[10] The rather vague language of the bill portended the difficulty that would come in implementing it.

Actual establishment of the Freedmen's Bureau had been delayed until March 1865 because of the internal administrative battle over control of the agency. The Treasury and War departments each wanted the new bureau under their auspices, but the War Department, headed by Edwin Stanton, finally claimed it. Unfortunately, the problems of starvation, destitution, and chaos following the war, coupled with difficulties caused by Yankee speculators and exploiters crowding into occupied areas of the South, did not wait until the bureau had found a parent agency. Other problems stemmed from the fact that no special funds were to be allocated for the bureau, since it was administered by the War Department. The bureau was therefore unable to pay adequate salaries and was forced to draw heavily on military personnel. The situation allowed for the possibility, too inviting for some, of graft in collecting fees. Military storehouses provided supplies of food and clothing when needed.

The Radical Republicans were concerned to keep the agency under their control. Their choice to head the bureau was Oliver O. Howard, former commander of the Union's Army of the Tennessee, a man the Radicals felt they could bend to their purposes. William McFeely has shown that, while Howard is remembered as a great Christian soldier who sympathized with the freedpersons, he lacked the will to fight for the basic economic and social reforms needed. Particularly demoralizing was his work in the crucial months of presidential Reconstruction when the bureau's policies were being formulated. While the problems grew to epidemic proportion, Howard, unfamiliar with the situation, was forced to rely on the advice of others, agreeing now with one and then with another of the factions involved. Ironically, the bureau actually came to be used by

President Andrew Johnson, "with the compliance of Howard, to subvert radical purposes and advance conservative ends."[11]

The plight of General Rufus Saxton and agents such as John Emory Bryant, whom he handpicked for the bureau, most clearly exemplifies the internal struggle to determine the policy of the Freedmen's Bureau. Saxton believed strongly that blacks should be given land of their own; during his command of the experiment at Port Royal, South Carolina, he had struggled to give the former slaves permanent possession of the land they farmed there. Saxton himself had been a possible candidate for commissioner of the Freedmen's Bureau. Since General Howard had visited Port Royal and seemingly approved of Saxton's methods, however, Saxton willingly supported Howard's appointment. Howard in return named Saxton assistant commissioner for Georgia, South Carolina, and Florida.[12]

Saxton's concern that blacks be given permanent land titles or be allowed to buy them in a protected market was shared by a few persons such as Mansfield French in Port Royal, Thomas Wentworth Higginson in Massachusetts, and Senator Charles Sumner in Washington. The plan was fiercely opposed by many others, including President Johnson. Admittedly the issue was not simple, for it involved the constitutional question of federal jurisdiction over land and the status of the defeated South. Under the Constitution of the United States, the punishment of traitors could not extend beyond their lifetime to descendants. If former Confederates were defined as traitors, their confiscated property would therefore be only a temporary possession of the government. Lincoln had not taken a hard stand on the issue during the wartime debate, but for Johnson the matter was plain: "The war . . . was not a war between Governments, but . . . the overthrow of traitors."[13]

The complexity of the question did not obscure the morality issue for Saxton and others. Blacks had earned the right to the land, such people believed, because they had worked it for generations. A committee from the American Missionary Association expressed a similar view to President Johnson early in the summer of 1865, while the matter of land for the former slaves was still being debated. Emphasizing federal responsibility for the persons who had been freed, it suggested using public lands covered by the Homestead Act if blacks could not remain on land of their own where they were.[14]

The Homestead Act, it might be assumed, was the ideal solution. First proposed in 1864 and passed in 1866, the Southern Homestead Act was an attempt to extend the original Homestead bill of 1862 to include public and confiscated lands in the South with other acreage open for settlement. The bill, however, never fulfilled its potential of giving blacks an economic base for freedom. (It was used only to a limited extent, as in the case of one colony of blacks who traveled from Georgia to Arkansas.) Through a combination of mismanagement, white opposition to blacks' ownership of land, and the inability of blacks to raise the necessary capital for an initial investment, the Southern Homestead Act was for the most part a failure. Likewise, blacks had little opportunity to settle western lands. There was prejudice against blacks in the West, where residents opposed the migration of former slaves, and Southern landowners feared that their labor force would vanish. In short, the blacks' chances to become economically independent were few and far between.[15]

In Georgia the consequences of this oppressive combination of prejudice and fear could be seen soon after the war. A group of planters met in Savannah early in June 1865 and expressed their anxiety in a letter to General Howard. The slaves' idea of freedom was "fanciful," they wrote; "control of the planter[s]" would be "lost" without restraints for the former slaves, and labor would cease. To prevent starvation and chaos, these representatives of the old regime made the following suggestions: (1) "military or other physical force" should be employed to enforce discipline and labor; (2) the Freedmen's Bureau should issue public orders requiring laborers to remain on plantations and on farms to harvest crops; and (3) no government rations should be given to those who deserted plantations between planting and harvest times for the crops.[16]

The planters expressed a prevalent prejudicial view of what the former slaves were likely to do with their freedom; they also anticipated some of the worst social and economic problems in the defeated South. Unfortunately, the Freedmen's Bureau did not have single-minded direction to meet the crisis. Agents on the local level became experimenters, while officials in Washington debated policy. Howard's first order reveals an open-endedness destined for failure when he said, "Do all that behooves the Government in answering the question, 'What shall we do with the Negro?'" Saxton translated this directive when he wrote to John Emory Bryant in the summer of 1865: "Persons under your charge must be protected in all their rights, and encouraged in their industry, schools will be established wherever it is possible." Recognizing the obvious lack of policy guidelines, he continued, "The Freedmen's Bureau is but just starting on its mission and we have no past experience to guide us in the performance of the peculiar and delicate duties which pertain to it." In light of this deficiency, Saxton defined the problem facing the bureau. We must, he said, "rely in a great degree upon the earnestness and good judgment and sense of justice of those who have its interests in charge. Let us strive so to conduct its affairs that it shall be a power in the country and a blessing to those in whose interests it was established."[17]

Saxton had signed the orders, dated May 1, 1865, that appointed Bryant, then almost thirty years of age, to the post of "General Superintendent of the freedmen" in the city of Augusta, Georgia, and vicinity. Bryant arrived without Emma Spaulding Bryant, who stayed in Maine with relatives. Bryant apparently had ideal credentials for work with the bureau. Not only was he from the North, which Saxton preferred, but he was relatively familiar with the life-style and capabilities of the Southern Negro because of his work with Saxton in the Sea Islands during the war. Furthermore, one might assume that his military background would help him ease the potential strain between military and civilian personnel in the bureau, though this could easily be a false assumption. Many military persons staffed the Freedmen's Bureau, but not all were like Bryant in meeting Howard's primary requirement of having sympathy for blacks. Martin Abbott states that the military personnel used in South Carolina held views that were not consonant with Howard's aim. Rather, the military personnel there resented the extra work the bureau required.[18]

The historiography of the eras of slavery and Reconstruction as it attempts to define racism and paternalism illustrates the difficulties that confront twentieth-century writers who attempt to understand the nineteenth-century mind. Chapter 2 discussed attitudes toward slavery as distinct from attitudes toward blacks; now, after the Civil War, a similar compartmentalization continued. It is important to distinguish between the benevolent regard of a Higginson or a Bryant and the bias of a confirmed racist. But to regard the former as paternalistic raises other questions. As the word has been defined by Eugene Genovese and more recently by James Oakes, "paternalism" connotes a stable order of prescribed classes, with blacks assigned to a lower class than whites. This definition well fits the attitudes of paternalism in the New South, but it cannot encompass the radical ideology of Republicans such as Bryant. More will be said later about this dilemma. In any case, Bryant himself seemed at times to suffer from what C. Vann Woodward has called "the old sickness endemic among the crusaders"—racism.[19]

During the war, Bryant, like many other officers, for a time enjoyed the services of a personal valet, a former slave named Jim. Accompanying the captain to Maine on one occasion and being left alone in New York, Jim took the opportunity to "miss" his sailing time for return to South Carolina. Bryant continued to await the arrival of "my boy Jim" throughout his stay at Port Royal. He remarked to Emma Spaulding, "Beneath his dark skin is a soul which perhaps has been entrusted to me. He has a mind which I will try to develop and send him out to do good to his own race." There is no record that Jim ever returned. On another occasion, Bryant offered to send black servants, a couple whom he described as "smart and good people," to his fiancée's family. He planned to keep them for his own household if his future bride approved.[20] There is no confirmation that she did or that they ever engaged such servants.

These nagging stereotypes notwithstanding, John Bryant continued to gain education on the issue firsthand. Soon after arriving in Augusta he attended a meeting of former slaves at which his old friend Mansfield French and others preached. Bryant wrote of the great solemnity of the blacks and of how, after the benediction, "they could hold in no longer." There was singing, jumping, and clapping of hands. "It was a wild thrilling sight. I wish you could have seen it. These people are smart. They know what freedom is as well as I do and they are as happy as I should be to become free if I had been a slave. It does my soul good to witness their joy. They almost consider Mr. French and myself their deliverors [sic] and wherever we go they all want to shake hands with us. Everywhere there was the uniting of families. Oh! such happiness."[21]

All was not happiness, nevertheless, as John was soon to learn. In the first months of the bureau's existence, it was concerned mostly with the problems of starvation and disease among the throngs who were living in filth and inadequate housing. Poverty-stricken blacks crowded into the cities. For some, newly freed, the city was a place to look for relatives from whom they had been separated by slavery. For others, the city meant enjoyment of a mobility unrestricted by white persons, where "freedom was free-er." Vagrancy was a real problem, and many whites, such as the planters quoted above, were convinced that this proved what they had long contended: "Negroes would not work without compulsion and could not work without white supervision."[22]

Saxton's orders to Bryant advised that blacks should remain on the land and begin "at once upon cultivation of their old plantations now abandoned by their rebel masters." The former slaves were to be given the option, however, of going to the seaboard. Bryant was to carry out "such measures for the benefit and protection of the freedmen as may seem best to you or as the Government may from time to time direct." The option of the seaboard represented the coastal lands that had been given to blacks under the provisions of General W. T. Sherman's Field Order 15 in the last months of the war. Sherman had designated the coastline and riverbanks thirty miles in a belt from Charleston to Jacksonville as an area exclusively for Negro settlement. Under Saxton's extended jurisdiction, these new lands along with the Port Royal acreage were to be given to blacks with "possessory title" in farms of not more than forty acres per family. Blacks were to be protected by the military until they could protect themselves or until "Congress shall regulate their title." Rumors of the land provision in the bill that created the Freedmen's Bureau and actual designation of the coast for black settlement by Sherman sent the former slaves streaming toward the seaboard. As one observer reported to General Howard, the "big question of blacks everywhere is: How can we get land of our own?"[23] They crowded into the cities, seeking transportation to the shore.

Nothing more graphically illustrates the prevailing confusion in Georgia than Bryant's dispatches to Saxton through the summer of 1865. JEB described "much suffering" in the city of Augusta, where he set up a hospital but desperately needed a doctor. The resources of the military commissary from which Bryant obtained supplies, he rightly feared, would not be "enough for the destitute and suffering." There was frequent difficulty in coordinating civilian and military authority, as illustrated by the red tape that prevented Bryant from obtaining supplies and providing quick transportation for blacks. Even direct orders from General Saxton had to be routed through certain channels. At one time Saxton's aide and brother Willard Saxton wrote, "I do not understand why transportation should be refused when proper requests are made. . . . I will try to have it made all right." Apparently Saxton began to doubt the wisdom of his order giving blacks a choice as to where they would settle. On June 12 he wrote, "Why must the freedmen go to Savannah? Leave [them] where they are if possible." Bryant, as the agent on the scene, was pained "to see suffering caused by my inability to get transportation."[24]

Through the summer of 1865, Saxton held resolutely to his plan to settle the former slaves on confiscated lands and to make permanent the titles already held. Howard seemed to uphold him in this decision for a time, but by autumn the blacks were being dispossessed by President Johnson's order that land must be returned to pardoned Southerners. Agents of the bureau were urged to dispel "the erroneous idea" that the government intended to "distribute lands" and were directed to encourage blacks to sign contracts agreeing to work on the lands owned by whites.[25]

Validating these contracts represented an important aspect of the bureau's work in protecting whites from blacks who did not live up to their contracts and preventing the former slaves from accepting unfair wages and working conditions. John Emory Bryant gained immediate notoriety when his formulation for establishing fair wages was published in Georgia newspapers. He outlined responsibilities for planters and freedpersons alike and warned that failure to honor contracts was a "grave offense." As one of only a few bureau agents on the mainland in Saxton's jurisdiction, he was immersed in case after case of contract disputes.[26]

White Southerners did not always appreciate such activities, believing that bureau agents want to "interfere in our domestic affairs," as one diarist, Ella Thomas, expressed it. Mrs. Thomas was unable to face the "insolence" of blacks who delivered a message to her home on one occasion. "I went into the room . . . where Mr. Thomas was reading the note," she wrote, "and found it was a summons from the Yankee Cap. Bryan[t] in Augusta summoning Mr. Thomas to appear before him to answer to the demand of these Negroes for wages." Another irate Georgian complained to Washington about being brought before "the Star Chamber Court of John Emory Bryant, saviour of the freedmen." Mrs. Thomas commented in a later entry, "The Negroes suddenly emancipated from control were wild with their newly gained and little understood freedom. Cap Bryan[t] of the Freedmans Bureau aided as much as was possible in sowing broadcast the seeds of dissention between the former master and slave and caused what might have continued to be a kind interest to become in many cases a bitter enmity—the Negro was the all absorbing theme which engaged all minds." She continued passionately, "The Negro and Cap Bryan[t]!—The Negroes regard him as a Savior. (They are just beginning to discover the cloven foot.) Someone once remarked to Andy Johnson that 'his name stunk like carrion in the nostrils of the Southern people.' A strong expression but I know of none which will so well express my sentiments for the man who thus presumes to interfere in our domestic affairs."²⁷

So widespread and pernicious did Bryant's reputation among white Georgians become that Charles Stearns, novice planter and self-appointed Yankee missionary to blacks, traveled from his nearby plantation to Augusta to check out the notorious agent. "Whoever else among the Northerners might be decent men," Stearns understood from what he had been told, "Bryant was the impersonation of depravity. . . . At length [an associate] and myself ventured to pay him a visit, not without many misgivings as to his true character, as we had heard so much said against him." He went on to say, "We returned from our visit perfectly satisfied that Col. Bryant's only offense was that of defending the rights of the colored people; and as such, our hearts immediately warmed towards him as to a true defender of the principles of Christianity, as manifested in his self-denying labors." Stearns admitted that "without a doubt, Col. Bryant had faults, as who is wholly destitute of them?" But he was "persuaded that the greatest crime [Bryant] then committed, was in defence [sic] of those who had none to plead for their behalf."²⁸

The Freedmen's Bureau was indeed to protect the civil rights of the former slaves, intervening in cases where courts had not been reestablished or where the testimony of blacks was not allowed. Often a single agent or a court of three persons (one chosen by the planter, one chosen by the black or blacks, and the bureau's agent) improvised as a court for minor offenses. Bryant found in the fall of 1865 that in numerous cases the bureau had to defend the rights of blacks, and he asked Saxton to provide a special legal counsel for the bureau in each city. "My reasons for making this suggestion," Bryant wrote, are that "this [legal] dimension of the service is immense and necessarily increasing and requires agents of legal ability." Bryant was sure that Northern lawyers who had the Negro's interest at heart could be encouraged to come South. "A class of men will be engrafted into Southern society who will assist in changing public opinion at the South. Unless something of the kind is done I fear for this poor downtrodden people, when the military authority is withdrawn." Moreover, he found it "impossible to attend to the legal business and at the same time attend to the other duties required of me."²⁹

One of the severe problems of the bureau was the inadequate number of agents for the many tasks required. Saxton, concerned more with qualifications than with numbers, deliberately appointed a limited number of agents. Abuses were rampant simply because the difficulties were severe. One observer for the bureau visited Augusta and wrote that the people were "beaten" and that they submit "but mostly in a grumbling manner." Too many of them "vent their spleen" on the Negroes, and "there are constant outrages, mainly by planters, but some by negroes. The agent of the Bureau here, Capt. Bryant, is overwhelmed with such cases and with other work. I have stayed here this long in order to get his status defined and acknowledged by the military authorities. One of the most [word illegible] troubles are the opposition and mean tricks of the military. I have been contending with them ever since my arrival."[30]

The problems would have been immense in even the best-run branch of the organization. In Saxton's vast operation for all of South Carolina, Georgia, and Florida, troubles abounded, and Howard soon reduced Saxton's jurisdiction. Already in July 1865 there were complaints that Saxton was overextended and understaffed. One agent telegraphed to Howard, "Nothing has been done in South Carolina save by military authorities. Things are going by default. Gen. Saxton should be here & S.C. is [as] much as he can positively attend to."[31]

It would be too facile to conclude, however, that the complexities of a three-state area were unmanageable. McFeely has noted another reason for Saxton's loss of authority and has outlined the extent of the general's personal sacrifice. By the fall of 1865, agents of the bureau who were too radical for President Johnson's taste were gradually being moved out of their positions. Some were quietly transferred to the Washington office; others were offered military promotions with substitute assignments. According to McFeely, when Saxton was presented with the choice, he refused both options. Unwilling to see the Freedmen's Bureau change policy and cease to give blacks their much-needed economic base in landownership, and loath to betray his personal promise to them, Saxton dramatized his stand by insisting that he be fired. He " 'would not touch [other options] with a thousand foot pole.' He flatly refused to deprive the freedmen of the last service he could render them—the publicity attendant on his being removed for taking their part in the struggle for land in the South." In one of his last official statements before he was removed by Howard, Saxton stubbornly insisted, "I find no limits to the time the possessory titles under Gen. Sherman's order were to run."[32]

The question of land for the Negro was rapidly becoming nonnegotiable. Saxton was one of the last officials to fight the tide, and by January 1866 he was no longer an official of the Freedmen's Bureau. Saxton's removal had obvious—and ominous—implications for John Emory Bryant. Saxton's replacement would immediately seek to undo the "harm" done by JEB's abrasive style and by his clear sympathy with the blacks.

General Davis Tillson, formerly bureau superintendent for the district of West Tennessee, was appointed assistant commissioner of the Freedmen's Bureau for Georgia in December 1865, replacing Saxton. Tillson had actually been in the state since early fall, as acting assistant commissioner, following up the report that Georgia, with the "largest black population of any Southern state," was in a "more demoralized condition" and in "need of more attention" than any other state. Tillson, a native of Maine, had served under General Howard in the Army of the Tennessee. Despite the recommendation that someone "besides officers from the Army of the Tennessee" be appointed to the bureau, Howard continued to draw from the leadership of the group he knew best. Furthermore, Howard knew that Tillson would please President Johnson, since Tillson had been recommended by a friend of Johnson's in Memphis. During the summer of 1865, Tillson himself corresponded with Howard about his appropriate place within the bureau.[33]

The planters in Georgia were also pleased with Tillson's appointment. So sympathetic with the whites was Tillson that Howard had to warn the new appointee, "Try not to alienate the negro by too apparent endorsement of the wishes of their former masters." One cannot say without qualification that Tillson disregarded the need of blacks. He seems rather to have possessed a paternalism that failed to see any possibility of altering the existent class structure of the South, though he admitted that new laws "regulating labor [would] drive the freed people to seek land and homes of their own." As he put it, "This desire on their part resembles an instinct, and is almost uncontroleable [sic]. I hope Congress will take some wise action which shall enable all well disposed and industrious freed people to gratify this very natural and [word illegible] wish." Tillson nevertheless insisted on written labor contracts and forced the freed men and women to accept contracts made for them if they had not found work by January 10, 1866. The *Augusta Daily Chronicle and Sentinel* cheered on the day of the deadline, "Time will soon pass when idling and loafing about the streets will be tolerated by the authorities."[34]

The major reason for delay among the former slaves in signing the contracts for 1866 had been the persistent rumor and last hope that land would be given them at Christmas 1865 or on New Year's Day 1866. One reporter observed that those newly freed "understand that the Government is their friend and protector," but there is great disappointment that there will be no land to distribute, "as they had certainly been encouraged in such hopes." They are extremely desirous of securing land, "but as there is no land except in the possession of the whites and as they are not very willing that the colored people should be allowed to become land owners[,] great obstacles are placed in the way of their doing so besides that which in most cases their poverty would offer." Even among blacks the "idea that lands will be distributed is rapidly losing hold. The hope will soon disappear." Thus, though many whites displayed paranoid fears that there would be riots when the former slaves were disappointed, the holidays passed uneventfully.[35] Supporters of land distribution such as Rufus Saxton were gone from the Freedmen's Bureau, and local agents such as John Emory Bryant were forced to use other means to carry on the struggle.

Early in January 1866 Bryant received notice that he was "dropped altogether" as an agent of the bureau because Tillson was hiring "no civilians but clerks." He had anticipated the dismissal, but he was unwilling to let the matter rest. Believing that Saxton might still carry some weight in the hierarchy of the bureau, Bryant wrote to the general and asked that he be allowed "to act as counsel for the freedmen before the military and civil courts" in his old districts. He expected to receive no salary for this but would "receiv[e] fees from them in payment of my services." Bryant claimed that his life had been threatened and was in danger because of his "radical" stands on behalf of blacks and that he therefore needed the protection of some association with the government. He maintained that his records proved he was "someone who is truly a friend to the freedmen . . . I am a true friend of theirs." He further reminded Saxton, "I have fully sympathized with you in the policy you have carried out." Bryant's evaluation of Tillson, on the other hand, was predictable: "I fear that Genl. Til[l]son tries too hard to please southern men and believing that, no act of his would give them more pleasure than my removal from all connection with the Bureau." He then went to the heart of Tillson's attitude, as he saw it: "I think Genl. Til[l]son will labor with zeal to give the freedmen justice but I judge he has but little sympathy for them as a people and will not labor personally to elevate them."[36]

Saxton was unable to grant Bryant's wish to remain associated with the Freedmen's Bureau, but JEB refused to accept the fact that he had been dropped from the rolls. Perhaps with Saxton's encouragement, he continued to identify himself with the work of the bureau until the summer of 1866, when Tillson made it impossible for him to do so. Tillson was soon to have his fill of John Emory Bryant.

The policy concerning the political activities of bureau agents had always been vague. Theoretically, their work with blacks was not to be political, but at the same time they most closely linked the freed slaves with the national government. While legislators in Washington debated the role the bureau should play in securing rights for blacks, it was an easy step for agents in local situations to instruct their clients in new political concerns.[37] Bryant lost no time, in his new tenuous relationship to the bureau, in acting on his belief that blacks should seek ways to secure their rights. Freed from his former tiresome duties as bureau agent, Bryant the political organizer went into action. Under his leadership, the Georgia Equal Rights Association and its newspaper, the *Loyal Georgian,* were born in January 1866.

On January 10, 1866, representatives from the black population of Georgia met in convention in Augusta. Thirty-eight delegates from eleven counties gathered on the morning of the first day; leaders expected the number present to be "greatly enlarged" in the evening. A broadside urging attendance purported to address individuals interested in mobilizing blacks for political action. (Bryant noted later that no whites had responded to the call.) Blacks other than official delegates were welcome as observers, as were General Tillson and the mayor of the city. The latter two individuals received special invitations to attend, as did "the various ministers of the city." Bryant, also a "visitor," participated actively in the proceedings. As might be expected, contemporary spectators as well as later historians charged that Bryant directed the activities of the convention. The issue involves the matter of black autonomy and remains difficult to assess. Certainly the former bureau agent enjoyed the confidence and trust of the Georgia blacks present and took a strong leadership role. After some floor discussion he was elected president of the newly formed Georgia Equal Rights Association (GERA), described as "friends of impartial justice in Georgia." As Bryant himself recalled in his speech before the council of the GERA in April 1866, he was elected because the convention was "desirous of securing the practical assistance of white friends."[38]

That a group of blacks in Georgia was able to meet in an orderly convention and make concrete decisions doubtless had a great psychological impact on both black and white citizens in the state. The *Loyal Georgian* called it "the most remarkable incident in the history of the state of Georgia." After having first adopted strict rules of order, the convention heard a congratulatory speech by General Tillson. Tillson's remarks outlined the meaning of freedom, pointing out that for blacks it would not include suffrage, a limitation that Tillson defended on the basis of their lack of education. (He noted, however, that this deficiency did not disqualify white voters.) The burden of Tillson's remarks was that blacks must work to be worthy of any privileges. Their first duty was to cultivate "kindly relations" between themselves and whites, with success in such relations requiring "a kind and conciliatory spirit" on their part. Tillson did not miss the chance to praise the officers of the Freedmen's Bureau and the bureau's mission. He underlined his insistence on work and labor contracts, which he expected to enforce. The tone of the speech was much like that of a later black leader, Booker T. Washington, as Tillson urged blacks toward "patient, kindly industry," so that "sooner or later your rights as a people will be freely conceded."[39]

Tillson left a series of "General Orders" that were read to the convention after he departed. The orders were endorsed by the delegates, who were well aware of the importance of the Freedmen's Bureau for their protection. Equally aware that the bureau would not endure forever, the delegates addressed a poignant plea (possibly written by Bryant) asking the Georgia legislature to enact laws that were fair and just. Referring to their own faithfulness during the recent war and before, they appealed to the legislature's "wisdom, sense of justice, and magnanimous generosity." The "dust of our fathers mingle with yours in the same grave yards"; this is your country, "but it is ours too . . . ; your fathers fought for it, but our fathers fed them."[40]

These petitioners had no ambition merely to fill a niche in some paternalistic scheme. With eagerness they predicted to the solons that their youth "will be aspiring to the positions of doctors, lawyers, ministers, army officers, and every capacity in which they can represent the interests of their people." The appeal also mentioned specific needs such as jury duty, civil treatment on railroads, and suffrage.

Again, this group was conscious of the limitations of the Freedmen's Bureau. The afternoon session that day focused on pressing needs of blacks in the state, needs not being met by Tillson's agency. "Owing to their large numbers [of complaints], it is almost impossible for [the bureau's agents] . . . to adjust every grievance which occurs through the various counties." The delegates were urged to form care committees "in every town and neighborhood" for relief of suffering and "to see after the education of our children."[41]

The issue of education was clearly a concern of the convention, but not the primary focus. The committee on education made a report (which was unfortunately not printed in the proceedings), and as noted above, the members were enjoined to encourage education once they returned home. G. L. Eberhart, "Supt. of colored schools in the state," addressed the convention and reported an enthusiastic response among freed men and women to the opportunities for education across Georgia.

The primary business of the convention came on the third day, with the election of officers of the newly created Georgia Equal Rights Association. The question of leadership was important to those present, and the matter of having a white president was debated. Nevertheless, the majority report of the nominating committee was adopted, and John Emory Bryant was elected president of the new association by unanimous vote. Other officers elected were recording secretary, treasurer, and vice presidents from each county represented.

On the fourth day of the convention, the new president addressed the assembly. He spoke immediately to the issue of white leadership and promised to work hard and not to betray their confidence. He stated the purpose of the GERA, which was "to aid in securing for all, without regard to race or color, equal political rights." Bryant optimistically predicted that "a large number of the white race, friends of freedom and progress" would join with those in attendance. In this first speech before the group, Bryant gave a brief history lesson, covering such American milestones as the Declaration of Independence, the Constitution, the causes of the Civil War, and the end of slavery. Skillfully, and not inconspicuously, he underlined the role of the Republican party and linked the party's goals to those of the newly formed association. Then, echoing Tillson's words, he urged the blacks to be industrious and, where possible "with respect," to cultivate friendly relations with their old masters. "You ask political, only political equality; conscious that social equality does not exist." He promised to aid them in securing "fair compensation" for their labor and then enjoined them to uphold their part of the bargain by diligent work. Bryant also seemed hopeful that the performance of blacks would win converts to their cause. "The best men in the state," he continued, "intend to be just, and although justice in their estimation may not mean equal political rights, yet exemplary conduct on your part will perhaps induce them to advocate even those."[42]

At its conclusion, the convention passed a series of far-reaching resolutions that were justified by the "duty" to "define our position" and that embodied the tone of optimism and goodwill that Bryant's speech had set. The resolutions asked for full legal or civic equality for blacks, condemned "vagrancy and pauperism among our people," claimed the right of trial by a jury of peers and just compensation for labor, and claimed the recognition of black men's "full dignity of manhood." Concerning the all-important land question, the convention asked that the government sell land to blacks at prices they could "pay without embarrassment."[43]

The constitution of the GERA reflected the concerns of the first convention as outlined in its resolutions. It adopted the motto "Peace and good will to all" and outlined officers' duties at the state and county level. The primary purpose of the association was to create an organization that represented black males, giving them a lever for political and civil action. To carry out this purpose more effectively and to facilitate grass-roots participation, the officers divided the entire state of Georgia into districts.

Bryant was probably correct in assessing the event as remarkable, though not so much in the sense that he meant. The comment perhaps reflected his ambiguous racism and at the same time his increasing appreciation for the ability of blacks. More remarkable, beyond the meaning he intended, was the fact that he and the GERA were well ahead of the majority of Republican leaders in Washington and preceded by more than a year the official birth of the Republican party in Georgia. Still, there was Bryant, defending equal rights and expecting blacks to move into professional occupations, work cooperatively with whites, and become productive citizens.

The GERA's council, composed of the president and vice-presidents, met in April 1866 with twelve counties represented to conduct business and to follow up on the January resolutions. The gathering gave President Bryant a chance to reiterate his vision in another flowing speech that most white Georgians would doubtless have called an effort to "stir up bad blood," a fact that Bryant himself acknowledged in his address. He prepared his listeners for opposition but urged them to perseverance. One urgent item of business was the association's newspaper, to be discussed below. Another matter requiring action was the association's constitutional provision that it have a political representative in Washington. At this April 4 meeting, Henry M. Turner was chosen to be the lobbyist. Turner had been one of the invited participants at the January convention. Born in South Carolina of free parents, Turner became one of the state's outstanding black leaders. He had served as the first black chaplain in the Union army and later rose to the rank of bishop in the African Methodist Episcopal church. He remained active in Georgia politics for a time and continued to be a good friend of Bryant's, though he eventually became disillusioned with Republicanism.[44]

In his letters to Bryant from Washington in April 1866, Turner soon reported some ground for disappointment. He indicated that the few Democrats whom he had seen "treat me scornfully." Still, he was able to meet with some prominent Republican leaders, who assured him that "Mr. Johnson shall execute that civil rights bill, or leave his seat. They also say there is more on hand, when they get ready to enforce it, and they will do it." Turner suggested to General Howard that copies of the Emancipation Proclamation, civil rights legislation, and other pertinent information "should be . . . distributed like tracts" to the thousands of blacks in the South, a plan Howard seemed to accept, though there is no evidence that he acted on the suggestion. Turner was eager to have copies of the GERA convention's proceedings sent to him in Washington, so that he could inform the legislators of "our efforts."[45]

The initial relationship between the GERA and the better-known Union or Loyal League was tenuous, though the two organizations had somewhat compatible aims. The league had been created in the North during the war as a society to support Lincoln, his unionist policies, and the entire war effort. After the war the Union League moved south, though it was somewhat changed in character. As the league became instrumental in organizing blacks for political action, most white Unionists in the South gradually dropped out, unwilling to be associated with activities among blacks.[46]

Bryant himself claimed to have received the charter for the Union League in Georgia. This claim must have referred to JEB's "commission from the Union League of America," issued on September 16, 1868, giving him "power to install subordinate councils within and for the said state of Georgia." But Henry P. Farrow, a Southerner and Unionist, was the recognized head of the league in the state. Bryant, on the other hand, had immediately turned his attention to the organization of the GERA. It is tempting to speculate on the competition that might have existed between the two men and their organizations. The seeds of later political rivalry between John Emory Bryant and Henry Farrow may have been sown here in the early months after the war.[47]

Nevertheless, cooperation was clearly in the best interests of all. As early as April 1866, the council heard that a chapter of the Union League in Macon wished to unite with the GERA. The council's action was to approve its affiliation as a "subordinate association" and to ask the Savannah Union League to join as well. The meeting of the entire Georgia Equal Rights Association in October 1866 took action toward an even broader goal when a committee was appointed "to confer with the Union League, for the purpose of uniting all the friends of equal rights in one convention."[48] The members of the committee later reported, however, that they were unable to agree on a plan of union, specifically with Savannah, and the merger was not effected until 1867.

The educational work of the association, noted above as a concern at the January convention, was handled through what Bryant, in the beginning, called the Georgia Educational Association. But by October 1866 an expanded name for the entire organization showed the added emphasis on education: The Equal Rights and Educational Association of Georgia. Blacks were eager to learn and to pay what they could for their own schools. Bryant, as president of the GERA, advocated education as a significant means for advancement, and he felt that the most effective means of educating blacks was through their own efforts. Perhaps Bryant came to this belief from observing the inadequate work of the Freedmen's Bureau. Crippled as it was by lack of funds, the bureau was forced to rely in large measure on the work of Northern missionary societies, with the bureau aiding these voluntary efforts with the use of buildings and supplies when possible. The schools of Savannah, Georgia, were a "model for other cities," since they were both self-supporting and under black control.[49]

To accomplish this same goal throughout the state, Bryant planned to organize the Educational Association in each county, creating committees that would establish schools. Students and their parents would pay operating and maintenance expenses insofar as they were able. Bryant encouraged the training of black teachers rather than continued reliance on overcrowded schoolrooms with a single white teacher. Other observers concurred in this need for normal schools to train black teachers.[50]

But not all educators agreed with Bryant. G. L. Eberhart, superintendent of Georgia schools and on Tillson's payroll, preferred Northern white teachers, despite the opposite preference of blacks. According to Bryant, Eberhart "had little confidence in the ability of the colored people to organize associations and support teachers." Nevertheless, even General Howard supported the project of the GERA for schools, and the Georgia bureau worked with the GERA for the most part. Howard's letter of endorsement is one of many that Bryant obtained from prominent men as he traveled in the North seeking monetary aid for educational work in Georgia.[51]

The nature of education offered to Southern blacks after the Civil War has recently received close scrutiny. According to at least one historian, the philosophy, curriculum, and intent of the American Missionary Association (AMA), which was a major force among the Northern societies and later with the Freedmen's Bureau as well, was not "to liberate" but "to bind" the former slaves; that is, to instruct them in the merits of a paternalistic society and acceptance of their place in it—on the bottom of the structure.[52]

While John Emory Bryant had worked with the AMA at Port Royal and while he continued to correspond and cooperate with the AMA in building schools in Georgia, his vision of education apparently did not agree with this alleged philosophy. He did expect education to be the key to black achievement, but in educational programs he did not intend to bind the race to a prescribed and limited role. As already noted, he expected education to lead to real social mobility. In addition to Bryant's own glowing accounts of his efforts for education, various records do confirm that the Georgia Educational Association of the Georgia Equal Rights and Educational Association was complimented on its efforts, first with the Freedmen's Bureau and the AMA, and, in time, with the public education movement. Remembering the faith in education that permeated JEB's youth, it is entirely consistent that he now believed that education would "unlock all doors" for blacks, just as it had for him.

Not surprisingly, some people rejected Bryant's leadership. In 1867 Bryant would uncover a scheme of Eberhart's to use the popular reputation of the GERA for his own advantage. After calling a convention with the sponsorship of the association, Eberhart planned to unseat President Bryant and to remove his influence from educational work, even as Tillson had successfully removed him from the Freedmen's Bureau. Uncovering the effort spurred Bryant on to a political maneuver, the sort of coup he loved to concoct. In a letter to E. P. Smith of the AMA, he reported that, "when I found . . . [Eberhart's] plans [to discredit the GERA] were well laid, and that he was backed with considerable influence, I feared that the cause [of education for blacks] would be seriously injured." Therefore, Bryant claimed, he moved that there be a slight change of name to "The Board of Education of the Georgian Education Association" and a combination of "all the friends of the education of the colored people into one organization." He accomplished both by electing to the newly created board all "those men who had opposed our Association." "I secured," he went on to claim, "the election of Genl. [John R.] Lewis as President of the Board, becoming myself simply a member." Bryant triumphantly concluded, "Thus all opposition to the Association was killed." Apparently, the tactics of Eberhart were exposed as well. Others concurred with Bryant that Eberhart did not really have the interests of blacks at heart, for he was replaced as educational superintendent of the Freedmen's Bureau the next month.[53]

In his account, Bryant had naturally put the best face on what may have been his ouster. One must note, however, that (1) by the time the change occurred, his political involvement *was* compelling and time consuming; and (2) he supported a valid choice for the GERA's new leadership. The wisdom of Lewis's selection was borne out by his continued involvement in education. In addition to his post of assistant commissioner, which began in October 1868, he held the position of the Freedmen's Bureau's superintendent of education for Georgia.

Bryant's decision in 1867 to focus on the rising political tide of Republican politics did not diminish his support for education. In his correspondence he assured Smith that he could guarantee that five black associations in his region alone would support teachers the AMA might send. He would, he said, "continue to do what I can."[54]

But the incident with Eberhart would come later. For the present, John Emory Bryant was the president and preeminent spokesman for the GERA and editor of its newspaper, the *Loyal Georgian*. The paper provided a voice for the association and added a measure of cohesion to its activities.

The paper came into being early in 1866 through GERA's purchase of the *Colored American,* a newspaper "established by an enterprising colored man in . . . Augusta." The Union League had purchased the *Colored American* and published it until the GERA was formed. According to Bryant, a debt of $370 accrued by the older publication was assumed by the GERA, another tantalizing detail in the uncertain relationship between the two groups. If the league supported the new newspaper, the help must have been minimal, for the *Loyal Georgian* continued to be in financial trouble throughout the entire first year of its three-year existence. Bryant had originally anticipated that the black community would support the paper by subscriptions, but these proved inadequate. Other fledgling Republican newspapers in the state experienced the same difficulty.[55]

Trying to broaden the base of the paper's support, Bryant sought funds from sympathetic Northerners. Likewise, Henry M. Turner, the GERA's representative in Washington, attempted to interest congressmen in subscriptions. Both envoys for the *Loyal Georgian* found more "interest" and verbal "support" than actual money and subscriptions.[56]

Happily, it was possible for the *Loyal Georgian* to exert some influence over the freed men and women, even though most of them were illiterate. The paper, a weekly, was simply read aloud to many black congregations on Sundays after the church services. This practice provided a forum for ideas, knit blacks together, and served as a means of educating them regarding their new rights and responsibilities. Bryant estimated that as many as "two or three thousand" attended these meetings in "many of the counties." In 1867 he reported that the paper was read in this way in "about fifty [of 131] counties." He further claimed that the GERA had little difficulty in locating "one or more" readers among the black population in each county to perform this service.[57]

As the association's official organ, the *Loyal Georgian* had as its stated aims to advocate "the cause of justice and equal rights; to labor to secure for all citizens equal civil and political rights; to labor to educate the people of the state; [and] to assist . . . in the transition from slavery to freedom."[58]

It should be noted that, as Bryant pressed his sanguine philosophy of equal civil and political rights, legislators in Washington were debating the nature of citizenship and whether freed slaves should be guaranteed political rights. Bryant did not wait for legislative direction from the national party but relied on the local press to push forward the educational movement of the GERA and Republican ideology as he understood it. In the first issue of the paper, on January 20, 1866, the editor sounded very idealistic and confident about the future of race relations: "We do not propose to discuss the question of slavery; we shall so far as our influence extends, strive to bind up the bleeding wounds which it has left. . . . We shall labor to secure for *all* good wages and kind treatment." Then, addressing the question that he imagined had arisen in the mind of his readers, editor Bryant acknowledged, "There are many lazy white men, and, also, many lazy colored men, but we believe that human nature is the same in both cases. We shall especially encourage education and improvement among the colored population. . . . [We] shall use our influence to settle any difficulty that may arise [between blacks and whites]. . . . Our effort shall be . . . to assist in making Georgia the most prosperous and wealthy state of the South." In this editorial, Bryant continued the hopeful and conciliatory tone of his own speech to the GERA, in which he had closed with an appeal to all Georgians: "The truest philosophy and the wisest policy is to accept the situation and breast the storm. . . . We recommend to every honest heart and pure mind to consider the claims of these people and give them a patient hearing."[59]

Some people in Augusta and in Georgia did not share Bryant's optimism; they would interpret his interference with established customs as arrogance and would consider the conciliation he expressed as meant for another time, another planet. Outrages against blacks mounted, and one black woman noted, "Our friends in Congress are wasting time and breath, and all the bills they may pass will do us no good unless men are sent here that will see those laws enforced. . . . God knows it is worse than Slavery. The negro code is in full force here with both Yankees and rebels."[60]

Just as some Southerners made life unbearable for the former slaves, so they made it extremely unpleasant for many Northerners by ostracizing them from community and social life. Teachers with missionary groups, some agents of the Freedmen's Bureau, and other Northerners such as Bryant faced close to total rejection by most whites. The wives of the carpetbaggers faced special problems of isolation, since they had neither the political associates their husbands enjoyed nor the dedication to a profession that motivated the teachers. Emma Spaulding Bryant joined her husband in Augusta in February 1866. Homesick at first, she found little to make her feel welcome.

An unfortunate series of events, reaching a climax in July 1866, began on April 20 with the mysterious poisoning of the Bryants' dog. Then on April 27 a seemingly harmless incident brought the seething animosity between Tillson and Bryant to a head. Emma Bryant and the children of one of the black schools were to place flowers on the graves of Union soldiers, but town police, their action sanctioned by Tillson, prevented the children from entering the cemetery. Mrs. Bryant wrote despairingly in her diary, "O Southern loyalty!" Tillson later denied that he had opposed their putting flowers on the graves, objecting "simply to the *time and manner of doing it.*" He claimed merely to have suggested that the children wait until another day when they could have armed escort; he wanted "*to promote harmony and kindly feeling* between the races." Charles Stearns, Yankee planter, remembered it differently: "There was no excuse for the pusillanimous conduct of Gen. Tillson . . . in refusing to protect the colored people in strewing flowers upon the graves of the Union soldiers. . . . for this dastardly conduct he was rightly denounced with unmitigating severity, by Col Bryant." Stearns went on to explain that Augusta whites did not object to the Northern white teachers' decorating the graves, "but no procession of 'niggers,' for this purpose, should desecrate their really beautiful cemetery."[61]

Bryant's denunciation did not go unnoticed. On April 30 an unknown assailant attacked him from behind with a club, in a "most cowardly and brutal manner." Emma Bryant recorded in her diary on June 20 that the ladies she passed on the street "spoke insultingly," and the next day John was refused service in a soda shop. Soon afterward, Emma Bryant left the sultry Georgia tempers and summer heat for a cooler Maine. She wrote wistfully to John the following fall, "I sometimes think of our enemies with the hope that they will sometime know us better and dislike us less." And again later, "I sometimes wonder whether the time will *ever* arrive when we shall be on friendly terms with the Southern people. If it can be, without any concession of principle on our part, I would be glad but it seems scarce probable to me." It seemed that Bryant's cousin in Maine had not been far from the truth when he had warned, "People say that with your ideas which you so boldly advance that your enemies will kill you and I am sometimes afraid that they will."[62]

A newspaper account of the assault, identifying Bryant as an agent of the Freedmen's Bureau, found its way to General Howard in Washington. He immediately wrote Tillson, asking for a complete account of the incident.

Tillson confirmed the fact that Bryant had indeed been "attacked in a most brutal and cowardly manner, as stated." But he added, "Capt. *Bryant* is *not* an officer of the Bureau, or in any way connected with it. . . . I am compelled to state, that Capt. Bryant's course recently has been such as could benefit no one but himself, and well calculated to provoke hostility. No officer of the Bureau is in any danger whatever of being attacked in this city, so long as he conducts himself as a gentleman."[63]

Tillson and Bryant had clearly developed widely divergent concepts of the place blacks should occupy in society and how best to help them. While Bryant was pursuing politically oriented activities and giving "radical" advice, Tillson was urging blacks to settle down, work for better wages, and cease to "struggle on alone" for their own property, the land question being "of no practical value." He felt, on the other hand, that preserving the goodwill of the Southern planters was the first priority for stabilizing the South. "For without their aid," he wrote, "with their sullen indifference, even 50,000 soldiers cannot sufficiently protect the freed people of Georgia."[64]

Perhaps both men were partly right. In any case, the conflict between them erupted into verbal feuding as the summer progressed, again arousing Howard's interest in what was happening in Augusta. According to Tillson's version, Bryant had printed a "false and malicious statement misrepresenting the official conduct of [another agent] and myself," a charge that received wide circulation. Tillson felt that Bryant had written stories about him in the press that were "devoted to producing an impression in the North, very likely for political purposes." Bryant maintained that, prior to that reproach, Tillson had "publicly asserted that I [Bryant] have deceived the colored people of this city and vicinity, and that I have charged them exor[b]itant fees for assisting them before the court: I pronounce these charges false." Tillson had also "publicly made the assertion" that Bryant had "been guilty of illicit connection with colored women," which he also vehemently denied. Tillson felt justified in fighting his fellow Down-easter with any weapon: "I don't like killing skunks," he confided in a private letter to General Howard, "but being compelled to enter the contest I propose to [word illegible] the crowd. Those who may be incidental[l]y hurt must stand from under."[65]

Bryant suggested that an impartial committee, similar to the ad hoc courts of the Freedmen's Bureau, be assembled to settle the charges between the two men, "with the understanding that the finding of this committee may be made public if either you or myself desire it." Tillson rejected this suggestion, maintaining that Bryant was "a disturber of the peace and dangerous to the safety of the community." Denied the opportunity to clear his name, Bryant threatened to publish his request for a trial in the *Loyal Georgian* and to brand Tillson's allegations against him as lies. To prevent the publicity and "apprehensive that the threatened publication, if permitted, would lead to violence and probably to bloodshed," Tillson put the office of the *Loyal Georgian* under armed guard until he himself received the next paper issued and could reassure himself that Bryant had not carried out his threat.[66]

Tillson claimed that he "should have arrested" the radical editor but had restrained himself, awaiting the action of a grand jury. He was able, however, to send Howard an article from the *Loyal Georgian* bearing the caption "Let Us Rally Around the Flag," in which blacks of the city were asked to bring in contributions "for Bryant," though Tillson did not specify the details of the cause for which Bryant solicited. "Could anything better establish the truth of what I have before written you," Tillson queried, "that this man is living off the negroes. . . . A reaction is already begun, many colored people are already suspicious of Bryant, who is now engaged in collecting money in the colored churches for his private use." Tillson apparently never considered the possibility that Bryant's work with the GERA and the *Loyal Georgian* might be of genuine benefit to the blacks of Georgia. JEB himself sent the same clipping to Howard and denied that the solicitation had been made by him. The request turned out to be a letter signed by a black man and addressed to the freed men and women of Georgia, asking for contributions to aid their old friend.[67]

The uproar between Tillson and Bryant coincided with the visit of Generals James B. Steedman and Joseph S. Fullerton, presidential advisers who were touring the South for President Johnson in the summer of 1866. Distrustful of the work of the Freedmen's Bureau and unsure of his control over it, Johnson attempted to block the passage of a new Freedmen's Bureau bill that sought to extend the life of the agency and to provide it with appropriations for its program. Johnson carefully picked the two men to make the report. Fullerton had served under Howard during the war and had been on the general's staff in the bureau for a time. He had made the trip to Georgia in the summer of 1865 and had severely criticized Saxton's work as ineffective and inefficient. While he was in the bureau, Fullerton consistently urged Howard to yield to presidential attitudes concerning the agency, and after leaving Howard's staff he worked more directly for Johnson, for example in the mission to the South.[68]

The manner in which Fullerton and Steedman conducted their investigation produced a barrage of complaints from agents of the Freedmen's Bureau throughout the South. They wrote to General Howard that the presidential envoys made their visit "brief and pleasant but very superficial." Their report was replete with "inaccuracies"; it "greatly falsified facts." Several agents accused the examiners of choosing "no loyal white citizens" to question but only "the most radical Southern men." Perhaps a few blacks were called on, but "no leading colored citizens"; the former slaves were "not fairly represented." One newspaper charged that "President Johnson seems to have sent out [Steedman and Fullerton] to collect information damaging to the Freedmen's Bureau"; another agent, feeling misjudged, summed up the outcry: the visit of Steedman and Fullerton was "unfair," and their report could not possibly be accurate "unless they be gifted with the powers of intuition."[69]

In Macon, Georgia, Steedman and Fullerton conducted an open meeting that attracted a crowd of one thousand. Hundreds more could not get in. In something of a circus atmosphere, people heard "witnesses" speak for and against federal policy. Though the judges denied that they had come "to wipe out [the] Bureau" and claimed that they were merely obeying orders, Steedman elicited from one witness the opinion that the "rich white/former masters" were still the "best friends" of the former slaves.[70] Before the tour and the report were completed, however, Congress had passed the new Freedmen's Bureau bill over Johnson's veto, and the two investigators hastily concluded their futile mission.

Steedman and Fullerton not surprisingly gave the bureau in Georgia a fairly positive evaluation, for Tillson, a "staunch supporter of Johnson," was moving the bureau there in the direction the president desired. A minority report was more critical, stating that some agents in Georgia "incited turbulent spirit among the blacks." It might be assumed that John Emory Bryant as a former agent was considered one of the troublemakers. Tillson, on the other hand, was called the "most capable" officer the investigators had met.[71]

General Tillson's plan for the bureau had endeared him to white Southerners as early as the fall of 1865, when he spoke to the Georgia State Convention and promised that the bureau would not require social equality between whites and blacks and that it would not allow blacks a life of ease with no work. He proposed soliciting the help of some two hundred native Georgians to serve as bureau agents in Georgia. While the need was great (Saxton had purposely restricted the number of agents to ensure high standards in their qualifications), the background of the appointees would obviously make it less likely that the civil rights of freed men and women would be protected. As one newspaper reporter commented after hearing of the plan, "Any disinterested man who will read that address carefully, *must,* and *will,* see that it is a low effort to pander to the barbarous prejudices of the traitorous slaveholder, from beginning to end." If Tillson was a friend of the former slaves, he concluded, they should "beware of friends." Further testing credulity, Tillson asked Governor Johnson to "instruct the justices of the peace and ordinaries of the counties to act within their jurisdiction as agents of the Bureau." As Tillson explained, "the Administration of justice through unusual channels necessarily occasions dissatisfaction."[72]

The "dissatisfaction" among freedpersons that might be expected under this system apparently did not concern Tillson. It is not surprising that former slaves seeking justice, with the cards thus stacked against them, welcomed the professional services of John Bryant and considered him their friend. One black minister wrote to JEB asking for protection from "officers of Tillson" who had threatened to revoke his preaching license if he maintained his membership in the GERA. Other blacks, he wrote, were too intimidated even to celebrate Independence Day on July 4. He pleaded with Bryant to do something: "But the people was a fred to do mutch and if there can be any[thing] don to stop these things we will be glad if you would do so." Despite Tillson's allegations, Bryant continued to have the support and trust of most blacks. H. M. Turner, after hearing of the battle with Tillson, wrote Bryant from Washington that he needed only to ask if he lacked money or aid, for "you have friends in this state by hundreds."[73]

While the civil case that Tillson initiated against Bryant was pending, the council of the Georgia Equal Rights Association met in July 1866 to review for itself the charges against the president of the organization. Its findings were that Bryant was completely innocent of defrauding the former slaves and of misconduct. While endorsing Bryant, however, the council did recognize the potential danger to the association's viability if it became embroiled in controversy with the Freedmen's Bureau. The members therefore asked that the *Loyal Georgian* henceforth not be used as a forum for the personal conflict between Bryant and Tillson. Silenced temporarily and awaiting his formal hearing, Bryant traveled in the North during August and September 1866, attempting to gain subscribers and contributors for the needy *Loyal Georgian*. He almost surely attended the Union League Convention at the end of the summer of 1866, since he was in Philadelphia at the time. With Tillson's chief critic out of the state for a while, one observer wrote in September, "The Bureau is in the hands of old proslavery secessionists who look after the interest of the white man [and] not those of the freedmen."[74]

Emma Spaulding Bryant, away from her husband and concerned about the proceedings in Georgia, hoped that Bryant's travels would bring him to Earlville, Illinois, where she was visiting her father and sister. Following his itinerary, she planned for their reunion and expected to travel with him back to Georgia. There are indications that pregnancy may have been one reason she left Georgia so hastily in the face of hostility there. Without mentioning grief, she later confirmed that the pregnancy had been terminated, presumably by miscarriage, and that she was feeling better. By September 1866, however, Emma realized that she would not see her husband before he returned to Augusta. In her letters she compared Bryant with Tillson, whom she considered a "hypocrite," asking that John never "in political scheming be induced to take yourself or encourage in others any step inconsistent with Christian dignity of character." She added, "I had rather that we would live poor all our days than you should do so." She hoped his decision to concentrate on the *Loyal Georgian* "may be temporary," until finances allowed him "to lend your energies to the law." Finally, she reminded him of the danger he faced in Georgia. "Be sure and use every caution while you are in Augusta, won't you? Do not go out *alone* in the evening," she wrote.[75]

In October JEB returned to Georgia without Emma to face the grand jury and charges of "deception toward colored people and [charging] exorbitant fees." Again, the charges could not be proven, and the case against him was dropped. Thus released, Bryant concentrated on solving the *Loyal Georgian*'s financial problems. Though its debt had been reduced by contributions of $1,426 from the North, the paper was still not solvent. Bryant scraped and attempted to borrow an additional $2,000 to support it, even trying to borrow from his father-in-law in Illinois. (The family was distressed to learn of his financial plight but could not help.) Bryant next proposed that the creditors of the *Loyal Georgian* form the

Loyal Georgian Publishing Company and sell stock in the company as a means of financing publication. The stock was sold, and operation of the paper continued with Bryant as managing editor. Bryant had originally planned to have a black man and a white man serve as coeditors, thus emphasizing the aim of equal rights, but for unknown reasons the plan was abandoned.[76]

Tillson himself meanwhile faced removal from his post in Georgia, though he was "retained in the service until December 1st," 1866, in order to settle once and for all the nagging question of dispossessing blacks on the coast. A new investigator from Washington had evaluated Tillson's effort and had found it "not altogether satisfactory to the colored people, and I think so far as I have seen, they have some cause for complaint." The number of civil agents appointed by recommendations of citizens should be reduced; they may be "respectable citizens," but "I could not ascertain that their political antecedents and loyalty to the Government were especially considered [in their appointment]."[77]

Another reason to question Tillson's leadership was the abuse of federally funded transportation for black workers in Georgia. Instead of using the privilege to benefit blacks, only "Negrobrokers and employers" were aided. Howard's second investigator reported that agents, "slavebrokers before the war," were gathering up unenthusiastic blacks and transporting them at governmental expense to plantations that contracted for them. The workers "do not settle down but work only one year or less," and are "anxious to return" to the place from which they were taken. The report implied that Tillson both knew of and may have benefited himself from this practice, which, in the investigator's opinion, "should be greatly restricted." The bureau's policy of relocating black laborers in the Washington area had been suspended in April 1866 after similar abuses.[78]

Some people certainly would not miss Tillson. One teacher in Georgia wrote to Bryant, "Would to God that candor and justice had influenced the Republicans and General Tillson [had] shown up in his true colors. . . . The manifold acts of injustice perpetrated by him, have tended to miss the good effects of the best institution [Freedmen's Bureau] ever formed for the good of a people, and to cause that people to wish it had never existed." Change was at hand, however, for in Washington the Radical members of the Republican party were winning the battle for control of Reconstruction. Even General Howard would lose effective authority when the bureau came under military command in 1867.[79]

In Macon a large group of blacks, well exceeding the number who had gathered in Augusta in January, convened the second meeting of the GERA, now called the Equal Rights and Educational Association of Georgia, and welcomed Bryant home on October 29, 1866. In his "annual address" as president, Bryant reviewed the activities of the year, highlighting the organization of "subordinate associations" in fifty counties. In reporting on the financial situation of the *Loyal Georgian,* Bryant urged and received approval for the stock company, the Georgia Publishing Company (first called the Loyal Georgian Publishing Company), which he had formed to bear the expense of the association's publishing venture. Likewise, he did not miss the opportunity to blame Tillson's "false" charges against him as one reason why contributions from individual members of the GERA had proved inadequate for supporting the paper.

President Bryant continued by projecting aims for the work of the GERA in the next year that included a greater effort in education and a reduced emphasis on politics. Elated over the passage of the Fourteenth Amendment and anticipating the new Reconstruction legislation of 1867, he also instructed the delegates on the means and potential of congressional authority. With another short history lesson, he reminded the convention that the Civil War had been fought primarily to save the Union; equal justice for the former slaves must now be guaranteed by the (Republican) Congress.

Bryant doubtless foresaw that the Union League and the Republican party would take up the political function formerly carried by the GERA, and as previously noted, this October meeting brought a move to unite the GERA with the Union League. But for the time, he urged the neophyte political activists to "lay low," discuss education at their meetings, and see what the new year would bring from Washington. Bryant himself stated to the convention that "there are . . . , in Georgia, three parties who think alike, the Republican party, the Equal Rights Association, and the Union League." The final merging of these organizations did not come until 1867, and with it renewed encouragement to political participation. But Bryant could report, even in October 1866, that the *Loyal Georgian* was the only newspaper in the state that represented all three groups, and the Georgia Publishing Company could rely on the support of both the Union League and the Republican party.[80]

Impatiently awaiting the changes that the pending Reconstruction Acts

Title page of the *Proceedings of the Freedmen's Convention,* Augusta, Georgia, 1866. (Courtesy of Duke University Library.)

would make in Georgia, Bryant acted after the convention to make permanent his own commitment to the state. In conjunction with an old army friend, Captain C. C. Richardson, Bryant established a law firm in Augusta and in December 1866 completed, via the state of Maine, the formal procedure for being admitted to the bar. Thus ensconced as a citizen of Georgia, but without his wife in residence with him, Bryant anticipated a public-service future for himself and success that could bring "position and money."[81] He also saw a political career as an avenue for helping the "degraded race" whose cause he had adopted. Politics, he expected, would provide a more effective platform for his radical ideas than he had previously found. As the presidential phase of Reconstruction passed into the congressional phase, JEB's metamorphosis from abolitionist Yankee to carpetbagger was complete.

‖ Four

Congressional Reconstruction

I have done as much as I can do for the Republican party of Georgia.

The events of presidential Reconstruction had proven to Northerners that little had changed in the South. Furthermore, with the election of former Confederate leaders to national office, it appeared that the political power of the South might return intact. The stage was set for Congress to define a new policy for governing the rebellious states. The Reconstruction Acts of 1867, which remanded the South to five military districts, were designed to retard Southern reentry into the federal legislative system and to effect a change in attitude among the defeated Southerners.

Specifically, the goals of congressional Reconstruction lay in two areas: politics and social order. The first, political goal was to develop a party organization that would guarantee Republican strength in the former Confederacy. The Republicans ultimately failed to establish lasting political gains or to effect permanent changes, which has made the effort seem in retrospect "an ephemeral experiment," a mere parenthesis in Southern history. In reality, however, the Republicans responded to an existing and ever-emerging context, and Southern politics were never the same after the Reconstruction experience.[1] The situation in Georgia proved to be a prime example of the struggle between past and present and revealed both the power of the existing conservative political attitudes and the short-sighted divisiveness of the Republicans, which limited their effectiveness and achievements.

The second area, of social order, was never a primary target of most

Republicans, and progress here was even less apparent than in the political realm. Party organizers such as Bryant were forthright, as has been shown, in saying that blacks could not expect social equality. The question of how to achieve any lasting change, however, was thrust upon the Republicans both in the South, as they worked for political ends, and in Washington, as some legislators began to realize that their laws, and even constitutional amendments, were meaningless without some alteration in the ordering of the postslavery society. Yankee settlers were sometimes changed into carpetbaggers by the desire to improve conditions as they found them, while carpetbaggers with only political ambitions soon found that social goals were often prerequisites to their success.[2]

It also became clear that blacks would not be able to enjoy new opportunities without the cooperation, at least in part, of their former masters and other collaborators who had supported slavery, even as Tillson had predicted and as President Johnson's plan had assumed. The war, for the most part, had done little to alter the judgment of these Southerners that blacks were innately inferior to whites and were qualified for only menial labor. The best humanitarian ideals of former abolitionists and Northern legislators conflicted not only with their own political priorities for Reconstruction but also with the resistance of white Southerners who found the social implications of the changes wrought by the Republicans utterly abhorrent to all their values and self-understanding. Racism was at least part of the reason that Georgians were constantly roused by press and oratory to bitter denunciation of Republican "Radicals" and to violent retaliation against blacks who usurped "power." Indeed, the seeds that blossomed a few months later in the activity of the Ku Klux Klan were sown in the early days of congressional Reconstruction. As one witness explained in 1868 in his testimony before the Fortieth Congress's Committee on Reconstruction, "The Cause and origin of the resistance in Georgia lies in the minds of the people on account of the war and its results, of which the prime was emancipation, and the changes wrought in society by these causes, as well as the very active agitation which some political leaders who were dissatisfied with the existing state of things have created."[3]

THE POSSIBILITY OF REPUBLICAN POWER

Soon after the Reconstruction Acts were passed by Congress in March 1867, the Republicans in Georgia were apparently in a favorable position. Many party leaders felt that the black vote was the key to their political success in the state, and even during the years of presidential Reconstruction, they had begun to mobilize blacks for political participation by instructing them in their rights as citizens. As has been noted, such instruction obviously did not overlook the role of the Republican party in freeing them from slavery. Other leaders saw the future of the party in cultivating the Unionist and former Whig vote among the white electorate, which could be accomplished by attracting business capital to the state for investment and future industrialization. The party, while not officially constituted in Georgia until 1867, was well represented in the state soon after the war by agents of the Freedmen's Bureau, military men, Southern Unionists, and Northerners who had gone South seeking opportunities in business or politics.

One of these future Republicans was John Emory Bryant, who had a great deal of influence among blacks in the state. His work with the bureau and primarily with the Georgia Equal Rights Association had made his name familiar and his Republican principles clear to everyone. The groundwork had been laid for the party by the activity of the GERA and the Union League. These embryonic political structures merged their work in 1867 and then were superseded altogether by local Republican clubs. The GERA's political work encompassed and focused its activities on education, as seen in chapter 3.

Under the protection of military rule after March 1867, the work of officially organizing the Republican party began in earnest. The *Loyal Georgian,* official newspaper of the GERA and edited by Bryant, published frequent instructions for organizing these local clubs. On May 3, 1867, following a Republican gathering in Macon (a strong GERA center), the *Loyal Georgian* published the party platform that had been discussed and suggested that an acceptable constitution for the clubs would be based on these principles: equal political rights and privileges; equal right to property and defense of persons; taxes based on property only; equal right to vote and to serve on juries; rejection of torture as punishment; protection of Union veterans and their dependents; recognition of the national debt and cancellation of the Confederate debt; right of people to change the Constitution, laws, and legislators; dignity of labor; free schools and churches; and supremacy of God.[4] Many of these provisions were later incorporated into the state constitution that was ratified in 1868.

Bryant had continued to reside in Georgia without his wife, Emma

Spaulding Bryant. The year 1867 proved frustrating for her, since she yearned to be with her husband but received little encouragement from him to come south. John's long-awaited visit to Illinois had never materialized, and in January 1867 Emma traveled to New York in the hope of catching him there, since he shuttled often between New York, Washington, and Augusta. The plan succeeded, but after a reunion, presumably cordial, Bryant left her in New York, where she stayed for the remainder of the spring. Her sister urged her to stay in Illinois for another summer, but Emma refused. Maria Eberhart, wife of Superintendent Eberhart in Georgia, who was apparently unaware of John's disagreement with her husband, invited Mrs. Bryant to visit her in Pennsylvania. "Now that Mr. B. is south I know you can come," she wrote warmly. Emma did not record her response, but she did choose to spend most of the summer in Maine.[5]

Republicans convened in Atlanta on July 4, 1867, to launch formally the Union Republican party of Georgia. At that time, the party declared itself in alliance with the "National Republican Party of the Union," pledged support for the measures of congressional Reconstruction, called for the establishment of free schools, declared itself for the rights and dignity of labor, and promised to maintain the free and equal rights of all males.[6] Soon afterward, party leaders constituted the state central committee of the Union Republican party. The committee consisted of four representatives from each of the state's four congressional districts in addition to the committee's chairman. Foster Blodgett, businessman and former mayor of Augusta, was the first chairman of the committee, and John Emory Bryant was its secretary. Bryant was the only Northern-born member in the top-level party leadership who had gone to Georgia after the war and therefore drew a disproportionate amount of hostility from native Georgians.

The central committee, dominated by Bryant and his Augusta friends, was known collectively as the "Augusta ring." Besides Bryant and Blodgett, the group included Rufus Bullock, an Augusta businessman, and Benjamin Conley, a council member and also a former mayor of the city. Conley was a native of New Jersey but had lived in Georgia since the 1830s. The control of the ring over party strategy and direction was not absolute, and other factions within the party perhaps received more popular support. Joseph E. Brown, who had been Georgia's governor during the Civil War, led a large group of southern whites who accepted the fact that "we are a conquered people, and must submit to whatever terms the conqueror imposes." They were determined to make the best of Reconstruction and to cooperate with Republicans. Brown was branded "traitor" and "scalawag" by many Georgians. The Democratic press labeled his cooperation a "low-down game" and sarcastically predicted, "Who knows but we shall yet find him a ruler of Egypt and the vendor of grain?"[7]

Brown was a shrewd politician and from the start managed to make his support a necessity for Republican success in the state. For Brown the key to Georgia's future rested with neither Democrats nor Republicans per se but in attracting capital to the state for industrial expansion. He promised early in Reconstruction that he would "connect with whatever national party shows the most disposition to act upon just and true principles and to aid us in developing our section." In the last analysis, Brown believed, leadership would be decisive. He considered it "impossible to build up and maintain a party . . . without the aid of leading Southern men who know our people and sympathize with them." As for blacks, they would "vote with their masters" anyway; "the intelligence and wealth of the state . . . will always control tenants and laborers."[8]

Another leader, Henry P. Farrow, head of the Union League in Georgia, also commanded a strong following. Farrow was a native of South Carolina and had supposedly served reluctantly as a conscript in the Confederate army. After the Reconstruction Acts were passed, Farrow also openly acknowledged that Southerners were "a conquered people" who had "forfeited the right to legitimate government."[9] Unfortunately, there are few sources on Farrow's early work with the Union League. As noted above, competition between Bryant's leadership and Farrow's may have laid the groundwork for future trouble.

Through the summer of 1867, JEB resisted his wife's repeated suggestions that she join him in Georgia. Visiting in New Haven in August and September, she attempted to keep current with the political intrigues he described and offered encouragement. Emma seemed to feel that John's financial situation accounted for his delay in sending for her. Recalling the difficulty of the previous year, she wrote, "Those were dark days, darling, when I was with you in Augusta." She realized that he was "struggling under a heavy burden," and she urged him to "trust God." As the constitutional convention required by the Reconstruction Acts drew near, she wondered how it would affect their coming winter schedule. "I am anxious to know whether you will be a delegate to the convention," she wrote. "Am very glad that [it] is not until I can be with you."[10]

But Emma was overly optimistic. The state constitutional convention provided a testing ground for the various factions of the party, and the carpetbagger had no intention of being distracted from it by family matters. He had relinquished the leadership of the GERA, an organization now primarily concerned with education, and indeed was elected to the convention. Emma visited with her brother, Greenleaf, and his wife for several months and then went to Washington for the winter, ever hoping that John would ask her to join him. He professed loneliness over the Christmas holidays and continued to write frequently but did not change his mind about her coming. Only Emma's letters from this period remain. They tell of her increasing impatience with the separation and of her unhappiness caused by his lack of financial support for her. No, she wrote, she was not "losing confidence in him," but she was "puzzled and hurt" that he failed to remember his promise.[11]

The contours of a strange pattern were beginning to emerge, perhaps the most paradoxical of the indexes to the carpetbagger's conscience. Totally caught up in Republican politics, John failed to translate his professed love for Emma into money that would improve her well-being. In the winter of 1867–1868, his energies focused on a new constitution for Georgia.

Although Republicans dominated the convention, which was held in Atlanta from December 1867 to March 1868, the body could hardly be described as radical. Those seated included 46 staunch Democrats, in addition to others elected as Democrats, and 99 Republicans. The latter included scalawags, Unionists, carpetbaggers, and blacks. Richard Hume's breakdown of the delegates is perhaps more illuminating: 113 Southern whites, 12 outside whites, 33 blacks, and 11 whites he could not classify. Of the 113 Southern whites, Hume finds that 47 voted with the Radical Reconstructionists on most issues, 43 could be designated as conservative, and 23 as unaligned. The moderates clearly held the balance of power.[12]

The Democrats had followed a questionable strategy of boycotting the election of delegates. In so doing they not only forfeited a commanding voice in the convention but almost sabotaged it, since the Reconstruction law had required a majority of registered voters to elect delegates.[13] (The law was subsequently changed to require election by a majority only of those voting.)

The convention maintained a temperate atmosphere largely because of former governor Brown's leadership. Though he was not a member of the convention, his presence was felt, and his views were made known through personal and written messages and a public address. One key victory for the moderates concerned the freedmen's right to vote and to hold office.[14] The franchise committee, which Bryant chaired, dealt with this explosive issue as well as with the rights of former Confederates. The convention readily accepted the committee recommendation to guarantee voting rights for the freedmen but it opposed mass disfranchisement of former rebels and the right of freedmen to hold office. Moderates from both parties feared that these radical proposals would lose support for the Republican position.

Brown was instrumental in the defeat of the report's tenth section, which guaranteed that "all qualified electors . . . shall be eligible to any office in the State." Even before the convention Brown had supported the adoption of voting rights for black males, believing that their vote could be controlled and seeing their potential value for Southern representation in Congress. Beyond the specific rights required by law, however, he would not go. He maintained that Congress had not conferred upon the freedmen the right to hold office and to sit on juries. In an address Brown asked the convention, "Who authorized you to confer upon the negro race greater rights and privileges than Congress has required Georgia to secure to them?"[15] Brown's position was supported by other moderates and led to the modification of the third section, to avoid disfranchising former Confederates, and to the defeat of the tenth section. The immediate need for votes from white farmers of the state outweighed the future value of blacks' participation in government. Sufficient unto the day were the dangers at hand. Ironically, the black members of the convention themselves, confident that suffrage automatically brought the right to hold office, voted to defeat the tenth section.

Bryant had worked to keep the franchise committee report intact and had warned black delegates to support the tenth section—to no avail. Later, H. M. Turner admitted that the blacks erred in not heeding this advice. Still, by the end of the convention, Bryant's overall contribution had been recognized, and he gained the editorial approval of "Joe Brown's voice," the influential *Daily New Era*: "When Mr. Bryant first took his seat in the Convention he was looked upon with distrust by a large class of our citizens, but we are pleased to be able to state that this feeling no longer exists, and the people have discovered in him a spirit of concession and an ardent wish to serve the State in a manner well calculated to promote its present and future prosperity." The writer continued, "The Convention, as a body, have manifested the same disposition, and this endorsement cannot, with fairness, longer be withheld."[16]

The moderates had made the constitution more palatable to Georgians by a relief clause that promised the cancellation of debts contracted prior to June 1865 and by defeating the tenth section of the franchise clause. Republicans could thus appeal to the hard-pressed farmers, while the question of whether blacks were eligible to hold office became deliberately vague; the franchise clause could be interpreted to suit any audience. Brown, for example, campaigned for ratification of the new constitution in the south-central Wiregrass counties by emphasizing its silence on the matter. "I am asked whether the new Constitution gives the freedmen the right to hold office," he said in Marietta. "I reply, in my opinion it does not.... Our black friends should be patient.... The civil rights bill passed by Congress made them citizens of the United States. But this only conferred upon them civil rights, not political rights.... I admit, however, that the [Georgia] constitution does not prohibit the Legislature from conferring the right in [the] future if they think proper."[17]

Amos Akerman, a member of the constitutional convention, in testimony before the Congressional Committee on Reconstruction in December 1868, explained the mixed motives of the Georgia convention: "I think some who voted against [the tenth section] did so for the purpose of excluding colored men from holding office: I think the majority did so because they believed they had the right without it.... [Also,] one motive was to enable the constitution to be differently interpreted upon that subject in different parts of the State."[18]

Though the moderates, led by Brown, had their way in defeating the tenth section of the franchise report, the vote did not split neatly along radical/moderate lines. Even the Augusta ring did not hold together. Philosophical differences emerged that later became full-fledged divisions within the party.

Bryant steadfastly supported his franchise committee's report, but Rufus Bullock, Foster Blodgett, and Benjamin Conley all voted against the tenth section, which removed officeholding rights for blacks. Likewise, on the earlier vote on exemption and debt repudiation, Bryant moved to reduce the amounts allowed—in the face of the Bullock position to keep it high. In both cases the Bullock faction seems clearly to have been seeking the most salable constitutional package.[19]

Bryant's willingness to stick to principle rather than heeding political expediency was consistent with his previous actions. He had hitherto maintained a firm commitment to black civil and political rights. In this instance he correctly perceived the danger for them if the convention defeated the tenth section of the franchise clause.

The reason for Bryant's vote to reduce exemptions is less clear, but perhaps, as a lawyer, he was persuaded by Amos Akerman's argument that the clause was on shaky constitutional grounds.[20] Or perhaps Bryant was seeking a compromise between the two extremes, one that would not lead to greater disappointment later.

Though they had differed on aspects of the constitution, the Augusta ring did unite in selecting their gubernatorial candidate, Rufus Bullock. Their methods in selecting him, however, did nothing to win them lasting friends. Bullock, a businessman and railway executive, had moved to Augusta from New York in 1859 and, although he was viewed with suspicion by some Confederates, was generally well liked. He was probably selected to represent the group because he had not held elective office before and did not have the political odium of the newly-arrived Yankee. In addition, his position with the Southern Express Company gave him important and far-reaching business contacts. These very reasons also made Bullock a dubious choice, for he had no solid political base. Just as he had failed to support the officeholding clause in the constitution, his tenuous commitment to humanitarian goals would quickly be forgotten in his struggle to maintain power.

At least two other men had desired the Republican nomination for governor—Judge Dawson A. Walker of the Georgia Supreme Court and Henry Farrow of the Union League. Joseph Brown publicly backed Walker, but indicated privately to the Augusta ring that he could support Bullock. As early as November 1867, a number of Farrow's supporters had urged him to run for governor. In January 1868, league officials asked that each county meeting "pass a resolution expressing your preference for [Farrow] and directing your delegates to support him."[21]

An ugly event tangential to the power struggle going on within the party was the murder of Colonel C. C. Richardson, radical member of the constitutional convention and law partner of J. E. Bryant. Richardson had been accused of voting twice in the Republican caucus, an offense not taken lightly with such high stakes. He apparently believed his accuser to be Captain E. M. Timoney, "formerly of the U.S. service" and secretary of the Union League in Georgia, an active supporter of Farrow's candidacy.

Richardson sent Timoney an evidently accusatory note, hand delivered by Colonel H. T. McDowell. Timoney, seated with Farrow in a public restaurant, refused to read Richardson's note without an introduction and Farrow refused to introduce the two. McDowell left the restaurant and returned later with Richardson. When personally confronted by Richardson, Timoney stood up, twice shouted, "Take it back!" and then shot Richardson, who died a few days later. Farrow's role in the murder is unclear, though McDowell claimed he had seen the murder weapon in Farrow's office an hour before the shooting. The *New Era* claimed that the feud between Timoney and Richardson revolved around the political struggle between Farrow and Bullock. The cold-blooded shooting did not endear Farrow to JEB, who lost a strong friend and ally. Bryant's support of Bullock presumably displeased Farrow.[22]

In view of the following that Farrow and Walker commanded, the Augusta ring feared that they would be unable to determine the party's choice for governor in a new nominating assembly. Bryant had advance warning that Farrow would attempt "to pack [the] convention [in order] to nominate himself for governor." To avoid such a possibility, the officers of the central committee canceled plans for a new meeting and announced that Republican delegates to the constitutional convention— who did not include Walker or Farrow—would themselves act as a nominating assembly. Farrow, convinced that the move was made to forestall his own success, later wrote, "When Blodgett saw that I would get the nomination over Bullock he withdrew the call & resolved the constitutional convention into a nominating body."[23]

The noisy protest of a large group of Republicans the night before the nominating meeting did nothing to defeat the plan, and on March 7, 1868, Bullock became the Republican nominee for governor. Brown promptly pledged his support to Bullock, and a week later Farrow did likewise. After his nomination, Bullock attempted to pacify the losers by promising Brown a chance at Georgia's seat in the United States Senate and Farrow an appointment as the state's attorney general. In addition, Farrow was later appointed attorney for the state-owned Western & Atlantic Railroad, a post that guaranteed him three hundred dollars per month while Bullock was in office.[24] For all the eventual surface unanimity, the raw power employed in securing Bullock's nomination revealed factionalism as an inherent weakness in the Republican party of Georgia, a foreboding of future, more serious strains on party unity.

Despite the internal struggle for power in the party, Republicans were determined to join forces in order to succeed in the crucial election of April 1868. At stake were the newly written constitution, control of the state legislature, and the governorship. Even before Bullock's nomination was secure, the *Loyal Georgian* had published complete organizational plans for the coming election, and the Augusta ring worked together in the closest harmony to ensure success. Bryant, ultimately a successful candidate for the house of representatives from Richmond County, traveled over the entire state to hold mass meetings and to make speeches. If his strategy in 1868 was like that reflected in 1867 letters concerning his city campaigning, he urged blacks to ignore advice from their old masters. In rhetoric that, again, could be described as "stirring up racial hatred," Bryant admonished his "colored friends of Augusta" not to support at the polls "men who have called you 'niggers,' and said you were a cross between the monkey and the human species."[25]

The Democrats, led by General John B. Gordon, popular Confederate war hero, could not agree upon strategy. They failed to rally the people in any viable opposition to the Republican platform of "Bullock, Relief, and Reconstruction." Brown campaigned effectively for the Republicans, assuring his followers among Georgia's farmers that the party could aid them in their plight. Despite Brown's private doubts that Bullock could be elected, the election turned inexorably toward Republican victory, with Bullock defeating Gordon by a vote of 83,146 to 76,099.[26] The outcome was unaffected by predictions from both Democrat Benjamin Hill, former Confederate senator, and Republican Amos Akerman that Congress would reject the relief clause in the Georgia constitution.

Both sides used fraudulent election tactics, and each side accused the other of substituting or destroying ballots and of deceiving the inexperienced freedmen. Election managers (usually Republican) appointed by Military Commander General George C. Meade attempted to protect their voters from intimidation by changing election sites to county towns. The polling period was four days, an extended time that unfortunately allowed a greater opportunity for fraud. Federal military detachments were small and often undisciplined. In addition to perpetrating overt deception, landowners threatened to fire black laborers unless they stayed home or voted Democratic.[27]

Under the leadership of the Democratic nominee, General Gordon, the Ku Klux Klan made its first appearance in Georgia in connection with the

April elections. Begun in Tennessee as a social club, the organization quickly became a terrorist group intent on thwarting Radical Reconstruction goals. Georgia was a prime candidate for Klan activity because of the deep racial prejudice *and* the potential for Republican success. The murder of George W. Ashburn, categorized as a Southern white because of his fifty years in the state before the war and as a scalawag because of his support for the Radical Republican issues in the constitutional convention, was well publicized by the Northern press, partly because the Klan had warned Ashburn and claimed responsibility. The trial of those accused and acquitted of the crime served to keep passions high. There is evidence that Gordon withdrew his support of the Klan as it became increasingly violent and as his control over it lessened. Rather than disband, however, the organization grew stronger during the summer months of 1868. By the time of the presidential elections in the fall, terror and intimidation would be a key factor in the Republican defeat at the polls.[28]

THE REPUBLICAN ADMINISTRATION'S FIRST EFFORTS

On election day in April, the Republicans swept the field. Besides electing Bullock governor, the voters ratified the constitution and gave the Republicans a majority in the Georgia Senate and House of Representatives. In both houses, however, the moderate Republicans held the crucial balance of power. The senate was composed of seventeen Radical Republicans, ten moderate Republicans, and seventeen conservative Democrats. In the house the Radical Republicans held seventy seats; there were twenty-five moderate Republicans and eighty Democrats.[29]

Before they could enjoy the fruits of their labor, dissension erupted among the victorious Republicans. Others also were disenchanted with Bullock and his methods, but the quarrel with John E. Bryant most seriously damaged Bullock's administration and broke up the Augusta ring. The simplest explanation for the split is that the division was over patronage and that Bullock's political debts made him vulnerable to unrest within his own ranks. Bryant complained that in several cases strong Republicans who had toiled for the new governor were refused appointments.

But something more fundamental occurred when he objected vigorously to Bullock's relations with Foster Blodgett, whom Bullock was supporting for U.S. senator. Blodgett, a confirmed secessionist before the war and a Confederate soldier, had blithely taken the test oath that he had never "given aid or comfort to the enemy." Henry Farrow, as early as January 1868, had attempted to document Blodgett's perjury, probably to remove him from consideration for a governmental position. Soon after the election, Farrow and moderate Republican Joshua Hill sought out Bryant and warned him of Blodgett's background.

It seems unlikely, but Bryant claimed that he "knew nothing of [Blodgett] prior to May, 1867"; after that time he was swayed by the fact that Blodgett was "one of the first southern-born" to support the Republican party. Following Hill and Farrow's warning, Bryant conducted his own investigation, which revealed that Blodgett's record was "even worse than [they] had represented it to be." He promised to support Blodgett no longer, apparently believing that his standing with Bullock would be unimpaired by the decision. But there Bryant was wrong. Even as his own denunciations of Blodgett increased to include "drunkard and liar," he discovered that the man was Bullock's "evil genius," his "intimate friend" who held great influence over the governor. Bryant seemed baffled by the relationship of the two, since he himself claimed to have first put forth Bullock's name for office and to his knowledge Bullock was "indebted to Mr. Blodgett but very little."[30]

John Caldwell concurred in Bryant's evaluation of Blodgett. Caldwell, a native of South Carolina and a courageous Methodist minister in LaGrange, Georgia, had left his church after twenty-six years of service because he was unpopular for advocating the reunion of its Southern branch with the Northern and because he had worked for black rights. Caldwell later served as district superintendent of schools for the Freedmen's Bureau in the western part of the state, and he was appointed a federal judge. Called to the mission of Reconstruction politics because of his belief in the evil of slavery, he had served in the constitutional convention and was a newly elected representative in the state legislature. He was also a national committeeman from Georgia, having been appointed at the Republican National Convention in Chicago in May 1868.

Caldwell had supported Bullock's candidacy for governor and, like JEB, claimed that "the beginning of the breach between the governor and myself arose in consequence of his persistent determination to secure the election to the U.S. Senate of a man who at the time was under indictment for perjury." Discovering that Blodgett was, in addition, under warrant for a personal "outrage" perpetrated as a secessionist, Caldwell warned

Blodgett at the convention in Chicago (where Blodgett allegedly "stayed drunk") that he would not support his candidacy to the Senate. Caldwell interceded on Blodgett's behalf in Chicago to prevent his arrest there and to avoid embarrassment to the Georgia delegation; Blodgett later thanked him for his assistance. The minister's subsequent remembrance of that revealing incident was that he answered, "Yes Mr. [Blodgett], I kept you out of jail last night, and now I must be candid with you and say that I will keep you out of the United States Senate." Caldwell made good that promise by joining with Bryant to lead the opposition to Blodgett's nomination.[31]

Both men were important to Blodgett's success. Their refusal to support him apparently infuriated Blodgett and Bullock, with the result that Caldwell and Bryant were eliminated from any consideration for political appointment. Some historians have doubted that they acted solely out of conviction, yet neither man seems to have gained from their stand. Bryant claimed it was a matter of conscience: "It was in my interest personally to support him. He promised to assist me in any way he could if I would do so."[32] Bryant claimed that he and Caldwell could not endorse the plan that Bullock and Blodgett finally revealed for the state of Georgia.

The motivation, however, was at least a combination of personal pique and concern for the state of Georgia. It is likely that Bryant had overestimated his own status in the Bullock camp. Whereas he had been important during the election because of his alleged influence with blacks, Bullock probably saw Bryant as expendable afterward. The black leadership had shown both a measure of independence and signs that they could be led away from the carpetbagger. Bullock was correct in his assessment, for many blacks continued to follow the governor against Bryant's good advice for their benefit.[33] They discovered their error too late, as will be seen.

Another factor, perhaps, was that both Bryant and Caldwell had demonstrated at the constitutional convention *their* willingness to resist Bullock's leadership, a fact that he had surely noted. The Augusta ring had nevertheless held together through the election, and Bullock had benefited from Bryant's endorsement and work for the party. JEB thought that he would benefit from his efforts after the election. Bullock and Blodgett were principal stockholders in the Georgia Publishing Company, and Bryant fully expected that, if he supported Blodgett for senator and Bullock for governor and they came to power, the *Loyal Georgian* would become the administration's voice and would receive the lucrative plum of being designated official printer. "I based my calculations to pay my debts upon the assistance I should receive from these men when they should be elected. . . . I expected to get money through the aid of Bullock . . . and Blodgett. . . . Had they been good and honest men as I believed them to be when I first knew them they could have easily given me the needed assistance." When Bryant was rejected after all, he claimed that he feared the schemes of Bullock and Blodgett would "plunder the state" and "ruin the party." Simply put, "When I knew Blodgett would betray me if elected I determined to defeat him."[34] The timing of that decision in relation to Caldwell's enlightenment in Chicago is unclear, but in any event the governor had aroused a formidable foe in John Emory Bryant.

Bullock's "plan" for Georgia seemed to be no more than to hold power by whatever means he could. He would increasingly rely on federal intervention in the face of a crumbling coalition locally. He faced the first test of his strength in the summer of 1868, when the newly convened Georgia legislature in Atlanta was to elect U.S. senators. Having made the decision to oppose Blodgett, Bryant in May 1868 corresponded with party leaders about his own candidacy for the Senate. The answer, as expressed in one letter, was "Your place in the Legislature *cannot be filled*, and, therefore while the Radical Yankee Georgians would be pleased and proud to see you in the Senate they cannot spare you from the state." Undeterred by this diplomatic discouragement, Bryant was still "running for the Senate 'in earnest'" in the summer, and his wife wrote that she was anxious to know the result of his "senatorial contest."[35]

It is unclear when Emma and John were reunited in Georgia; a dearth of surviving letters from the first months of 1868 may indicate that she joined him soon after their lonesome Christmas of 1867. In any case, by July she was writing to him from their home in Augusta and was hoping to be with him soon in Atlanta. Their correspondence at this time reflects a warm relationship, although the usual problems of money remained. The landlord had been asking for the overdue rent. In addition, Emma had other bills to pay, and how would she pay for the trip to Atlanta? Two dollars "would be enough," she wrote in July. One reason that Emma wanted to be with her husband was that she was again pregnant. "I fear the same disaster as befell me two years ago [when she miscarried]. Shall try to be careful." Shortly afterward, Emma joined John in Atlanta, where he was pursuing his party's nomination for senator.[36]

Bryant's entry into the race made public the breach within the party, and some Republicans were critical of "his course in refusing to abide by the party nominations for senators." By July 1868, party leaders had discounted Bryant's candidacy. One wrote to Bullock, "I regret exceedingly the condition of the party. . . . Capt. Brayant [sic] is constitutionally ineligible [sic] and it will be impossible to strike either Brown or Blodget[t] without injuring the party. Can you not appease Capt. B[ryant]?"[37] There is no record that the governor even tried; he continued to endorse Blodgett.

After failing to block Blodgett's nomination, Caldwell and Bryant moved their fight to the Georgia legislature, where Blodgett did not intend to lose. It was "common rumor" that pressure was brought to bear and that Blodgett used "the patronage of the Governor to buy men to support himself for Senator," but still his bid was unsuccessful. To the delight of some Democrats, Joseph E. Brown, Bullock's candidate for the second Senate seat, was also defeated, though both Bryant and Caldwell supported him. Elected instead were the candidates of the moderates and conservatives: Joshua Hill, a Georgia Unionist before the Civil War and a moderate Republican, and H. V. M. Miller, a one-time Bullock man who had returned to the Democratic fold. Bullock nevertheless redeemed his promise of political office for Brown and appointed him to the Supreme Court of Georgia. Blodgett took the powerful post of superintendent of the state-owned Western & Atlantic Railroad while he bided his time and waited for another try at the Senate seat.[38]

The governor continued to ignore any debt to Bryant, despite the latter's election as chairman of the state's Republican executive committee. Yet in the legislature as well as in the party's councils, the representative from Richmond County made his presence felt. His committee appointments included the Manufacturers, Judiciary, and Privileges and Elections committees, while he chaired the Public Education Committee.

Bryant had long considered education the key to improvement for blacks; under his leadership the Georgia Equal Rights Association had emphasized that goal. Now, by working to realize the state constitutional provision for free public schools, he attempted to redeem the promise he made when he relinquished his office in the GERA. As early as 1821 the Georgia legislature had contributed to the support of the state's schools and academies and in 1837 had created a "full fledged public school system." Unfortunately, economic crises and then the Civil War had prevented its full enactment. Bryant's efforts to broaden the earlier concept of "public" met with only limited success. By the time the new school act was implemented in 1870, Democrats had modified the requirements to a system that segregated black and white pupils.[39]

There is some evidence that Bryant sought to temper his radical image by cultivating good working relations with members of the Democratic party, even when he disagreed with them. One such effort brought the comment that "no one—not even his [JEB's] bitterest opponents, cannot but admire the kind manner in which he spoke of the dissenting members of the Committee, and the patriotic purposes he had in view." The efforts of Bryant the diplomat, however, were largely unappreciated by Southerners, who saw him as an obnoxious carpetbagger. Fellow legislators openly scorned the attempts of Bryant and others, such as Caldwell, to bring about change for the state, while the Democratic press continually editorialized on what it considered Bryant's "inflammatory and revolutionary" remarks on the floor of the house. Often the reporter for the legislative sessions would not cover Bryant's speeches, explaining scornfully, "We will not attempt to give the remarks of this haranguer, . . . as we drem [sic] them unworthy to appear in public print."[40]

The matter of jury selection illustrates the sort of issue that so inflamed the native Georgians. The legislators deemed the basic qualifications for jurors to be "intelligence and uprightness," but when Bryant offered an amendment that the ruling should not exclude anyone "on account of race or color," there was an outcry. One representative, who frequently challenged Bryant's views, charged that Bryant "would have us believe that there is but one honest class in the state of Georgia and that is the negro." Furthermore, he went on, "I challenge him to give an instance where the rights of the negro has been injured by the people of this state. . . . If you get honest white men [on juries] . . . they will be sure to give the negroes their rights." Bryant's amendment was ruled out of order, and when it was raised at another similar discussion a few days afterward, it met the same fate. Later on, the native white solons concluded that "Mr. Bryant had but one idea and that was that the state of Georgia was made exclusively for niggers and New England carpet-baggers!" Meanwhile, earnest Republicans such as John Caldwell, in sympathy with Bryant's efforts, confided, Bryant "is the most talented, active, energetic and influential leader in the party in the 5th dist," but the two parties are "so nearly equal in number in the House [of Representatives] that we could carry forward no effective legislation."[41]

The impasse was due not only to the parties' being so nearly equal but also to the failure of party discipline, as evidenced by Caldwell's own defection. The criticism of Caldwell and Bryant for revealing the governor's weakness extended to Democratic newspapers, one of which claimed that the party had been "sold out by pretended friends." The defeat of the governor's candidates for the Senate had shown that Bullock's grasp on his "Republican" legislature was slippery. The assembly proved its independence in the summer of 1868 by defeating Brown and Blodgett and also by refusing to purge itself of former Confederate members, disqualified by the Fourteenth Amendment, as the governor requested. General George C. Meade, then commander of the Third Military District, which included Georgia, declined to come to Bullock's aid by intervening in the matter, which he considered beyond his jurisdiction and potentially hazardous to tranquillity.[42] With his refusal, the governor began to look for other means of eliciting federal assistance.

A third show of the legislature's defiance strengthened Bullock's claim that he needed support. While campaigning for the new constitution, former governor Brown had predicted that, "if any black man should be elected to the Legislature, the respective houses will be the exclusive judges of the election and qualifications of their own members." The import of that statement was clear at last, when the legislators, in September 1868, over the protest of men like Bryant, who pleaded that this was "the age of progress," with "old ideas of the past exploded," turned out two senators and twenty-four representatives under the pretext that the Georgia constitution did not provide officeholding rights for blacks. Bryant, in his outrage, went on to stress that slavery was gone, "all persons were equal, socially, politically, and otherwise, the Bible sustains the proposition" (the reporter sneered, "Mr. B. has a *political* Bible, we presume"). Bryant continued, "If you turn out these colored members, you have the same right to turn out carpetbaggers" ("Agreed," added the reporter). "None of us are safe," Bryant went on. "The exclusion of these colored men is revolutionary, and is calculated to precipitate a revolution in the Government. . . . I say the Constitution of Georgia does give the colored man a right to hold office."[43]

The Negro legislators who had been betrayed were justifiably angry. Their sympathizers were impressed with "the clearness and boldness with which they [the blacks] expressed their constitutional rights" and their confidence that, although they might "be expelled now, they [would] come back again, and come to stay." Henry M. Turner, one of the ablest black legislators, was especially effective. He declared that "never before was man arraigned before a legislative body for an offense committed by God himself" and maintained that, until the controversy over eligibility, he had not fully calculated "the imbecility of the Anglo-Saxon race." "You may drive us out," he warned, "but it will light a torch that will never be put out."[44]

Taking Bryant's lead, Turner, with some accuracy, predicted, "After we leave, the next thing will be to turn out carpetbaggers and scalawags, impeach the governor, and upturn the whole State Government just inaugurated, and the result will be God knows where it will end." Turning to blacks, Turner continued, "I tell you, my colored friends, the white men are not to be trusted. They will betray you. . . . Black men, hold up your heads. Other men in times past have been persecuted, and thank God, they have risen above the prejudices of their adversaries." Turner then, in a last defiant gesture, requested permission to walk out of the chamber before the house adjourned. When permission was granted, he approached the speaker's desk, "raising his foot and brushed the dust therefrom (in derision) and retired."[45]

Shortly after the expulsion, Turner was instrumental in forming in Macon the Civil and Political Rights Association for blacks. The disillusionment of the black legislators had been reflected in Turner's words that "the white men are not to be trusted." This condemnation did not include Bryant, whose staunch defense of the legislators earned him a spot on the speaker's podium, if not a leadership role, in the new association.[46] Black leaders were coming of age.

Bullock determined to turn the outrage to his own advantage. Indeed, it suited his purposes so well that Democrats accused him of instigating the expulsion, though the black legislators refused to see Bullock's hand in the action and continued to support the governor. Twenty-two white Radicals in the house and three in the senate did not vote, but Bullock later claimed that members of his party abstained because the outcome of the vote was inevitable. Caldwell observed before the vote that the issue was "greatly demoralizing" to white Republicans. He had accurately predicted that "more than half" would "either dodge the question or vote with the Democrats to exclude them." Only a few Republicans, such as John Emory Bryant and Amos T. Akerman, continued to plead against expulsion and voted against it. But Bullock attempted to benefit from the injustice by using it to argue that Georgia was not properly "reconstructed."

He petitioned Congress to repeal the bill that had allowed Georgia to reenter the Union. With reimposed military rule, Bullock hoped to purge the assembly of former Confederates, as he had wished to do earlier, and reinstate the black legislators, thereby making his majority more secure.[47]

Bullock faced obstacles to carrying out this plan, but the events of fall 1868 seemed to strengthen his contention that the situation in Georgia was unstable. Reaction against the expulsion of blacks from the legislature had already given the state a bad reputation in the North. A race riot in Camilla, Georgia, on September 19 seemed to prove that there was no order in the state. The Ku Klux Klan, spurred on by the Republican victory in April, was determined that the November elections would have a different result. The infamous night riding began in earnest in the fall, with black and white Republicans beaten, humiliated, shot, and sometimes burned alive. It was, according to reluctant witnesses in the congressional investigation, the "lawless and violent" element of Southern society that would not tolerate "black and scalawag rule." "The object and spirit of the people of the state is to put the negro in a semi-serf condition." They will "not consent" that blacks "should occupy any other." Political leaders who had early spawned this ugly reaction later disclaimed it.[48]

In response to the reign of terror, Bullock did little. Proclamations outlawing "secret societies" and rewards offered for information leading to arrest did nothing to deter the Klan. Indeed, Bullock's rewards were so ineffective as to become the butt of jokes in the Democratic press. The *Athens Southern Banner*, for example, once printed a long list of criminal acts and Bullock's offered rewards but then reported an "omission of Bullock: the murder of *Abel* who was barbarously and feloniously assassinated by a KU-KLUX by the name of CAIN," friends report that he now resides "in Nod."[49]

Even with the presence of U.S. troops during "military Reconstruction," there were never more than a few regiments in the state, and they could do little in their scattered details to secure the countryside. President Grant was never comfortable with sending troops and feared that he would appear to be a military dictator. But without the military, Bullock was helpless. Instead of sanctioning the formation of a black militia to act in defense of the former slaves, Bullock maintained that the state was beyond his control and asked for another federal military intervention. To repeated personal requests for relief from violence, he later instructed his secretary to say, "No answer—nothing can be done."[50]

The work of the Republicans united for the Grant-Colfax ticket was conducted by a divided party structure. Caldwell and Bryant, who had claimed the party was "thoroughly reorganized and ready for active work" in August after Bryant was chosen to be a Grant elector, complained in October that they "worked day and night" as members of the State Executive Committee but that Foster Blodgett, the chairman of the State Central Committee, did nothing. Blodgett, according to them, was "a man of very small ability; . . . a trickster," who "accomplishes by trickery what others labor months for." A private letter from O. O. Howard indicated that some agents of the Freedmen's Bureau, enumerated by name to Bryant, could be counted on to assist the effort for Grant. "Each will do quietly all in his power to aid you," Howard wrote, "taking care to do nothing inconsistent with their official position and duties."[51]

Emma Bryant worried for John's safety as he traveled during the campaign. She realized that "God allows his people to suffer martyrdom in a good cause," which they both considered his work. "God bless you darling, make you a good soldier of the Lord and your country," she wrote. Frequently she did not know where he was on any given night.[52]

On election day the vulnerability of the Republicans was made manifest, as Grant received only 57,134 votes in the state to the 102,822 votes of Horatio Seymore, the Democratic nominee. Counties that had been carried by the party in the spring now fell to the Democrats from a combination of disillusionment and intimidation. Some white voters did not believe that campaign promises made in April had been fulfilled, while black voters encountered a volley of obstacles, including the threat of force, actual violence, and the charge of unpaid taxes, including the poll tax, which had been suspended by the governor. In one report, only 137 out of 1,500 potential black voters were ruled eligible. In addition, much of the baleful work of fear had been done before the polling day. The freedmen largely stayed away, having been warned of the deadly consequences of voting the wrong ticket. The Republican vote, as compared with that during the April election, was reduced by drastic proportions in this manner, and Georgia fell to the Democratic column.[53]

GEORGIA'S THIRD RECONSTRUCTION

Internal Republican dissension was growing over black expulsion and what should be done about it. Bullock seemed more convinced than ever that federal intervention to reinstate the black members by force was the only answer, while others feared that a new military presence would splinter the party irreparably by causing the defection of native white Georgians. Party officials such as Bryant, who opposed Bullock on this issue, were in the uncomfortable position of unwittingly providing evidence that seemed to bolster the governor's case. JEB had documented many violations during the presidential elections with which to protest the defeat of the Republican ticket in Georgia, and Bullock found in his work perfect evidence to support the case against Georgia before the congressional committee on Reconstruction in Washington. The testimony of ousted black legislators, whose support Bullock still enjoyed, was also impressive.[54]

While Bullock paraded his witnesses and statistics before the congressional committee, Republicans back home began organized public protests against the governor's leadership. Horrified that under his plan Georgia would be remanded to a third reconstruction, they held rallies, wrote editorials, and generally made political noise. One typical gathering in December 1868 drew up "resolutions pledging fealty to the Republican Party, but opposing any further Congressional interference in Georgia."[55]

John Emory Bryant took an active and vocal role in opposing Bullock. His own personal grudge by this time surely played a part in this, as well as his continued condemnation of Bullock's right-hand man, Foster Blodgett. Convinced that the two of them were destroying the chances of Republican success, Bryant was quite willing to lead the defectors.

The split in the party led to a shift in terminology. "Radicalism" now meant identification with Bullock's plan for a third reconstruction venture in Georgia. Bullock's own weak record on "radical" measures for aiding the freed slaves was not yet fully comprehended, even by black leaders. Meanwhile, men such as Bryant, truly visionary regarding rights for blacks but now willing to form new coalitions to prevent Bullock from maintaining power, were dubbed "moderate" Republicans. This terminology would prove not only confusing in distinguishing one party faction from another but detrimental as well to Bryant's reputation as a staunch Radical Republican.

But for the present, he was seemingly in solid company. In a long letter, Joseph Brown also warned Bullock against seeking a new congressional intervention and a return to the status of "provisional government" under military rule. "It would hardly be wise," he wrote, "to go back and undo what we have done." If all were undone and reorganized, and the test oath applied, it "would raise such a storm, and so embitter the feelings of our people, that at the election two years hence, when the people govern by ballot," Republicans would be overthrown. Brown's advice instead was to unite with the moderate wing of the Democratic party to form a coalition of "leading men in the state." Though Brown's idea was not one that Bryant would have embraced in 1867, he now seemed willing to consider it. As an additional deterrent to Bullock, he and Akerman traveled to Washington to testify before the congressional committee, hoping to counteract the effect of Bullock's story. Confronted with contradictory evidence on the situation in Georgia, the committee left the case pending.[56]

In February 1869, the state treasurer, Nedom L. Angier, a native of New Hampshire who had lived in Georgia for twenty-seven years before the war, joined the dissidents when he began to uncover certain irregularities in Bullock's handling of funds. Angier's disclosures brought public outrage over Bullock's "high-handed" use of some thirty-five thousand dollars in unappropriated funds. The Democratic press was ready to cheer the discovery. "The governor has been guilty of usurpation of power and malfeasance in office," editorialized the *Augusta Daily Press*. "His least enemy has not colored too lightly his official conduct. Nothing but the interference of Congress can save him. On that thread he hangs all his hopes. It is not [to protect] the rights of the negroes specially, but to shield himself from the consequences of his own acts, that he is urging that the state government be overthrown." Bullock claimed that he used the money legitimately, although without authorization, to pay the rent and purchase furnishings for the Kimball Opera House, which then housed the Georgia legislature. In a counteroffensive, Bullock likewise charged Angier with misuse of state funds. Nevertheless, these and other accusations of corruption stemming from Bullock's close association with Hannibal I. Kimball, railroad executive and capitalist, continued throughout Bullock's term of office. Indeed, Linton Stephens, brother of Alexander H. Stephens, would characterize Bullock and Kimball (predictably) as "unprincipled adventurers, hunting in couple, to plunder the public. I have knowledge of both of them, obtained in the course of professional business. Whenever one of them appears in a matter there is reason to suspect, at least, that the other is standing behind his back. . . . They are a pack of swindling adventurers."[57]

The dissension among Republicans and internal criticism of the Bullock administration delighted Democrats. Most Georgians could not or would not distinguish one Republican from another and were unimpressed with the subtle differences between Bullock's plans for the state and those of the so-called moderates. "One doctrine is as objectionable as the other," wrote one editor. "We cannot join with some of our respected contemporaries in patting such men as Bryant and Caldwell on the back." Furthermore, the divided leadership left blacks unsure of which direction to take. For the present they followed the governor and trusted the strategy of seeking federal force to protect them.[58]

Just as he was attempting to establish the credibility of his wing of the Republican party, in February 1869 Bryant came under one of the bitterest attacks of his career. When the *Atlanta New Era,* under the editorship of Samuel Bard, was given the franchise for state printing, a howl went up that Bryant had accomplished the victory and would receive a kickback from the profits. The reason for this barrage is unclear, since JEB had no particular connection with the *New Era.* While Bryant had supported Bard's election as printer in the previous summer, 1868, it is difficult to see how, at this juncture, he could have benefited from the assignment. The suspicion possibly had arisen in August 1868, when Bryant introduced a bill in the house that would allow the governor to designate which papers would be printed as official. Certainly by that time he had known that the *Loyal Georgian* would not receive the business, as he had once hoped. "This printing fraud is what first opened our eyes to the corrupt notions of Bryant," the editor of the *Daily Press* wrote. "If there is anything he will not do for money, we should like him, or some of his friends to tell us what it is; and Sam Bard is about two degrees worse than Bryant." Despite the fact that the charges were never officially considered and there is no evidence that Bryant was personally enriched by the appointment, the bad press against "Bryant & Co." persisted.[59]

The struggle for dominance among Republicans continued to center on Blodgett as Bullock's man and Bryant as leader of the faction opposing the governor. Although Blodgett had maintained his hold on the chairmanship of the Republican central committee, Bryan had dominated the anti-Bullock executive committee since the summer of 1868. The tension between the two mounted until a showdown occurred at the meeting of Republicans of Richmond County on February 27, 1869. The underlying issue was support for Bullock's idea to recommit Georgia to military rule, while the actual business of the meeting was to elect delegates to the state Republican convention to be held March 5, 1869.

Blodgett masterminded the majority report that called for complete endorsement of the governor's proposal for a third reconstruction of Georgia. The caucus selected delegates but omitted Bryant; he was left "shivering in the cold," according to a hostile press. In an attempt to prevent the pro-Bullock members from completely dominating, Bryant then submitted a minority report in which he "spoke at considerable length in definition of the distinction and the probable effect of the two doctrines upon the party." He further asserted his own loyalty to the Republican cause and charged conspiracy in his being omitted from the list of delegates to the state convention. His efforts to reassert his leadership, however, fell on unsympathetic ears, as Blodgett controlled the meeting. The chairman impatiently took the floor in the "demolition" of Bryant. "Blodgett said it was the *third* time he had heard that speech, and the third time he had fought it. Sarcastically [he] admitted Bryant's good Republicanism; believed that he was at one time a good Republican, but thought that he had fallen from grace." Blodgett's remarks were "lustily cheered throughout," and before the conclusion of his speech, "Bryant was observed to take up his carpet-bag and seek a more congenial atmosphere, and, we suppose, more harmonious spirits."[60]

The "Skowheganite," as the *Daily Press* mockingly labeled Bryant, had reached the low point of his political career. The "cards had been dexterously manipulated against him." Ironically, after he suffered this scorn of his fellow Republicans, black and white, the Civil and Political Rights Association of Georgia, organized the year before in Macon, at which Bryant had been speaker, met in Augusta. Bryant's relationship with the black leaders was at its nadir. They had chosen, unwisely it would later appear, to follow Blodgett rather than Bryant. Leaders such as H. M. Turner would later recognize their error, but for now even Turner was pointed in excluding JEB from their meeting. Disillusioned with whites, he was proud of their association as "purely a colored organization." Somewhat disillusioned himself, in March 1869 John Bryant resigned as chairman of the Republican executive committee, despite the fact that more and more white Republicans began to dissociate themselves from Bullock's campaign.[61]

In the meantime, with Bullock's plan for Georgia pending in Congress, the Democratic party in the state was seeking its own strategy to subvert the governor. The "centrists" planned to cooperate with the Republicans just enough to regain control. The expulsion of the Negro members from the legislature seemed the most reversible part of the damaging evidence that Georgia was resisting federal policy. Perhaps reinstatement would clear the state's reputation and foil the scheme for a third reconstruction. As Democratic state executive committee chairman Elbridge G. Cabaniss later stated it, "I am willing to see the negro members reseated . . . not because I favor the abstract principle of their right to hold office, but to avert a calamity [another military reconstruction] which we have reason to fear is now threatening us." He went on to explain, "I am not afraid of their getting into office hereafter. The wealth and intelligence of the voters will surely rule & not the ignorance of the African. What I want is to get from under Radical rule—and when we get the government of our state fully in our hands, we can soon right matters." With that strategy clearly in the minds of some, in February 1869 the Georgia legislature passed a joint resolution asking that the state supreme court hear and decide a test case on the right of blacks to hold office. The assembly pledged to accept the ruling as binding.[62]

With the same confident faith in future control, and further to demonstrate progress in Georgia, some Democrats were willing to ratify the Fifteenth Amendment, which granted black males the right to vote. Bullock was now in the awkward spot of opposing this move. Perhaps aware that such an action would lend legitimacy to a legislative body he had ruled illegitimate and fearful that his own demand for military assistance would seem unnecessary, Bullock actively sought to prevent ratification. In the house, though only Republicans voted to ratify, a majority of Democrats ensured approval by a 64–53 vote. But in the senate the governor garnered all his forces and defeated the amendment by another skillful use of both votes and abstentions.[63] Such a blatant attempt to restrain the state's apparent progress toward full restoration proved to be too much even for some of Bullock's close supporters. Sam Bard, for example, editor of the *Atlanta New Era*, finally broke with the governor over his efforts to defeat the amendment. Bullock's desperate moves to control the state were losing him friends faster than he gained them.

Bullock's erstwhile friend, John Emory Bryant, had for the present removed himself from the political struggle with the governor but apparently felt that the Republican party owed him at least a patronage position for all his previous work. In a move seemingly devoid of logic but, one surmises, compatible with Bryant's combative lust for revenge, the carpetbagger set his sights on Foster Blodgett's job as postmaster in Augusta. JEB probably hoped to embarrass Blodgett by publicizing his record, since Blodgett had been suspended in January 1868, pending the outcome of his perjury trial. Or perhaps he thought simply that Blodgett would not contend for the position and that the plum should be his. Bryant, in any case, claimed that he believed the field was clear for the appointment.[64]

While he had been fighting political foes, Bryant's wife, Emma Spaulding Bryant, had remained with him in Atlanta. In March 1869, with JEB in Washington pursuing the position of postmaster, she awaited the birth of their child. Her plaintive letters reveal her fear of dying while he was away. Still, she was anxious for his "success" in the capital. When the baby was born with fatal brain damage, without John's presence to comfort his wife, she urged him to hurry to her if he would see the baby boy alive. But Bryant was further "delayed" and never saw his son. Two weeks later he was still absent while Emma attempted to regain her strength and wondered about her future. Would she have other children? Would she find work? She confessed that "none could fill the void left by our first born." Charles Stearns, carpetbagger in rural Augusta, whose wife, Etta, had died only recently, wrote the Bryants and offered permission to bury the infant "where my wife is buried." Now faced with the tragedy of personal loss added to his seeming political defeat, Bryant only awaited the opportunity to retire from public life. When the anticipated appointment as postmaster of Augusta came on May 18, 1869, he resigned from the state legislature the same day.[65] He took office in July 1869 but served only until January 1870, as will be seen.

Bullock could possibly have had Bryant out of his way, at least for a time, had he allowed the appointment as postmaster to stand. General Alfred Terry, who had assumed command of the Department of the South in May 1869, urged the governor to accept Bryant's appointment, citing JEB's service to the Republicans and the need for "party unity." But the feud now was too personal to be breached. Rather than allowing it to stand, Bullock and Blodgett waged a personal attack against Bryant, worked to have Blodgett reinstated, and endeavored to prevent congressional confirmation of Bryant's appointment.[66]

This kind of campaign was a mistake, for it drew Bryant back into the heart of the battle against the governor. Bryant sought the backing of every influential Republican he knew in his struggle to be confirmed as postmaster of Augusta. His correspondence was filled with letters to persons such as President Grant, General Horace Porter (Grant's secretary), Postmaster General J. A. A. Creswell, and General O. O. Howard, Bryant's old boss and head of the Freedmen's Bureau. Prominent state Republicans such as Amos Akerman, soon to be appointed to Grant's cabinet, and J. W. Clift, representative of Georgia's twelfth district, wrote letters to Washington on Bryant's behalf. One of Akerman's letters revealed the charges that the carpetbagger was bucking: "It would be a gross injustice not to [confirm Bryant]. . . . He was one of the most ze[a]lous and consistunt [sic] of the extreme Radical wing. He was one of the clever who voted with me against striking out the clause which explicitly gave the right of office to all voters, a clause which (if it had remained) would have saved us from many of our subsequent troubles." Akerman continued, "I am annoyed to hear that Senators are being told he is not a true Republican. . . . [I understand] he is charged with responsibility for unseating the colored members, whereas he was their main champion in debate and stood firm in their cause to the last, voting against their exclusion when many of our party faltered. . . . The charges are as ridiculous as to say that Garrison was no abolitionist."[67]

Akerman defended Bryant's motive in seeking a paying position by saying that it was understandable, since it was difficult for a Republican "to hero in the usual callings of life" in the South. Surprisingly, some men other than politicians gave Bryant their support. Even though Foster Blodgett had served two successful terms as mayor of Augusta (1859–1861) before the war, his Reconstruction appointments as postmaster (1865–1868) and mayor (1867–1868) plus his association with the Republican administration had lost for him much of his native following. Holding two positions simultaneously was in itself a violation of the city's code; Blodgett further angered the citizenry by promoting ordinances that more than doubled his salary as mayor (from two thousand to five thousand dollars), even as he retained his federal yearly stipend of four thousand dollars. A newspaper in Griffin, Georgia, was therefore willing to give Bryant a backhanded compliment when a reporter commented on a gathering of radical whites and blacks: "We saw that energetic and promising genius, J. E. Bryant, of carpet-bag notoriety, and present postmaster of Augusta, whom, by the way, we could almost forgive for all his devilment, because he 'euchred' Blodgett out of the Augusta post office."[68]

In his own letters asking for support, Bryant outlined his diligent work for the party over the years. He tried to show also that the postal position would be necessary if he were to publish a Republican newspaper as he wished to do. The *Loyal Georgian,* his first effort, had been suspended at the end of 1868. He now proposed to continue the publication under a new name, the *Georgia Republican,* and he gave it the founding date of July 17, 1869. A neighboring paper noted sardonically a few days earlier, "It is rumored that Bryant is about to start a new Radical paper in Augusta." Ever sanguine, Bryant pledged that he would use the paper to unite the Republican party in the state, maintaining that "the leaders who have done the work of building the party" backed his efforts. Bullock and Blodgett were still after him, but Bryant took possession of the post office in Augusta on July 21, 1869, and asked for five months to prove what he could do for the Republican cause. One might assume that his wife joined him in Augusta, since no letters chronicle their separation, but she perhaps remained in Atlanta. An old fan of Bryant's wrote enthusiastically when he first received the *Georgia Republican*: "I am vearey glad to see that you or not dead yet & ar Abeleell to Spaek for your Selft I have ben vearey sorreay & sad when I was tauld that you had left the party & was a working a gaints the party & now I find This is not True & so I fills much bettre Than I have bin a for som tim." Bryant gave his own assessment of the situation in a later letter. "When I commenced the publication of the *Georgia Republican,*" he said, "my influence in the party was almost entirely destroyed."[69]

In order to sanctify his new existence, perhaps to rebuild a political base and to underline his moral commitment to blacks, Bryant began two new organizations in Augusta: a chapter of the Young Men's Christian Association (YMCA) for blacks and the Mechanics and Laborers Association. Because he had made promises as he sought the general's support for his position as postmaster, JEB dutifully reported his new efforts to O. O. Howard. According to Bryant, the Mechanics and Laborers Association would take up the work of the old GERA, assisting blacks "in their own elevation through education." The new association had made the *Georgia Republican* its official organ, the editor said, and it sought cooperation with all the groups at "work for the freedmen," including the Freedmen's Bureau and the AMA.[70]

Howard requested another evaluation from bureau agent John R. Lewis, superintendent of the bureau's schools in Georgia and Bryant's successor as president of the GERA, but currently a supporter of Bullock.

In a confidential reply to Howard, Lewis maligned Bryant's motives. In truth, he said, the man "must ever be before the public eye." Though he did not pass judgment on the YMCA chapter, Lewis suspected that the "labor convention's" main purpose was to "make capital for Bryant . . . and other individuals." These "oft repeated conventions and assemblages are a nuisance and a drain on the people & I am sorry to see them," he wrote. It was the old conflict between Tillson and Bryant revisited. Howard concluded that the carpetbagger should resign from his position as postmaster, a request Bryant respectfully declined for the time being.[71]

Bryant's return to grass-roots politics and his work among a new group of blacks in a new convention invite a reappraisal not only of his motives but also of the uncomfortable situation in which freedpersons of Georgia found themselves. The split in the Republican party placed them in the awkward position of needing to choose sides, and, as has been noted, their leaders at least had stuck with Bullock. They reasoned that the power of the governorship provided their best avenue to security and equality. The plan for a third reconstruction did not bring dismay, for it meant new support from Washington, a benefit to them as they perceived it and as past experience had confirmed. Furthermore, Bullock was attempting to convince all who would listen that Bryant's motives were base and his commitment to their civil rights a sham. Future assessment would compare records and show that, when Bryant was postmaster in Augusta, half of his appointments went to blacks, in contrast to their later realization that "the Bullock administration had neither the will nor the power to help them."[72] After Bullock was removed, Bryant quickly regained his black constituency.

As Bryant attempted to recoup his political life in Augusta, Bullock was fighting for his in Atlanta, with a major portion of the governor's time being taken in waging his battle for the third reconstruction of Georgia. The legislature, fearful that the issue of black expulsion would aid Bullock's plan, had given the matter to the state supreme court, over the governor's veto. In June 1869, in *White* v. *Clements,* the court ruled that blacks were indeed eligible to hold office. Chief Justice Joseph Brown voted with the majority in the decision, lending credence to Bryant's original estimation that Brown had not really favored expulsion. Republican and Democratic leaders urged the governor to reconvene the legislature in order to implement the ruling of the court that the blacks be reinstated, but Bullock refused. In response to the governor's resistance, moderate (that is, anti-Bullock) Republicans met on October 22 and drew up a petition asking that the blacks be seated and that Georgia not be subjected to further congressional intervention in her affairs. Bullock ignored the plea. Controlling the November meeting of the Republican executive committee with his black supporters, the governor overturned a recommendation to end Reconstruction in Georgia. The black Civil and Political Rights Association held rallies and wrote petitions to underline further their backing for the governor. Congress would meet in December 1869, a month before the next scheduled session of the Georgia legislature. If the state legislature did not act in special session, perhaps Congress would intervene.[73]

In an attempt to ensure just such intervention, Bullock had devoted the fall of 1869 to gathering atrocity stories from the Georgia countryside. Unfortunately, it was not a difficult task. The Ku Klux Klan, emboldened by success in the previous year, continued to ride in 1869, though on a diminished scale because it was an off-election year. The governor's correspondence was soon replete with reports of injustices to blacks and of the barbarous treatment they received at the hands of whites. He concluded in his letters to Washington that the state was not safe from the Klan's terror and that he was helpless to restore order. General Alfred Terry, commander of the Department of the South, was impressed by the report, concurred in Bullock's assessment, and himself requested that the state be placed under military authority again.[74]

It appeared that Bullock was on the verge of success. Though congressional members in Washington were becoming weary of the "Georgia Question," they complied when Grant asked for a bill that acquiesced in Bullock's demand. Bullock himself took the bill to the White House on December 22, 1869, and Grant signed it without even reading it.[75] Georgia was to be "reconstructed" once again. Congress had written the bill to Bullock's specifications: the 1868 legislature was to be recalled and purged of those who could not take the "test oath" or show removal of the disability; ratification of the Fifteenth Amendment was the precondition for readmittance into the Union; exclusion because of race of any duly elected official was prohibited. While nothing in the Reorganization Act explicitly remanded Georgia to military rule, provision was made for troops to be dispatched if the governor requested them. Bullock convened the legislature on January 9, 1870, and the process of "Terry's purge" began.

John Emory Bryant was on hand for the opening day. He had withdrawn his resignation from the assembly in a letter to Bullock on January 10, 1870. Later he explained that, following his conscience, he had rejoined the legislature to fight Bullock's policies, leaving the more lucrative position he had worked so hard to secure. If he had received an inside tip that the prospects for confirmation were remote, the record does not reveal it. The Democratic press in Athens reported the carpetbagger's version of his motives: Bryant "stands by his record as a Union soldier and Republican, and has resigned his post office in order to serve his State, and that no matter what anybody charges, he intends remaining in his party and doing what he can to purify it." The writer confirmed that Bryant "charges Bullock with corruption, with acting illegally in the organization of the Legislature; with trying to serve selfish ends; with being willing to jeopardize everything else for the sake of securing his own election to the United States Senate," an ambition Bullock would attempt to realize later.[76] Presumably, Bryant moved his wife back to the capital at this juncture, if in fact she left when he moved to Augusta.

Although Georgia was not officially under military rule, President Grant had assigned General Terry as "commanding general of the district of Georgia" at Bullock's request. Terry allowed Bullock's appointed civilian officials to carry out the reorganization of the legislature, a method that was later ruled illegal by the U.S. Senate's Judiciary Committee. The Georgia senate agreed to the reorganization, but the house revolted, protesting that Bullock's organizer, A. L. "Fatty" Harris, a nonofficeholding carpetbagger, had no authority to convene the house. A witness to Bryant's involvement reported that "Harris ordered the Sergeant-at-Arms to arrest Bryant. Great excitement. Bryant refused to be arrested, and declared that this was an attempt to intimidate members. Hinton and Blodgett's son were the parties attempting to arrest Bryant." The tension mounted when "a negro near by drew a pistol on Bryant. After several excited harangues among the Radicals . . . order was restored at length, Bryant quieted down, pale with rage, and nursing wrath against the other faction of the party." Anti-Bullock Republicans united with Democrats and elected Bryant chairman pro tem of the meeting to replace Harris. "Bryant, mounting a chair (for Harris and coadjutors kept him off the Speaker's stand) [after] a motion to adjourn to 10 A.M. tomorrow was made and carried, . . . declared the House adjourned." Harris, cool and undisturbed and ignoring Bryant's claim to authority, ordered that the roll call be continued.[77]

After fifteen days of investigation, "humiliation," rebellion, and delay, the purge was over, but who was actually in control was a moot question. Only nineteen members of the lower assembly and five in the senate were declared ineligible, significantly fewer than the forty in the house and eighteen in the senate that Bullock had predicted.[78]

Bryant was admired by some rather surprising observers during those days. Even the *Atlanta Constitution,* "long the nemesis of all Republicans," praised him for "the nerve with which he braved down the d—— brutal piece of tyranny." The *Athens Southern Banner* admitted that Bryant was "certainly showing an immense amount of zeal and pluck, and it is said that he has scornfully rejected the most tempting inducement to desist from his course." The editor later confessed that his admiration for the effort was halfhearted: "We sympathize with Bryant," he wrote, "because we believe he is honestly trying to make the Republican party respectable—a consummation which a Democrat has no sort of interest in."[79]

Capitalizing on the centrist spirit of cooperation between moderate Republicans and Democrats, Bryant became the anti-Bullock candidate for speaker of the house. Joe Brown and even Robert Toombs, Georgia's "unreconstructed rebel," attempted to win conservative support for Bryant's candidacy. In a much-quoted letter, Toombs said, "Bryant is the candidate of the Democrats. . . . and I and Joe Brown are trying to elect him! Rather a strange conjunction, is it not? But you know my rule is to use the devil if I can do better to save the country."[80]

Bryant recognized that Brown would play an important role in any coalition. Keeping President Grant informed through his frequent correspondence with the president's secretary, Horace Porter, JEB called Blodgett and Bullock "bold and reckless." But under "Akerman and others," a reorganization could occur to "save the state from bankruptcy and ruin." He explained that there was little difference between moderate Republicans and Democrats and that both looked to Brown "as their leader. . . . Brown seems really in earnest in his endeavor to defeat Bullock and his schemes."[81]

But some Republicans doubted Brown's direction and were even less enthusiastic than Toombs about the attempt at fusion politics. They believed that Bryant was being used. Bryant, one wrote, "seems to be foolishly selling himself and his party, if he can, to the opposition. Not a colored member goes with him in either House." Though Bryant "seems to believe" he could give a balance of power to Republicans, "he greatly over-estimates his strength. His best friends in all the State will drop him.

Passing through the halls of the House, I overheard a group of Democratic leaders cursing him in the most blasphemous terms, and then, in an undertone, saying, 'but we've got to use him; can then throw him out,' &c." Furthermore, he has told me, the writer continued, "he'd rather the whole Republican party in Georgia should be a failure than that Bullock should triumph. His more intimate advisers, I have seen, and know their character, and can assure you that no true Republican here stands by him."[82]

Based on previous Democratic schemes and Bryant's own record, this analysis was probably close to the truth of the matter. But the rank-and-file Democrats found the strategy hard to swallow, even if for political expediency. And the *New Era*, by now taken over by Bullock supporters, tried to increase the anxiety over the possibility of Bryant's selection as speaker: "Bryant . . . is an adventurer, to all intents and purposes. Not only this; he is the worst of his class. . . . What claim has he to the leadership of any party in Georgia? What has he been or done, that he should now step forward as a great champion of any party, much less the Democracy? These are pertinent questions for our Democratic and Conservative friends to ask themselves."[83]

When the vote came, Democrats did not rally behind the coalition candidate; many of them did not vote at all. Bryant's opponent, R. L. McWhorter, won the race 76 to 52. Proponents of the moderate anti-Bullock bloc in the legislature were disappointed. Perhaps realizing that his vengeance for Bullock had somehow violated his own integrity, Bryant, in his letters, was strangely silent on the entire matter. Perman has shown that Georgia's failure in fusion politics was not unique. In many Southern states Democrats quickly looked to new strategies. Bryant, for his part, returned to his indigenous ground as "Regular" Republican, to use Perman's term.[84]

Bullock, meanwhile, had not given up his plan to have Foster Blodgett elected to the U.S. Senate. His new attempt, this time with the reconstituted legislature, was more successful than the first, for the reorganized legislature declared the election of Hill and Miller in 1868 invalid. In all the confusion over Georgia's status, these two senators had never been seated in Congress anyway. Now Attorney General Henry Farrow's faithfulness to Bullock would finally pay off. To replace Hill and Miller, the legislature elected Farrow to the term ending in 1873 and Richard Whiteley to the term ending in 1871. Blodgett was chosen also, at last, to succeed Whiteley as senator from Georgia for the term ending in 1877. While there was precedent in Georgia for the election of senators to future terms, under state law the selection for the term ending in 1877 should have been the prerogative of Georgia's assembly in 1871. It is not surprising, therefore, that a delegation of anti-Bullock Republicans traveled to Washington to lobby against Blodgett's confirmation. Bryant, as the chief spokesman of this delegation, continued his personal campaign against Blodgett and Bullock. Failure to protest the situation in Georgia would, he felt, lead to "a wide field for political speculation."[85]

LOSS OF REPUBLICAN POWER

Bullock found it increasingly difficult to maintain the support of the president and Congress in the face of the strong lobby. The Senate, becoming suspicious of Bullock's schemes, ordered the Judiciary Committee to investigate the political situation in the state. This committee reported on March 2, 1870, that the Georgia legislature had been reorganized in accordance with the provisions of the Fourteenth Amendment and had ratified the Fifteenth Amendment, that the black legislators had been reseated, and that there was, therefore, no reason why the reorganization order should continue to be operative.[86] Bullock feared this report, for the readmission of Georgia and normal elections, which were scheduled for the fall of 1870, would surely mean the end of the Republican administration, as Brown had predicted. The governor's last chance to prolong his power was to extend the term of the existing legislators under the claim that they had not served a full term as a legitimate assembly. It seemed imperative that the body he had worked so hard to reconstitute should have a longer life.

Black Republican leaders continued to agree with Bullock's line, but the "prolongation issue" seemed to many others an illegal ploy, and it further alienated the governor from some white members of the party. Henry Farrow, now more visible as senator-elect, became uneasy about his own reputation and finally abandoned Bullock's cause. Such realignments received encouragement from outside Georgia. As one congressman put it, "Republicans everywhere in the North are glad of the defeat of the schemes having prolongation in view and are especially grateful to those Georgia Republicans who labor for that result." Congress, preparing to readmit Georgia, debated the prolongation issue under the Bingham Amendment, which would require state elections in 1870. Bullock lobbied desperately to ensure defeat of the amendment and paid spectacular "printing costs" to the *Washington Chronicle;* the paper in return published editorials favorable to the governor.[87]

Anti-Bullock Republicans, such as Colonel John Bowles, urged Bryant and others "to write the Reconstruction Committee and urge acceptance of Georgia" on the following grounds: (1) that Georgia was in "as good or better shape as any other Southern state," (2) that acceptance would "ease anxiety and give confidence to capitalists who are waiting to invest in the state," and (3) that Congress should "settle the question of the Republican party in Georgia." Bryant was willing to do this and more. In May 1870 he wrote to General Porter, Grant's secretary, urging the administration to change its support from Bullock to other state party leaders and to back a reorganization of the party in Georgia.[88] Besides his correspondence to Washington, Bryant continued to attack the "Bullock ring" in the *Georgia Republican.* Bullock, in another attempt to rid himself of JEB's effective opposition, chose June 17, 1870, as the date to accept Bryant's resignation from the state's house of representatives, the resignation Bryant had written on May 18, 1869, and had previously withdrawn in January 1870. Bryant ignored the gesture.

Legislators in Washington seemed "less eager to be seen with Bullock" now, and in the White House his influence was waning. One might have expected otherwise, since in June 1870, Amos T. Akerman joined Grant's cabinet as attorney general, a signal that Grant might be somewhat more sensitized to civil rights enforcement and the plight of Southern Republicans. But as a newly dubbed "moderate" Georgia Republican, though clearly "radical" in matters of racial equality, Akerman's displeasure with Bullock leadership had been apparent for some time, and he undoubtedly helped to change the president's attitude toward the governor. At the same time, Akerman was praising the Republicanism of Bullock's opponent, Bryant, in Washington, lending credence to charges made in Bryant's own letters. Without Grant's support and with Congress increasingly doubtful, Bullock's bid was hopeless. Eager to be rid of the matter, Congress passed a resolution in July 1870, readmitting Georgia to the Union and, with the Bingham Amendment attached, requiring legislative elections in 1870. Now Bullock could not prolong the term of his purged legislature. The governor left the capital in a cloud of accusations that he had used bribes and "improper means to influence the votes of Senators" on the resolution.[89]

Back in Georgia, Bullock faced the elections he so dreaded, while anti-Bullock Republicans also worried about losing everything. Akerman himself went to the state and attempted to fashion an election bill that would guarantee Republican control of the electoral process and perhaps thereby preserve the party, if not Bullock. The governor, who had promised to veto the bill if he was not satisfied with it, either saw some hope in that control or else felt his options were gone. After his reconstituted legislature passed the election bill, with Republicans again divided, he signed it into law on October 3, 1870. John Emory Bryant voted for the bill, which allowed for a polling period from December 22 to 24, election managers appointed by the governor, no elections at all where managers were not appointed, and no challenge of voters at the polls.[90]

Despite the controls, the attempt to save the party proved futile, since the outcome was once again decided before the election. In the fall of 1870 the failure of the two principal goals of Reconstruction was clearly seen in Georgia: the Republican administration was tottering and there was no perceptible movement on the part of white Georgians to sustain any change in the social order. Even decent whites who were becoming critical of the Klan's terror were afraid to make any gestures to aid in its restriction. The possibility of full black participation in the election was precluded long before December. Some of the freedmen had already learned that the prudent way to vote, if one voted at all, was Democratic. Many of those who braved threats against Republicans and attempted to vote anyway were turned away on the pretext that the poll tax remained unpaid (though once again it had been legally abolished). There were charges of corruption on both sides, and doubtless there were violations by both parties. Nevertheless, witnesses before Congress—as well as the outcome of the election—showed that Republicans suffered most.[91]

Before the election Bullock belatedly tried the strategy of making peace with the real powers in Georgia politics, those of "intelligence and wealth" whom the native whites in his party had been touting so regularly. It is still unclear whether the governor actually expected his new effort to win the election for Republicans or whether, knowing that he would be out of office, he was shrewdly looking to the future. In any case, he attempted to sway a coalition of Unionists and industrialists in order to divide the white vote, a plan former governor Brown had long ago urged him to follow.

In order to make his try at conciliation with Brown and the so-called moderates believable, Bullock moved to unlock the till of the state-owned railroad, the Western & Atlantic. The management of this road, which was under the direction of Foster Blodgett, had been heavily criticized because of Blodgett's failure to pay its profits into the state treasury. Under Blodgett the line had instead "piled up a debt of $750,000 in two years," no doubt to Blodgett's benefit. The new arrangement, obviously calculated for its political effects, was signed by Bullock in October 1870 and leased the road to a coterie of industrialists including Brown, who resigned his supreme court position, Kimball, and twenty-one others. In a startling switch, Benjamin Hill, staunch Democrat and vociferous critic of Republican and scalawag rule, suddenly embraced the Reconstruction amendments; the revelation that he was also a cosigner in the new railroad lease helped explain the conversion. The deal did not smell like a rose. Even Blodgett was apparently involved in some way; he later claimed that Brown and Kimball had promised him sixty thousand dollars "for services rendered the Western & Atlantic R.R. Co."[92]

Unfortunately for Bullock, once he had signed the papers leasing the road for twenty-five thousand dollars per month, he was expendable. After a respectable period of seven years, when he tried to remind the group of their debt, Bullock was brushed aside, since he was no longer "in condition to injure us," and, after all, "he had his opportunity." If an "old friend" betrayed him, well, "it was his own misfortune." As Brown was to remind the governor, "I admit that in the past you have done me several favors . . . but you must recollect that there is another side to the account, without which you would not have been in position to bestow favors."[93] Bullock, that is, owed his governorship partially to Brown.

In the fall of 1870, Bullock could only watch the impending doom of his administration. The elections of December turned out as might have been predicted. The Republican party lost its tenuous hold on Georgia politics, as the Democrats took a commanding majority in both houses of the legislature that would convene in November 1871. Bullock at last realized the helplessness of the situation and remained aloof and wary after the results were known. In regard to a new movement by the federal government against the Ku Klux Klan, he showed little willingness to cooperate. Local law enforcement could bring the disorder to heel, he claimed lamely, if only it would.

U.S. Attorney General Akerman, whose strategy required strong assistance within the state, was determined to end the Klan's reign, with or without the governor's aid. He appointed John Emory Bryant and John

Caldwell as special counsels in Georgia to assist in the Klan investigations. Bryant assured Akerman that his newspaper, the *Georgia Republican,* would actively support the KKK legislation, even though he would lose "patronage I have received from white business men," lest it appear that Republicans in the state "oppose the policy of the national party." The Bullock/Blodgett-supported papers opposed Akerman's efforts, according to Bryant. "The truth is," he continued, "Bullock is working for himself as usual, regardless of the interests of the Republican party." Bryant concluded that the governor was afraid to take an unpopular position against the Klan, since he faced a Democratic legislature in November: "It requires some nerve to take a bold stand in defense of that measure in this state."[94]

By this time, Bullock found himself beleaguered from every side, and his Democratic opponents were determined to impeach him. Bullock had apparently hoped that Brown, now with his influence refurbished, would oppose impeachment, but these hopes were dashed when Brown disclaimed any opposition to such a trial. The evidence shows that for the disclaimer Brown had been assured that the Western & Atlantic Railroad lease would be allowed to stand. In the face of the certainty of impeachment, Bullock fled the state in October 1871, a few days after Brown's position was known. One Southern newspaper reported that Bullock's "elegant piano and handsome carriage" were discovered at the depot after his departure and were impounded by vengeful Georgians before the "plunder" could follow the fleeing governor.[95]

The president of the senate, Benjamin Conley, became governor in a short-lived attempt to keep a Republican in the office, but he had little chance of being sustained for long. Grant refused a request for troops to bolster the administration. Conley's term was brief but long enough for Foster Blodgett to secure a blanket pardon for any crimes he might have committed.[96] Early in 1872 Democrat James M. Smith was inaugurated governor after a special election in which Republicans did not field a candidate. Republican Reconstruction was over.

Members of the party who remained in Georgia did not immediately perceive that their day had passed. Anti-Bullock Republicans such as Bryant painted optimistic pictures of future divisions of the white vote, with Unionists and blacks emerging victorious. They seemed to believe sincerely that, with the rotten apple out of the barrel, the remaining Republicans with their national principles would be acceptable to Georgians. Republicans would pledge to "the unionists to stand by the Constitution and the rights of the colored race, ignoring as far as is possible the blunders of the state administration."[97]

The reasons for the failure of Reconstruction in Georgia went beyond the "blunders" of one man—there was blame to go around. The mistake made by the early Radicals in the state was their choice of a questionable candidate to head the party. Whatever the final evaluation of Bullock's administration, it cannot be denied that he was forced, because of his shaky political base, to fall back on a strategy that worked in opposition to the humanitarian goals of Reconstruction. The expulsion of blacks, the failure to move effectively against the Klan, and the effort to defeat the ratification of the Fifteenth Amendment all show at best an opportunism susceptible to short-lived solutions; Bullock's goals and association with Blodgett and Kimball reveal, at worst, blatant corruption. Ironically, those who had the most to lose by following Bullock—black Republicans—stuck with him throughout.

Some historians have identified another factor in Bullock's failure as his inability to hold the allegiance of the Georgia power structure, epitomized in the person of Joseph Brown, and to divide the white vote of the state rather than to solidify it against Republican rule. Bullock's late and futile attempt to protect himself by this route evokes little sympathy, however, for success by this means would have been bought at too high a price. Bryant's own coalition with moderate Democrats must be questioned in the same light. As the New South industrialists later proved, the theory that "men of intelligence and wealth" in the state should always control the tenants and laborers did nothing to change the social order weighted against blacks.[98]

Perhaps the greatest failure occurred in response to the former slaves. Not only were the Republicans unable to guarantee a free ballot to the freedmen, but blacks were systematically excluded from any positions of responsibility within the party itself. As one black Georgian would remember, "Governor Bullock did not employ a single colored man in his office, save as porter"; even on the Western & Atlantic Railroad "not a colored man was appointed." The issue of patronage continued to rankle the black Republicans of Georgia in the 1870s and 1880s. "We are not over anxious to do all the voting and let our . . . white party associates . . . hold all the offices," one explained to Bryant.[99] This failure to recognize and reward the ability of blacks revealed the inherent racism that infected the entire Republican effort.

In the face of Southern resistance and questionable Republican strategy and commitment, factionalism within the party provided the deathblow in Georgia. Whatever the motives of those men who attacked Bullock's administration from within, such conflict was suicidal to the party's chances of survival. The white people of Georgia could see few differences among Republicans, and they quickly closed ranks when the party's nominal head faltered.

Yet, in 1871 John Emory Bryant was far from discouraged about the future of Republicanism in Georgia. The anti-Bullock wing, including Bard, Akerman, and Joshua Hill, now controlled the party, and Bryant had accomplished two of his major objectives: Blodgett was not confirmed in the Senate, and Bullock had fallen "of his own weight." Bryant had come out on the winning side and was in a position to plan Republican strategy and to bargain for a patronage job. At last personal motives were in harmony once again with political structure. Bryant cast the whole struggle in a rather grand light: "I have desired to see Republican principles triumphant in Georgia. I have desired to assist in accomplishing that result. I am I suppose as selfish as other persons, but I believe I am capable of disinterested labor for a course that my judgement approves. I have done as much as I can do for the Republican party of Georgia."[100]

‖ Five

Bryant and the Strategic Shift of Republicans in the 1870s

I am proud to lead a party advocating such noble principles.[1]

The end of Radical Reconstruction is generally understood to be 1877, when a new administration removed all remaining federal troops and when Southerners controlled state governments in the old Confederacy. In truth, however, President Grant, who never forcefully pursued the military option, had long ago reassigned most military units in the South, and Hayes did not remove a single soldier from the region. Also, Reconstruction regimes had been crumbling for years before. In state after state, Radicals had conceded defeat, faced with corruption in government, recalcitrant Southern opinion, violence or the threat of violence from terrorist organizations, and Democratic "Redeemers."[1]

In the 1870s the Republican Party was desperate for a new policy in dealing with the South. Saddled with the blame for the devastating recession of 1873 and for the graft that honeycombed the Grant administration, Republican leaders searched for a new means of securing votes for their party. As the move toward Democratic solidarity in the South threatened to reduce Republican strength, party leaders realized that there was no guarantee of a loyal black vote in the South. Indeed, as the Democrats caught the sweet scent of their foes' retreat, the Redeemers feared less and ridiculed more the Republican effort and joined themselves in the game of buying, cajoling, and otherwise trying to secure the black vote, or at least a portion thereof.

Col. Bryant on the Stump!

ROOMS OF THE REPUBLICAN STATE CENTRAL COMMITTEE,
ATLANTA, GA., October 19, 1877.

THE importance of the political questions under consideration make it necessary that our party shall be thoroughly organized throughout the State. It has therefore been deemed advisable to hold Mass Conventions at the following times and places for the purpose of taking steps to defeat the ratification of the proposed Constitution.

For the First Congressional District at
Savannah, November 6.
For the Eighth Congressional District at
Augusta, November 8.
For that part of the Ninth Congressional District, contiguos to Morgan county, at
Madison, November 10.
For the Sixth Congressional District, at
Macon, November 13.
For the Third Congressional District, at
Cuthbert, November 15.
For the Second Congressional District, at
Albany, November 20.
For the Fourth Congressional District, at
Columbus, November 23.
For the counties contiguos to Coweta, at
Newnan, November 27.

I will be present and address the people, (D.V.), and hope to have other public speakers address them also.
It is desirable that each County shall have a good representation in these Conventions, but they will be entitled to twice as many votes as they have members in the lower House of the General Assembly.
Republicans desiring information in regard to the Campaign, and in regard to tickets, should address me at Atlanta, and their letters will receive prompt attention.

JOHN E. BRYANT,
CHAIRMAN

Broadside of Colonel Bryant's campaign to defeat the ratification of the constitution written by the convention in 1877. (Courtesy of Duke University Library.)

Several factors influenced the Republicans as they plotted strategy. The first was a profound weariness with "the Southern question" and the eternal bickering of Southern Republicans. Military Reconstruction, attempted by uneven and vacillating policy, to be sure, seemed a failure. Republicans also had a desire to hasten the process of healing sectional differences that had retarded business growth. In fact, the crusading zeal had lost its spark for many, and industrial interests seemed much more important than reform. "The party of abolitionist radicalism had now become the party of vested interests and big business. . . . The contradiction was obvious." As historian William Gillette has stated, "Americans were yearning for peace, prosperity, constitutional order, civil government without army interference, a return to federalism, and national unity." More than anything, Republicans wanted to claim that they could deliver this bliss.[2]

Influencing the clamor for new party directions was a second factor: the growing impatience or intolerance of many Northerners for blacks. Discounting the obstacles that had been placed in their way, the "double talk, double standards, and double dealing," many Republicans were coming to believe that Negroes were not developing into responsible citizens rapidly enough; they were "not suited for equality." Charles Darwin's scheme of human evolutionary development, introduced at midcentury, was gaining widespread acceptance. It became easier, even for many educated Northerners, as Social Darwinists misappropriated Darwin's theories, to see blacks as inferior or laggard beings in the evolutionary process. Perhaps, after all, gradual methods of "civilizing" should be emphasized to prepare former slaves better for citizenship. Education and culture were needed rather than politics and protest.[3] Surely some compromise could be devised with responsible white leaders in the South; Southerners could again have the charge of their "second-class citizenry" and work out race relations in their own way. By such reasoning, former Whigs in the South might be lured from the Democratic to the Republican ticket; carpetbaggers and blacks could be eased out of office and power.

Republican Rutherford B. Hayes became president in 1877 and attempted to execute such a plan, which was considered by many a betrayal of blacks. Although Hayes was under pressure from both business and political leaders to end Reconstruction, it is still possible to conclude that he genuinely believed in the validity of his policy and was sensitive to the charge of deserting the former slaves. He immediately removed himself from consideration for a second term, perhaps to lend credence to his protestations.[4]

Whatever the national party's motive for adopting these strategic changes, they caused shock waves in the South, where Republicans such as John Emory Bryant still labored for Republican power. By 1877 JEB had already found from practical experience the necessity to shift Republican emphases; the drama of the 1870s can be seen in his struggle to reconcile the old ideology of Radical Reconstruction and immediate reform with the new Republican strategy of gradualism and retreat.

REPUBLICANS REGROUP

Those who remained in the Republican camp began to pick up the pieces in 1872. Bryant, for one, expected the party to work with new vigor for the principles of equalitarianism and full civil rights for all males. He also anticipated that he would step into an acknowledged leadership role. In the waning days of Bullock's administration, Bryant had masterminded an exiled Republican party organization, "under cover" until Bullock should be no longer a factor in controlling the central committee, and called it the "State Council of the National Guard." Included in this group, among others, were James Atkins, Georgia-born Republican, carpetbagger Volney Spalding, who assisted Bryant in publishing the *Georgia Republican*, and, of course, JEB himself, who was listed as the council's secretary. After Bullock's resignation, Bryant had secretly corresponded with party officeholders in Washington about a possible Republican candidate for the hastily called gubernatorial election held on December 19, 1871; he concurred that the attempt was futile.

The flurry of party strategy and correspondence did not result in Bryant's inclusion in the legitimate party hierarchy. Foster Blodgett, who had been discredited along with Bullock, held onto the chairmanship of the state central committee for a time after the governor had fled, a situation that irritated some observers. Bryant confided to a friend, "Blodgett is chairman of our State Central Committee. He promises to resign but unfortunately for us he belongs to that class that seldom die and never resign." The wheels did turn eventually, but the changes did not affect

Bryant. The new power structure that emerged within the party featured Henry P. Farrow, who had skillfully detached himself from Bullock at just the last moment and was now district attorney for Georgia.

Bryant was aware of the scorn with which he was regarded by many, though he tended to see it not as personal but as part of the general dislike of Yankee politicians by native Georgians, even by some in the Republican party itself. Hearing his complaint to that effect, a national officeholder responded, "I appreciate what you say in regard to 'Carpet Baggers' and the feeling in regard to them entertained by the natives. I was already well aware of that feeling, [although] there ought not to be any such feeling for if the Republican Party is to have any success in the future . . . it will be obtained by the sh[r]ewdness, indomitable energy, [ta]lent and brains of 'Carpet Baggers.'" Such sentiments notwithstanding, the animosity between Northern- and Southern-born would prove to be one of the most divisive antagonisms faced by the trouble-ridden Georgia Republicans.[5]

As for Bryant, certainly disappointed after the significant role he had played in the exposure of Bullock, he contented himself for the time being with rebuilding the party by resuming his Republican newspaper, which had fallen on hard times. Bryant was desperate for income and claimed to be deeply in debt. While waiting for Bullock "to fall of his own weight," back in 1871 he had begun another letter-writing campaign for a lucrative position. Ironically, this very course added to his reputation as merely a spoils seeker and increased the hostility toward him. The dilemma was similar to that of other Georgia Republicans who attempted business ventures in the South. At a later time the wife of one faithful member of the party wrote Bryant asking for a political appointment for her husband. She confessed that her husband was the only white Republican in the county, and his store was patronized only by blacks, who, despite good intentions, had "nothing but their crops, which is principally rice." Unable to make a living, the man would have to leave the state if no position were forthcoming. This poignant appeal clearly indicates a problem that went well beyond Bryant's particular case. The "politics of livelihood" and dependency on federal office, already noted, remained an unpleasant necessity of life for Southern Republicans. The situation was particularly acute after Democratic "redemption" and got worse with the Depression of 1873.[6]

As Bryant surveyed patronage jobs that might be available to him in 1871–1872, he considered Edwin Belcher's post as assessor of internal revenue for Georgia's third district. Bryant had held the post of assistant assessor in the same district for a short time in 1868 and claimed that he could improve the quality of work being done in the office. Later he would rather lamely deny what was clearly an intensive scramble for Belcher's position.

Unfortunately for Bryant's reputation as a friend of the freed slaves, Belcher was black and an able man who had served in the Georgia legislature; because of his light skin, he was one of the few not expelled. As a matter of fact, he was one of those held in contempt by H. M. Turner because of Belcher's denial of his black heritage—Belcher had been caught trying to pass for white. Perhaps Bryant sensed Belcher's vulnerability on this point or perhaps he had not forgotten that Belcher had yielded to Bullock's pressure and had signed a petition in 1869 that slandered the carpetbagger. Nevertheless, the ultimately unsuccessful attempt to seize Belcher's job created an unfavorable reaction to Bryant, and during the months of party reorganization in 1872, he wisely maintained a low political profile. "You have no idea of the feeling against you," one friend advised; "your fight on Belcher was very disasterous [sic]." Bryant would have to do much fence mending before he would emerge as a leader acceptable to blacks in 1876, clear evidence of his political durability. Long before 1876, Belcher himself had come to support the aggressive politician as before, probably believing that Bryant was, after all, the best or most available friend that the blacks of Georgia had.[7]

For the time being in 1872, Bryant declared his intention to retire from politics. That declaration elicited the desired expression of regret from coworkers in the party, such as M. H. Hale: "With regard to your retiring from active participation in politics, let me say for myself and for many others, if it be so I am sorry, we want your advice in planning and your energy to carry out our plans." Hale went on with exactly what Bryant himself felt was true: "You have much to congratulate yourself with at the present time[,] the flight of Bullock and Blodgett being discarded by the Senate and his displacement from chairmanship of the Committee but an acknowledgement that your course in reference to these men has been right and your stand today vindicative [sic] in the position you have henceforth taken, and today [you] ought to be more influential with the National Administration than any other Georgian."[8]

With such encouragement it was only a matter of time before JEB again answered the call to political participation. For the first three months of

1872, however, he concentrated on his law practice in Augusta and awaited presidential action on the suggestion made by friends that he take the post of deputy collector of customs in Savannah, a patronage position that paid a salary of $2,500 per year. In addition, he took such clients as Brown's Western & Atlantic Railroad, lobbying for subsidies on its behalf in Washington. Records show that he was promised 250 shares of capital stock for his efforts, as well as traveling expenses.[9]

This schedule still did not encourage real home life. Emma Spaulding Bryant had lived for the largest part of the past several years in Atlanta, as John's activities seemed to revolve around that city, Augusta, and Washington. In the fall of 1871, while her husband focused on the political demise of Bullock and the potential for a new party, Emma Bryant had gamely assisted with the publication, now sporadic, of the *Georgia Republican*. She was pregnant again and worried about the diet she was forced to eat at her boardinghouse; exposure to whooping cough gave her a valid reason to seek new lodging. "I know that you are unable to give much attention to home matters now and I will do the best I can till you return," she wrote him on one occasion. On November 16, 1871, a baby girl was born, a birth once again without father in attendance, though he had written not long before the event, "I feel anxious for you darling and want to be with you. With warmest love and kisses from Y[our] H[usband]." The child, named Emma Alice (Alice for a dear friend in Maine), was born in an unfinished farm house, "in a room that had a curtain hung up instead of a door to the room." She would be the Bryants' only surviving child, and Emma did not reveal any additional pregnancies.[10]

In his letters Bryant seemed genuinely involved in his family's welfare. "I wish I could be with you, but here I am in my office all alone," he wrote one night. "Tell me all about baby," he said on another occasion. "I love you darling and every day think how pleasant it will be next winter to have a home of our own." When a goat was needed to supply the baby's milk, the new father made all the arrangements. It was clear that both parents feared the loss of another child. "I pray that God may spare her to us," John wrote, "if it was for the best. He knows." Then, with less seriousness, he added, "It will be a joke if the goat does not give milk."[11]

With new baby and wife in Atlanta, Bryant showed his concern through letters but maintained his law office in Augusta. That his legal clients were chiefly blacks attests further to the difficulties facing professional white Republicans, bearing out the point made earlier. He was elated to win his first case. "The judge appointed me to defend a colored man charged with stealing," he wrote to Emma. "It was apparently a strong case against him but I succeeded in making a defense strong enough to satisfy the jury that the man was not guilty. . . . It gives me new courage."[12]

Bryant enthusiastically began this effort to reestablish his law career but hoped that his tenure in Augusta would be brief this time. He continued in the spring of 1872 to postpone moving his family to Augusta, claiming that he was "working hard to prepare a home where we can enjoy ourselves next winter." Keenly aware of the paucity of clients and of the hostility against Republicans, in fact he was marking time as he waited a return to governmental employ. The news he sought—that he had been confirmed by President Grant in the post of deputy collector of customs in Savannah—came in May 1872. James Atkins, collector and Republican ally, offered Bryant's name with the support of Amos Akerman, Joshua Hill, John S. Bigby, Joseph E. Brown, and Henry Farrow.[13]

Despite the relative financial security that the new post provided, he did not move Emma and the baby to Savannah immediately. "I should not dare to have you here," he wrote, "and I could not get a living in Atlanta, thus we are apart." Yet he claimed he was "disappointed" if he did not have a letter from his wife every day. Emma commented in the summer of 1872 that they had been separated for almost a year. She feared they would become accustomed to living apart. "Should our hearts ever stray from each other it would be a worse calamity than . . . death," she wrote. But John seemed unable or unwilling to change their life-style. When the opportunity to move back into politics came, he confessed his true passion: "I love political work. It is a pleasure for me to do it." Northern relatives, sympathetic with Emma's plight and his, could not understand John's perseverance. "I am not able to see what you can make out of staying in Georgia," one wrote, "but I think there is a chance for you west & I think I would go there before I would stay in Georgia & fite all of the time."[14]

One cannot conclude simply that the carpetbagger did not care about his wife. An incident during this period reveals something of their relationship. Apart from John a great deal, as noted, Emma was developing an independent spirit and an ability to cope with whatever domestic crises might arise. In Atlanta she did some sewing to mitigate her poverty and began to paint to ease her loneliness. In the summer of 1873, she traveled to Cleveland, seeking medical assurance that Alice, who was sick a great deal as an infant, would grow up without physical weakness. While in Ohio, Emma Bryant indulged in art shows and visits with artists and wrote her husband of treatments by another doctor for her own health. After sending Alice ahead with Bryant's sister, she intended to stop in Chicago before returning to Maine herself.

After reporting all her activities, Emma was stunned to receive harsh and belligerent telegrams from John in Savannah, who accused her of various improprieties and demanded that she return home at once. He did not approve of her being alone with this doctor for treatment ("his old phobia," according to Emma), and he was wildly jealous that she had accompanied the physician on rounds and had ridden in his buggy.

His words aroused Emma's wrath. In all her life she had "never been so grossly insulted until now." He need not write her again or ever expect another line from her "until you can assure me of your *unlimited confidence* in me and feel *sincerely repentant* for the terrible things you have said to me." She continued, "I have never lived with you on other terms than those of the most perfect *love* and *trust* and *equality. I never intend to live with you on other terms.*" Apparently Bryant apologized, for his wife's next letter began with the customary, "my darling husband." In following letters as they reconciled their differences, John explained that his reaction was based on his concern that the "freedom of the wife" could lead to "free love." For her part, Emma suggested that, since he acknowledged his own enjoyment of female company in her absence, he might "not consider my misdemeanor very grave."[15]

This exchange perhaps reveals more than Bryant's regard for his wife, but at any rate, he was most often without her and absorbed in politics—where Republicans in Georgia did indeed have an uphill struggle. Though Bryant held no party office, he joined in the strenuous but futile attempt of regular party members in 1872 to prevent a Democratic landslide. As with past elections, Bryant probably remained popular as a speaker at large meetings. Future campaigning would reveal that he had not lost his appeal to black audiences, but he did not hesitate to go on the stump to white audiences as well. The written word could also influence voters, and Bryant exhibited a faith in the power of that word by the sheer volume of printed material he produced throughout his career. He used pamphlets to defend character and actions, as well as to sell ideas, and he continued to believe that the newspaper was an effective and creative avenue for publicizing political views. At the time he moved to Savannah, with the now familiar promises and enthusiasm, he expounded on the potential role a Republican paper could play in revitalizing and uniting the party. He asked party leaders only for time to make good his word, writing in May 1872, "I will show surprising results by November." The paper he established continued his old *Georgia Republican* under a new name, the *Savannah Journal*. The Republican state convention, which met in August 1872, designated the *Journal* as its official organ, along with the *Atlanta Whig* and the *Oglethorpe Southwest Georgian*.[16]

At the August convention, the Republicans of Georgia were able to agree on a nominee to face Democratic governor James M. Smith in October, when state elections would be held. Their choice, Dawson A. Walker, was a former justice of the state's supreme court, who, like his old friend Joe Brown, had found accommodation with Republicans during Reconstruction. Naturally the party looked for Brown's support of the Walker candidacy, but they were disappointed. By 1872 Brown was seeking a way out of his Republican affiliation and refused to endorse Walker. Other Southerners also were less enthusiastic now and disillusioned by the opprobrium brought on the Republican party by the Bullock regime. Many who had joined with the Reconstruction forces, both for reason of principle and because of political ambition, lost confidence and respect in the party and "began to look with longing upon the greener (and more popular) pastures of the Democracy." The reform movement within the national party in 1872, reaching a climax in the Liberal Republican convention, provided an opportunity for Republicans of various views to express dissatisfaction. The Liberal movement represented the last, best effort of the centrist strategy of fusion.[17]

The loss of Brown was a severe blow to the Republicans, but his defection should not have been a surprise. Brown was ever mindful of shifting political winds, and there was little chance that he would go down with the sinking Republican ship. Moreover, the political philosophy of the Liberals was basically an elitist reliance on "men of intelligence and property," the strategy Brown had urged to no avail on Bullock.[18] When the national Democratic convention endorsed Horace Greeley, who was also the candidate of the Liberal Republicans, the bridge between the two parties was made. After the election a graceful transfer to the Democrats for

Brown and other dissenting Republicans would be possible. Recognizing their failure to transform the Republican party into a "Southern mold," they deserted it.

The Democrats and Liberal Republicans called for a withdrawal of troops from the South, for civil service reform, and for conciliation between the sections, all of which appealed strongly to Southerners. The irony that Greeley should be a candidate with Southern appeal, however, was not lost on regular Republicans. "How time flies and changes we see," one wrote to Bryant. "Greeley among the Demo[cra]ts and Rebels fishing for favors & votes as if they had never known all about Tyler, & Fillmore, and Johnson, & all the others that were traitors, including Benedict Arnold!"[19]

Many voters apparently noted the incongruity, but Greeley still took Georgia. Republicans gained an impressive 45 percent of the presidential vote in Georgia (62,550 votes for Grant to 76,356 for Greeley), but the overall turnout was low. The black vote was again an important part of the Republican showing, and as Democrats were also seeking the support of the freedmen, there was perhaps less intimidation at the polls than in previous elections. The "new departure" strategy of some Democrats was to accept black franchisement and to compete for their vote. Another protection for the black voter was the newly created National Guard units that Republicans such as Bryant had worked to organize, in anticipation of elections without the presence of federal troops and in response to numerous regiments of white militia authorized by Governor Smith. Despite their presence, there were the usual charges of fraud and disorder. In Savannah, Bryant himself protested at the polls the vote of a white man, presumably because he was not required to produce the receipt of paid poll tax, as were the freedmen. In the shoving match that ensued, Bryant received a nasty cut on his head from a billy club and was charged with inciting a riot and, since two loaded derringers were found on his person, with carrying concealed weapons. Ironically, two Democrats posted his bail; apparently the charges came to nothing. The effort to stay the tide was futile in any case. Grant won his second term but without Georgia; in the governor's race, Dawson Walker was badly beaten by Democrat James Smith, the incumbent.[20]

In the congressional elections Republicans retained three seats, the winners becoming the last Republican members of Congress from Georgia in the nineteenth century. One race, involving Andrew Sloan of the first district (Savannah), resulted in a contested vote that was not decided until March 1874. By the time Sloan was finally confirmed, a new election was approaching, and JEB had decided to seek the seat.

Bryant had chosen to run in a difficult year for Republicans. Not only was the depression well under way, but in Washington Congress was debating the unpopular civil rights bill that called for equal access for blacks to public accommodations. The issue of Reconstruction would be played down in congressional races all over the nation. Furthermore, his bid to become a candidate for national office met with mixed reaction, even among Republicans. In the district nominating convention, held in Savannah on May 20, 1874, a faction to stop Bryant's candidacy was led by Tunis G. Campbell, one of Georgia's black senators during Reconstruction and the first to be expelled from the state senate. Campbell's remarks before the gathering in Savannah were violent enough to cause Georgia's respected and talented black leader Henry M. Turner to rise to Bryant's defense. In an emotional speech that revealed his admiration for the carpetbagger, Turner maintained that he was "grieved" that Campbell should give "such willful misrepresentations of a man." Bryant, he said, had committed none of the "grave crimes" of which he was accused. "Thank God. I think I know the inside workings of Col Bryant's mind better than almost anyone else."[21]

Campbell referred to the constitutional convention in his remarks, accusing Bryant of being responsible for expelling blacks from the legislature and of supporting a poll tax, among other things. Turner deftly reminded the former senator that Bryant had been one of the few who argued against removing the section of the franchise clause that guaranteed blacks the right to hold office. "That was the cause of your being turned out," he reminded Campbell. As for the poll tax, Bryant had urged its defeat: "Turner, you are going to vote for that thing?" he had said. "It will ruin your race." Turner refuted Campbell's charge that JEB had become a Democrat with the facts of Bryant's campaign against Bullock when he "saw that [Bullock] was treacherous to our race, treacherous to the party and sending the State to bankruptcy and ruin." Turner concluded by saying: "I was with [Bryant] through reconstruction, I was with him in the Constitutional Convention, not in one house and he in another, but in the same house: on committees, in associations, in leagues, in equal rights associations, and I have never seen Bryant turn his back on the negro since I was born. I have never known him to desert our rights. That is the man we propose to send to Congress."[22]

The speech carried the meeting, and Bryant was declared the district's nominee for Congress by a vote of 38 to 8. Some people, of course, still had reservations about the candidate. "A distinguished Republican," wrote one friend to Bryant, "told [me] he had talked with you months ago and made up his mind you were working for the nomination and to run Sloan off the track . . . that it but came out just as he expected. . . . If you fail," he warned, "you will have all the blame of destroying the party in our district, after it was built up by Sloan." "The rebs will fight you more bitterly than they did Sloan," another wrote, and "with the lapse of each succeeding year the colored voters are less and less strongly attracted toward the Polls. However, you are a candidate much better calculated to bring them to the Polls than Sloan, & if they are not intimidated I conclude you will get more of their votes than he did."[23]

This letter indicates that Bryant perhaps based his candidacy on a desire to do more for blacks than Sloan was willing to do. The author of the letter, W. L. Clift, an officeholder in the Treasury Department in Washington, revealed that his support of Bryant was based on this understanding of the nominee's position. "I have not of late interested myself in the perpetuation of the Republican party," he confessed, "but I have interested and always shall interest myself in the election of Congressmen who can be depended upon to aid in securing equal rights for the colored man. In view of that fact I propose to make a little contribution . . . toward the payment of poll taxes for colored men in Savannah, and if there is anything else I can do to help you just call upon me."[24]

The poll tax, which Republicans had succeeded in suspending through a provision in the constitution of 1868, had been reinstituted by the Democratic legislature in the fall of 1871. As Bryant had predicted, it was a nuisance and a formidable barrier to black voters in Georgia both because of their lack of cash and because of their seeming inability to retain the necessary receipt of payment. Bryant, however, refused to use Clift's money for the purpose of paying the voters' taxes, because of "its future effects" on them. Clift yielded the point and offered the money anyway, to be receipted "as suits yourself."[25]

Sam Bard, former editor of the *Atlanta New Era,* who, with Bryant, had turned against Bullock, was ecstatic in his support of Bryant's candidacy: "I know you will do good and 'square work.' Of this I do not entertain the shadow of a doubt. Let the grand old party of liberty and human rights move forward and may the great God of Battles be with you and crown all your efforts with victory." Bard urged Bryant to go after the

Irish vote in the district, declaring that he had no doubt of Bryant's success among black voters. Bryant's political friend and sometime rival, Edwin Belcher, seemed to underline Bard's opinion when he offered his congratulations and his services for the campaign. Another supporter offered the backing of the Republican clubs he had organized in his county.[26]

Contemplating the effort before him, the candidate considered asking his wife to campaign for him, and he wanted her to look the part. Emma Bryant, with Alice on an extended visit with her family in Illinois, was more realistic. She would come, of course, but she would need clothes, and they were expensive. He must balance how he "want[s] me to look" with his "ability to send money." Apparently he reconsidered, for she did not join the campaign.[27]

Bryant based his platform on an appeal to the working people of the district, both white and black. "The Republican party declares 'that the laborer should be as independent as the capitalist,'" he said on one occasion. "It is true that the Democratic party makes war directly on the colored laboring man; but . . . if cheap negro labor is secured by Democratic legislation, the white laboring man will also be forced to work for low wages. If cotton is made by the large planters with cheap negro labor the price will be reduced so that the white man who makes the cotton by his own labor will be forced to compete with cheap negro labor."[28]

Bryant did not equivocate on equal rights for blacks, but he attempted to show the breadth of benefits for all citizens in the state under the Republican plan. He did "not advocate mixed schools; but . . . schools for colored children shall be equal to those established for white children." The party, he said, "does not advocate social equality, but it does demand equal rights for all citizens." Furthermore, "If the citizen is not protected by the State authorities . . . he shall be protected by the National."[29]

Not forgetting the local interests of Savannah and the former Whig vote there, Bryant supported "the appropriation of money to construct canals and improve our rivers and harbors." He claimed, on the other hand, that "the Democratic party opposes the appropriation of money for such purposes." He summed up his platform in this way: "In a word the Republican party would make Georgia richer, greater, and more powerful by making the laborer as free and independent as the capitalist, by establishing free schools that the masses of the people may be educated, and by developing the vast natural resources of our State. . . . I am proud to lead a party advocating such noble principles. I will try to do my duty."[30]

In light of Republican setbacks across the entire nation in 1874, Bryant probably should not be blamed for the defeat of the party in Georgia, where all three of the congressional seats formerly held by Republicans were lost. Despite the use of special ballots "impossible to counterfeit," Democrats were again charged with stuffing the ballot boxes and committing other fraud. One official observer testified that Democratic ballots had been substituted for Republican ones while he slept after an exhausting three days of wakefulness. Even so, JEB's attempt to contest the election came to nothing.[31]

Though Bryant lost the bitterly fought campaign, he found room for hope for the future. Clift, the Washington officeholder who had offered help to Bryant, was amazed at the defeated candidate's "wonderful confidence" and commended him for more success than Sloan had previously met among white voters, "a curious commentary on [Sloan's] supposed popularity with the whites." Still, Clift was less optimistic about Republican potential. "The time may come within ten years," he said, "when a wedge may be driven in the Democratic Party." Nevertheless, he would work only for the nomination of a "radical man, with the hope Providence would so change the situation as to make his election possible & I should do this on the ground that the election by the Republicans of any other than a pronounced Republican is no gain whatever."[32]

After the congressional race was decided and it appeared that Savannah would remain his residence for a time, Emma Bryant and little Alice, both of whom had been in Illinois for most of the past year, traveled to be with JEB in Savannah. Alice related in her autobiography that they lived in a boardinghouse where Emma would not allow John to walk the baby to sleep despite her screaming, which embarrassed him.[33] As before, their time together "at home" was limited. By January 1875, Bryant was in Washington mending political fences while his family stayed in Savannah.

Undaunted by the defeat in 1874 and not awaiting Providence alone, Bryant now was moving toward the election of 1876 and the year of his greatest influence in the Republican party in Georgia. Still not without his own detractors, with his pen he attacked the "Bourbon Conspiracy," criticizing the Democrats for attempting to "reconstruct the Southern states backwards." Bryant was aware of the importance of support at the national capital as well as at home. At his suggestion, Clift organized the Georgia Republican Association in Washington, composed of federal officeholders from Georgia and those involved in the work of the party in the state. Because of Bryant's influence in the party, as well as that of

James Atkins, collector of customs in Savannah, there was talk of the "Custom House Ring" and "Bryant & Co." running things. As always, there was a balancing viewpoint. William A. Pledger, the young and aggressive black editor of the *Athens Blade*, was beginning to take a leadership role in the Republican party. "Some of my friends . . . seem to have a distaste to the custom house clique," he wrote, "but I tell them to take [it] as a model."[34]

Pledger was rising to power at a critical point in the party's history. The Republican party in Georgia was clearly struggling for survival (which was not new), but its leaders were now also agonizing over its constituency. Blacks had been the mainstay of the party since the Southern strategy was first formulated after the war. The number of black voters had decreased dramatically since 1868, as has been demonstrated, but their numerical strength was still the majority of the membership—a majority that was not matched by leadership roles in the party's hierarchy. A new generation of black leaders such as Pledger was on the verge of confronting the white leadership over this issue, at the very time that longtime Republicans such as Henry Farrow were looking for new ways to define membership. One option was to reject black participation completely and to opt for a white-only party. Hints of this tack had surfaced as early as 1870 in Glynn County, on the southern coast of the state, where there had been a movement to establish a rival, predominantly white, Republican party, "with the majority of the colored vote left out."[35]

A related possibility was to seek cooperation with dissident Democrats, the Independents, who were talking about separation from the Bourbon mainline party. Farrow turned to this faction. The Independents of Georgia in 1876 were little more than a promise, but, in Farrow's view, one worth courting. While the Republican candidates were being demolished in the congressional election of 1874, Dr. William Felton of the seventh district, an Independent, with some help from Republican voters, defeated a Democrat and gained a seat in Washington. Perhaps a coalition between Republicans and Independents could harvest the white Unionist vote that Republicans were so sure existed. But at what cost? Former slave owner Felton was no crusader for black rights. His primary quarrel with the Democratic regulars had to do with their corruption, their oligarchic rule, and their warm reacceptance of Joe Brown.[36]

Not all Republicans sided with Farrow in wooing the Independents. Those still holding radical views on race supported a general move early in 1876 to replace the "appeaser" Farrow, who gradually had been losing their support. It looked as though JEB might succeed Farrow as chairman of the state central committee. Certain blacks felt that a forceful chairman could accomplish more for their race in the state. Pledger was furious with Farrow because he seemed unresponsive to blacks' need for patronage jobs. "You *white Republicans* generally have *white Republicans* to fill those places when vacant," he had written the district attorney. Another sort of letter went from Pledger to Bryant: "Nor need you be surprised if you're the next chairman of the State Central Committee. . . . In you I have the utmost confidence."[37]

In Washington, members of the Georgia Republican Association also discussed possible candidates and decided that Bryant could most easily defeat Farrow, who was reputed to be "tricky and unreliable." Clift held that Bryant was the "only aggressive man" in the Republican party of Georgia and "the most important man." The association had cooled to Farrow's leadership because of his dalliance with the Independents. Most unpalatable of all was Farrow's regard for Alexander Stephens, the old Georgia Unionist and vice president of the Confederacy, whom Farrow hoped would run for governor on a Republican-Independent ticket in 1882.[38]

Farrow's chairmanship was in jeopardy, but Bryant was uncharacteristically coy about being tapped for the job. There is evidence that he even defended Farrow for a time. One critic wondered about his "taking up for F[arrow]. I can't see how you consistently do this when you know Alex Stephens is his champion." Clift also worried about his resistance, fearing he was "committed to Farrow" and worried about his "reluctant consent." Eventually Bryant allowed his arm to be twisted, but he seemed aware of the difficulties ahead. He attempted to minimize the matter of patronage by claiming that he would have no offices to distribute, only work for "a glorious cause."[39]

The procedure for Republican organization in 1876, a presidential election year, was not unusual. The party held two conventions: the first in the spring to name delegates to the national convention and to elect new party leaders, the second in the summer to choose electors and to select a ticket for state elections. For the spring convention, held in Atlanta on May 3–4, Pledger had his followers well prepared. A gathering of two hundred delegates, three-fourths of whom were black, elected Bryant, unanimously and "by acclamation," he claimed, to the chairmanship of the state central committee, a post he had held for a time during earlier years of Reconstruction. The move to increase black representation to the national convention met more protest and confusion, but the delegation named included thirteen white and nine black members. It was headed by Farrow and Atkins, who were white, and by George Wallace and H. M. Turner, who were black. While Bryant was not chosen, it is questionable to what degree he tried to control the selection. Naturally the Democratic press reported a meeting composed of factions, with Bryant unable to determine the choice of representatives to the national convention (that is, unable to get himself elected). It is possible, however, that the new chairman was merely allowing rival interests to be heard and that he declined to go to Cincinnati because of this new position, as he later claimed and as his supporters believed. Bryant well knew the importance of holding the party factions together, and he needed Farrow's goodwill and Atkins's support to succeed as chairman. At this point he was still on good terms with Atkins. Throughout the summer he elicited Farrow's backing and sought to remain neutral in local fights, such as one among party leaders in Fulton County, where he urged conciliation between the disputing groups.[40]

The second of the Republican conventions, to choose electors and a slate for state offices, was held in Macon on August 16, 1876. With little enthusiasm and with less chance for success against the Democratic gubernatorial candidate, Alfred H. Colquitt, the rather small gathering named Jonathan Norcross its choice for the race to be held in October. A native of Maine who emigrated to Georgia in the 1830s and a pre–Civil War Whig, Norcross had been elected mayor of Atlanta in the 1850s. By 1876 a wealthy Republican, Norcross later gained the reputation of harboring hostility toward blacks as he led a move to make the Republican party of Georgia a lily-white party. For the present, he was a candidate who might appeal to the Unionist/Whig vote.[41]

Excitement for the convention was provided by W. A. Pledger, who had little use for Norcross. Since spring, the editor of the *Athens Blade* had been preparing for the Republican conventions, as he had said, "indoctrinating principles of self (race) reliance . . . among my people who are expected to be delegates." He was ready, he had written, "for the overthrow of the whitewashed Rep[ublican] official oligarchy." The first stage of his plan, in the May convention, had gone according to schedule; but now the selection of Norcross as standard-bearer, he feared, would give an entirely different direction to the party. In frustration Pledger rose to speak and, according to one reporter, "gave his brethren 'Hail Columbia' in a blistering speech over their past failures and bad management."[42]

The man Pledger had backed for party chairman back in May, John Emory Bryant, stood to answer the attack. Having spent the summer in organization at the grass roots and being somewhat taken aback by the charges, "Bryant defended the party but admitted that some of the republicans had done wrong." He blamed party deterioration more on the Klan and on Democratic fraud than on mismanagement. The dilemma of the Republican party was now manifested in this inner-party conflict, and as new state chairman, Bryant was caught in the middle. The movement to desert blacks was just beginning; the added pressures that would soon descend from Washington were not yet apparent. Meanwhile, blacks fully—and perhaps unrealistically—expected Bryant's leadership to effect beneficial change. Edwin Belcher, now in Bryant's fold and forgetting past grievances, complained with some bitterness in the summer of 1876 that he could not campaign in the fall elections if he were forced to leave the South to get work. "This is hard," he said, "when so many drones in this state are rewarded & the working men starved."[43]

Aware of the difficulty and contradictions in facing latent racism together with rising black expectations, JEB turned instead to his own career goals. At the district convention in early August 1876, he was again selected as the congressional nominee from the first district. Both Pledger and Norcross sent congratulatory messages, agreeing temporarily. Norcross was "truly glad" and Pledger was pleased to "congratulate the First District upon the selection of one whom I not only had confidence in but one whom I will take the stump for. . . . Bear in mind that you have in me an untiring friendship and [I] hope to manifest it this fall."[44]

Bryant, with his seemingly endless supply of optimism, plunged into another hopeless race for the congressional seat. Glad to reclaim his following among black voters, he no doubt welcomed Pledger's aid and continued on his own circuit with mass meetings and speeches. Nor did he neglect the whites of the district. "I am having a remarkable canvass," he wrote. "Everywhere I go the whites come out to hear me speak and I think I am making a good impression." In the attempt to appeal to whites, Bryant again emphasized the educational needs of the state. He was prompted by the chairman of the national executive committee to make "free common schools" the predominant issue, in the belief that education was "the answer to all problems."[45] The concern for education was not new to Bryant, of course, and he needed little encouragement to make it the basis of his campaign.

Emma Spaulding Bryant, again mostly alone in Savannah, had taken Alice to Maine in the summer of 1876 for another round of family visits. From there she wondered about "any chance" for a "fair election." Would "violence and fraud" control Georgia as before? If the Democrats won, she asked wistfully, would he "think of leaving Savannah and the South?" Emma's extended visit with relatives taxed their resources and embarrassed her. She alerted her husband that she must leave her brother's house by October, but she knew John would scarcely want family concerns in the midst of his political battle. "Do you want wife and baby as soon as that[?] I think we are sufficiently well trained not to look for much attention from you till after the election," she implored. But Bryant did not send the reassuring summons. Determined to impose on relatives no further but fearful of traveling to Savannah without John's bidding, Mrs. Bryant moved to Washington in November, hoping to catch her husband there. Letters implied his concern for her welfare, but apparently few funds were sent. By December she was in dire straits. In a curt letter that revealed her anxiety and growing displeasure with the situation, she demanded that he not ask about her needs again, since he did not send money to meet them. It is not clear how long she was forced to remain in Washington. Letters indicate, however, that by April 1877 she was in Savannah.[46]

John wrote infrequently in the fall of 1876, for he was almost wholly consumed with the campaign. Yet despite Bryant's efforts at party peacekeeping while his family members fended for themselves, all did not run smoothly in the congressional election. The hapless Republicans of Georgia needed more than a truce between the Pledger and Norcross followings. In a perfect example of the factionalism that plagued the party's effort in the South, three men who held grudges against Bryant began a vicious attempt to discredit him with charges of corruption and dishonesty comparable to the ones he had weathered under Bullock's wrath. (Not coincidentally, Bullock had returned to the state in May 1876.) In this case there can be little doubt that political vengeance motivated the conspiracy. James Atkins, who had worked with Bryant politically at least since 1872 and who was now his colleague in the "Custom House Ring," had wanted the nomination from the district for himself. Even after the convention named Bryant, Atkins attempted to have him resign, claiming that the new candidate had forced himself on the constituency. So much for their short-lived alliance, which Atkins had hoped would turn to his advantage. Thwarted by the response of the chairman of the county's Republican party that Bryant was "the obvious choice of a majority of voters," Atkins was primed for a fight. Ready to join him was Andrew Sloan, the man JEB had replaced in 1874 as nominee of the district. Bryant had not only beaten Sloan for the nomination but had also been instrumental in discrediting him in Washington when Sloan sought a federal post early in 1876. W. L. Clift, an influential Republican who displayed an acutely sensitive moral and political judgment, aided Sloan's political demise because, he said, Sloan was "bad." Bryant concurred and went further to specify the charge of drunkenness against Sloan. Always a crusading advocate of temperance, Bryant undoubtedly believed that the matter was extremely important in assessing Sloan's competence, but whether or not JEB's disdain for tipplers justified the attack remains questionable. Bryant used the same charge against Blodgett, which neither proves nor disproves anything, but makes one uneasy.[47]

The third member of the trio out to defeat Bryant, John G. Clark, described by Bryant as a "secessionist," was a stalwart of Bullock's and indebted to Sloan for his position as postmaster in Savannah. Belcher called the three men "crumbs—especially J.G.C. [John G. Clark] the 'white liner' who is trying to capture the party." But Clark had written of Bryant, "Gen. [John G.] Gordon and J. E. Bryant are typical men of their respective classes. They derive all their political power from and found their political hopes on the strifes of the two races. A bitter feeling between the two sections, the North and South, is the ark of their only salvation." The combination of personal and political venom would prove difficult for candidate Bryant to combat.[48]

By the spring of 1877, the charges against "the big Skowhegan chief," as one newspaper dubbed Bryant, had gone all the way to the president of the United States, a backhanded tribute of sorts that attested to Bryant's importance within the party. To this "Letter [printed as a pamphlet] to the President of the United States related to the character and antecedents of John Emory Bryant," not only Atkins, Clark, and Sloan signed their names, but all the enemies Bryant had accrued in his long career came forward to join the chorus against him. The list included Bullock's colleague Foster Blodgett (who would die in 1877 at age fifty) and General Davis Tillson, formerly with the Freedmen's Bureau in Georgia. Tillson claimed in the letter that he had "never known or heard of [Bryant's] holding a position of any kind where his vindictiveness and dishonesty did not get him into trouble." While the letter contained little except vague charges, such as Tillson's against Bryant's character, it was damaging to JEB's image as a candidate for office. One signer admitted later, to his chagrin, that he had allowed his name to be used without even reading the contents. The pamphlet had been written in September 1876 before the election, presumably in the same form it was sent to Washington, since Bryant's correspondence noted it and his planned response.[49]

Republican officeholders in Washington were angered by this assault on the party's congressional nominee. "But what a commentary upon the Republicans of Georgia!" one wrote. "Can we ever hope to accomplish anything?" Another indignantly called the pamphlet attacking Bryant a "shameless document & [one that] only means mischief, discord, confusion, [and will] work in[to] the hands of our enemies." Still another stormed in frustration, "Why do men in the Republican Party suffer such a thing to be done? Why could they not have found out all this alleged corruption before? Why was it left to publish to the world on the eve of an important, yes the most important election we have ever had in many respects.... I cannot understand all this. Is it not a dirty bird that fouls its own nest? ... For heaven's sake let the State Central Committee have a meeting and settle it. The Republican party of Ga. cannot carry any additional burdens."[50]

Friends of Bryant also expressed concern. "Be of good cheer," one wrote. "Your friends are Legions and like a stone wall." In his own defense, Bryant prepared an impressive pamphlet entitled "The Reply of Hon. John E. Bryant to John G. Clark, James Atkins, and Other Persons Who Have Attempted to Blast the Character of Mr. Bryant." In this rebuttal the besieged candidate showed that Atkins had supported him until the summer of 1876. He also exposed an attempt by Atkins to bribe one E. Yulee, a black newspaper editor, away from supporting Bryant. Yulee proved a poor choice for bribery, since Bryant himself had subsidized Yulee's paper for a time.[51]

The election in October 1876 was the last one of the century in which Georgia Republicans had any chance for success. The governor's race offered the least hope. There Jonathan Norcross was badly defeated by the popular Colquitt. Congressional candidates had been named in each district except the fourth and seventh (which saw Independents, with some

Republican support, go against the Democrats) and the ninth (where Benjamin Hill won unopposed). Though the Republicans showed strength in some areas, they carried only five counties. In the first district, David Porter, chairman of Chatham County's (Savannah) Republican party, had warned that "the campaign will be an up-hill matter, for though we have over 3,000 majority in the District it requires Republican unity to win success." The attack on Bryant, of course, subverted the essential formula. The candidate had continued to campaign despite the disruption, and he did make an impressive showing in some areas. Still, the overall result was less than spectacular, and in the final count he lost by a majority of over five thousand votes to Democrat Julian Hartridge.[52]

The poor showing was hardly surprising. The charges of corruption doubtless reduced the number of whites who might have voted for Bryant. And although he relied heavily on black support, blacks were less and less actively participating in the elective process. Many blacks, either apathetic or unable to pay their poll tax, were not even registered and therefore could not vote. Then there were the inevitable cases of fraud. One report to Bryant revealed that "somewhere in your district there was a sham Poll opened in a barn & the Negroes were sent there & of course the vote was thrown away. It was near the coast & the vote was near 500, in your favor, & some estimate it at 800." The Republicans could perhaps have overcome these handicaps with unity and organization. In the end they were at least partly responsible for their own defeat. A disillusioned H. M. Turner, now living in Philadephia and out of the Georgia hassle, wrote his friend JEB that the contest had come out "as I feared."[53]

The presidential election the following month, November 1876, brought the disputed contest between Samuel Tilden and Rutherford B. Hayes. In that battle, additional fraud plus an overwhelming rejection by whites of Reconstruction Republicanism took Georgia into the Tilden column. Ironically, those who voted for Tilden but got Hayes instead would find more to love than they might have dreamed in November. The Republicans had abandoned the Negro long before the election and were looking for a Southern accommodation.[54]

In the aftermath of Republican losses, the matter of candidate Bryant's reputation remained. The most damaging charge was one added by John L. Conley, Bullock supporter and son of Benjamin Conley of the "Augusta ring." Like his father, John L. had locked horns with Bryant; the skirmish had been over patronage. Conley despised Bryant and accused him of corruption going back to his days in the Georgia legislature. There, Conley said, Bryant had only pretended honesty and integrity but had sold his vote to the Brunswick and Albany Railroad Company for legislation favorable to the line. Bryant hotly denied that the recent discovery (Bullock again?) of "drafts or notes and letters" to him from the company had any connection with his vote; rather, he insisted that they represented a separate business deal.

The accused willingly moved to have the charges investigated by the state central committee in order to have his chairmanship of that body exonerated. The "Proceedings of the Committee," published January 10, 1877, indicate an attempt at fairness, with both sides of the dispute plus neutral parties, including J. Norcross and H. Farrow, represented on the board of review. Members called for the incriminating data against Bryant that had been promised by his detractors. Instead of producing evidence, the accusers denounced the hearing and then were suddenly silent. The committee therefore declared that "the conduct of [Bryant's] accusers is a vindication of him against their charges. There is no reason he should not continue to have the confidence and support of all earnest Republicans." One supporter in Quitman, Georgia, agreed: Bryant was, he believed, "the only man in the Republican Party to have the qualities of a bold leader." But by that time the election was history.[55]

After the ruling in Bryant's favor, Republicans in Chatham County removed James Atkins from the county's executive committee. But Atkins was still able to harass Bryant. In April 1877 the pamphlet attempting to discredit JEB was circulated in Washington. Also, as the superior officer in the customhouse in Savannah, Atkins had made things very difficult for his subordinate during the campaign by withholding his salary and, Bryant claimed, even by attacking him physically. Atkins in turn accused Bryant of threatening to strike him with a two-and-one-quarter-pound paperweight.

Atkins's primary charge, however, was political. He accused Bryant of replacing Andrew Sloan as congressional nominee from the district in 1874 for no good reason, and of creating factions in the party by his "destructive ambition." Bryant had accepted the congressional nomination again in 1876, Atkins had continued, knowing "well that his candidacy secures beyond any doubt the certain defeat of the party." Soon after Atkins wrote that condemnation of Bryant in August 1876, he began the process of replacing his deputy and all JEB's supporters in the customhouse. Bryant reciprocated by asking President Grant to remove Atkins instead. Obviously, things were at a stalemate in Savannah. It was Bryant who resigned from the intolerable position in January 1877, after the central committee's judgment in his favor. Only after his resignation did he learn that the Treasury Department had dispatched an agent to investigate the situation. The investigator was reported by Clift to be "against" Bryant before he began, and eventually he did decide the feud in favor of Atkins, though the charges directed at Bryant were very vague. Before the investigation of the customhouse was even completed, the Republican committee of Chatham County had passed a resolution of support for Bryant, endorsing him as chairman of the state central committee, commending him for his "work and principles" and expressing their "disapprobation of the infamous attacks made on him during the campaign." Bryant also discounted the treasury investigation and remained convinced that it had been biased against him. He continued in 1878 and 1882 to ask that the case be reopened.[56]

Bryant's round with Atkins was clearly a political power play with few innocents. Atkins simply had an undistinguished record, one that scarcely showed him to be of more exemplary character than the carpetbagger. A member of the Georgia legislature from 1868 to 1870, Atkins had narrowly escaped expulsion after he was charged with accepting a bribe. An investigation by the house brought to light new evidence of bribery, and a resolution for his expulsion (requiring a two-thirds vote) was narrowly defeated. When Atkins had been suggested as gubernatorial candidate for the Republicans in 1872, one party member wired the message: "Atkins has no influence less intellect. Bullock stripe. bad egg. won't do at all."[57]

Within the customhouse, as well, Atkins's difficulties were mounting. As early as 1873, an official in Washington had reported that "the expenses of the Custom House are increased whilst the receipts are diminished." Errors made by the statistical clerk were reported by Bryant in 1874; in response, his superior hoped that the clerk would "learn wisdom by experience and trouble you less." In 1876 Clift reported to Bryant that Atkins was "in trouble." "The balance against [Atkins] on [the] Internal Revenue Account is much larger than you wrote me & is causing him trouble," he confided. "I hear suit has been instituted against [him] on both his Bonds for $25,842.31 on his Colln. Acct. & $6,458.21 on his Distr. Acct."[58]

THE HAYES PRESIDENCY

Bryant was probably glad to leave Atkins with those charges while he himself enjoyed the confidence of the local Republican leaders. But national politics would soon impinge more closely on the state, and Bryant, as the durable but obnoxious carpetbagger on the scene, was destined to become an anachronism. Aware of the embarrassment, party officeholders in Washington sought to bring the big Skowheganite into camp. In April 1877, the Georgia Republican Association offered to make him the "head of the party in Georgia," a distinction he might have claimed anyway as head of the state central committee. The condition for such recognition was that Bryant publicly support the policies of the new Republican president, Rutherford B. Hayes, who had taken office in March. The need for unity within the party was obviously the motive for the effort to reconcile state and national priorities and leadership. After Hayes's disputed election had been settled, the new president attempted reconciliation with Southerners by ordering the transfer of remaining federal troops in the South to the nearest army barracks and by naming a former Confederate to be postmaster-general. Hayes, "an optimist as well as an opportunist," envisioned offering the inevitable—an end to Radical Reconstruction—with magnanimity; perhaps he would be remembered as "the Great Pacificator." Within his own party, however, there was much criticism of his policy, both in Congress and from Republican leaders in the South.[59]

Hayes was sensitive to the charge that he was deserting blacks, and he worried about the attacks on his policy. His aim was "to make southern Republicanism more respectable and thus more appealing," particularly to the old Whig element, by divorcing it from the taint of carpetbagger and black control. He wished as well "to remove race antagonisms, especially the political differences resting upon the color line, so that Republicans in the South would not need the protection of the Army." Once the race issue was removed from sectional politics, Hayes hoped that both parties would make an appeal for the black vote, "thus creating the circumstances in which Southern promises to respect freedmen's rights could be fulfilled." The Bourbon leaders of the South naturally assured the president that the rights of blacks could and would be recognized. But Bryant, belittling Hayes as naive, later said, "The President seemed to think that that crafty old Democratic politician, the Vice President of the Confederacy [Alexander Stephens] would tell him how to destroy the Democratic party in the South and build up a powerful Republican party, and thus in a few years solve the Southern problem."[60]

One concrete way in which Hayes implemented his plan was to appoint Democrats to some federal posts in the South. He selected Southern Redeemers for such offices as postmaster (in Louisville, Petersburg, and Memphis), in order to show former Whigs he was their friend. The reaction of one black Republican in Georgia to this policy was typical: "We are willing to suffer if such suffering shall be of any benefit to the cause which we have so near to our hearts. But we do not wish to be betrayed, bound hand and foot, and turned over to the tender mercies of our enemies, and this, too, by the very men whose elevation to power was brought about in large measure, through our instrumentality."[61]

The statement of support for Hayes, then, that John Emory Bryant signed in April 1877, took on significance in light of the new political situation. He was the chairman of the state central committee in Georgia and also was one of the Radical carpetbaggers whom Hayes was ready to drop from the party's leadership. The document confirming Bryant's conciliation to this new policy was an attempt to sanitize existing party structures, it seemed, since they could not be wished away. Bryant was not ready to sell out completely for the title "head of the party in Georgia." In deference to his conscience, at the bottom of the paper he wrote, "I do not approve of the policy of the President in . . . appointing Democrats to office in the South. In other respects I do approve of his policy." Then he added optimistically, "We will bring him to us in time."[62]

Attempting to influence the president, Bryant wrote to Hayes as he prepared to appoint a Democrat as United States marshal in Georgia: "I beg you Mr. President to remember the trials and enduring suffering of the Republicans of the South. No men in American politics have ever before endured as much. True some of them have not been good men but if some Republicans have been dishonest some Democrats have been murderers as well as dishonest. Republicans have been murdered for opinion[']s sake. I most earnestly beseach [sic] of you not to abandon us nor to promote over us the men who have for years denounced and vilified us." The problem, as Bryant and his colleagues saw it, was "to make Northern friends understand the true situation and the obsticles [sic] thrown in the way of Republicans asserting their political opinions. President Hayes' action will not relieve us in the least," one wrote, "but will tend to crush our efforts for free political action in the South."63

Hayes's directive of July 1877 had immediate repercussions for the party's fate in the South. Georgians interpreted this order to mean that "no [federal] officer should be required or permitted to take part in the management of political organizations, caucuses, conventions, or elections." A rash of resignations from the state central committee came to Bryant following this order. One Republican recognized that Hayes "evidently desires to disband the present Republican organizations in the Southern states, thereby giving a fair field for a re-organization of parties on a broader basis." Another official in Washington desperately tried to negate the disastrous results. He urged that the executive order should not "be held as forbidding members of the Republican committees from meeting with those bodies, and transacting the usual committee business. Whatever it may have meant originally," he continued, "or for whatever purpose issued, it is very certain that the Executive Department has now no desire to place any obstacle in the way of any appointee who, as a member of a party committee, aids in perfecting the party organization, and advancing the cause of opposition to the Democracy."64

Bryant, working in 1877 under the crippling effects of the order, turned to the medium he knew best for expounding what he considered "true Republican principles"—a newspaper. Having moved to Atlanta after he resigned the customs post in Savannah, Bryant worked to consolidate his interests with those of W. L. Clark, the editor of the *Atlanta Republican*. They and several other Republicans formed the Atlanta Publishing Company (later called the Atlanta Republican Publishing Company) in July 1877; the corporation was to own and publish the paper. Bryant had won Clark's gratitude in 1876, when he had aided Clark financially. At that time, W. L. Clift had commended Bryant for his action. "Nothing you have done since you ceased to be Editor of the Loyal Georgian has given you so warm a place in my regards, as your efforts in his behalf," he had written, and then he extolled Clark as one of "pure life and honest purpose" and not to be lost to the party.65

Bryant had apparently agreed in 1876, but alliances among Republicans were mercurial in this troubling time. Clark felt that the paper should continue in the fall of 1877 to endorse President Hayes's policy, while Bryant, stung by the directive that had undone his party structure, now openly criticized the president. Because he was perceived as opposing

Hayes's policy, in October 1877 JEB faced opposition to his chairmanship of the state central committee. Charges were made that he led "a small coterie" who wished to maintain "an organization almost exclusively *black,*" he had "kept up the 'color line,'" and was now presenting for office the name of one who erroneously claimed he was "a native of this state," one who would work to "resusicate [sic] the *black* party of Georgia, *a race party.*"66

Although Clark was not a member of the committee, he probably backed the effort against Bryant. Also, Clark accepted Farrow's strategy of linking Republican strength with Independent. Bryant had indicated to Hayes back in the summer that he would assist the Independents, but his inclinations now went in the opposite direction. Clark later charged that John Bryant had attempted to steal the *Atlanta Republican* from him. While that charge remains unconfirmed, Bryant did leave Clark to publish the *Atlanta Republican* alone. The Atlanta Publishing Company, on the other hand, under Bryant's direction, began issuing once again the *Georgia Republican* (later called the *Southern Advance and Georgia Republican*) in November 1877. Volney Spalding, a carpetbagger and member of the state central committee, Bryant's first assistant in the effort, envisioned that the company would "become a tower of strength to the oppressed by publishing a newspaper that will proclaim to the civilized world the wrongs and oppressions heaped upon the weak in Ga. until it be aroused to the enormity of the crime and the necessity of its corrections."67

As the rival Republican newspapers vied for readers in a Democratic state, the most compelling local issue in the fall of 1877 was the work of the constitutional convention. Most Georgians acknowledged that the constitution written by the convention in 1868 was a valuable document. Proponents of the new "Atlanta Spirit," even among Democrats, supported its protection of homestead and relief laws, state bonds, and prohibition of debt imprisonment. To the Bourbons it nevertheless represented the last evidence of their past humiliation. They saw it, according to one historian, as "the creature of bayonet reconstruction, [that] had been forced upon the commonwealth. Whatever merits it had were ignored in the resentment born of its origin and the manner of its enforcement."68 Bryant, one of those instrumental in framing the constitution of 1868, worked against the ratification of the new document, with little hope of success.

The separate issue of the capital, also to be decided, was another emotional one. The legislature had moved the capital from Milledgeville in 1868. Now a strong contingency from Milledgeville fought to have it restored, arguing that Atlanta was somehow synonymous with the villainy of Reconstruction.[69]

So divisive were the issues of reducing the homestead exemption and moving the capital that the Bourbons, fearing these issues would sink their entire effort, called for separate ordinances on these items. The Democrats who favored Atlanta needed the aid of the Republican vote, and Bryant was called upon to support the decision. Spalding was apprehensive, appealing to Bryant just before the referendum: "Things look squally in regard to the Capital question, & will require a very liberal outlay of money to defeat Milledgeville. I am becoming more anxious on your account, as the Democrats all acknowledge that it depends entirely upon you for the Capital at Atlanta, and I would not like to lose on that account. If you succeed you will be hailed as friend and savior of Atlanta in the Capital question, if defeated they will be just as ready to run against you." In the referendum, the reduction of the homestead exemption passed.[70] Bryant delivered the Republican vote, *against* the constitution, which was ratified anyway, and *for* the capital in Atlanta, which is where it remained. There is no evidence and little reason to think that Bryant's aid was ever acknowledged by his temporary allies.

With the Democrats firmly ensconced in Georgia and with national support for his philosophy and work undermined, some reconditioning was clearly in order for the big Skowheganite. Despite his endless optimism, Bryant had obviously been affected by the tedious regularity of Republican defeat in Georgia, and he worried about the native antagonism to carpetbaggers. Nor was he insensitive to the mores of Southern culture that had caused him to be ostracized and despised through all of his days in the South. While his focus had consistently been on political change, there is evidence that even in the days when Republicans were in power he had been aware of the unbecoming and self-defeating pose of conqueror. In one incident that reflected this awareness, Bryant had spoken harshly to the general responsible for a military band's playing the Northern pep song "Rally 'Round the Flag, Boys" in a gathering of Southerners. Bryant explained his reaction in terms of the insult that such a song represented to the former rebels. Comparing Southerners to the "gallant but oppressed" people of Poland, he had warned that Yankees could arouse in the defeated people "a hatred more bitter and intense than the people of this country have ever witnessed." If the North wanted southerners actually to "rally 'round the flag," Bryant had argued, "we should treat them as misguided brothers who have been wrong but honest." The sentiment was not shared by the general involved. "Your charity," he had written, "goes a little too far."[71]

While one may doubt that Bryant's comment was sincere, one must appreciate both the dimensions of his dilemma in 1878 and the abhorrence with which he must have been viewed by some Georgians. It is rather surprising that he continued to confront the issue of race and change at all. An unmistakable shift was brewing in Bryant's career, and as he anticipated it, it is perhaps significant that he reached back toward his earliest optimistic tenet, namely, that education could effect change. Ignoring for the moment the racism of the entire nation, Bryant began to think through his experience, what he called "the Southern problem," and ways by which whites as well as blacks could be included in an educational process there. He agreed with the American Missionary Association's assessment that the constitutional amendments and statute laws had destroyed the "superstructure of slavery" but had left its "foundation" untouched. The "antagonism of races, the ignorance of blacks, and the prejudices of the whites" were "embedded in the minds and hearts" of Southerners and "can only be overcome by education."[72]

As early as July 1876, Bryant had suggested to S. A. Darnell, the secretary of the state central committee, the basic line of his new thinking in regard to the Republican party. Its task was, he speculated, "as a fight between two civilizations, between American civilization and the European civilization of the South; that it is the mission of the Republican party to plant American civilization in the South." For Bryant, "a war was still being waged in the South—a war of ideas." The "feudal civilization" of the former slaveholding states was "totally different" from "the modern democratic, enlightened civilization" of the North. While Northerners believed in the "dignity of labor, in liberty and equality before the sovereign law," Southerners "cherished [European] ideas of aristocracy, caste," and "the right of one class to control another." As he outlined the case for President Hayes in 1877, "It is the mission of the Republican party to plant American civilization in the Southern States . . . ; to give school privileges to every child in the South of school age. . . . Then the people of the North and the people of the South will become one people."[73]

It is impossible to understand fully JEB's thinking as he immersed himself in this new rhetoric. As noted, he certainly faced the necessity of redirecting his energies, since the political doors were slamming around him. His anxious wife, almost ready to give up her share of "his wonderful confidence" but insisting that she could help in some tangible way, also sensed a turning point. "You cannot," she wrote him, continue "using up your energies at the lavish rate of the past four years with no material and pecuniary return. . . . The time is fast approaching when there must be some element of certainty in our affairs." Bryant seemed not to hear her. He was off on another crusade—or was he just neglecting her and his daughter while he enjoyed himself? Considering his intensity, it is difficult to dismiss him in this way. He seems, instead, to have been something of a Don Quixote. To Emma he wrote with some agony, "I do feel that I am passing through the last desperate crisis; but of course may be mistaken, God knows what is best." In another letter he acknowledged her role as supporter through it all. "You have," he wrote, "been so true to me in all my struggle."[74]

Beginning with his colleagues in Georgia, Bryant began to expound his thesis of Republicanism's "glorious cause." Considering his meager audience there, it is understandable that in 1878 he sought support from the national party for his version of gradual conversion through education. Leaving Emma in Atlanta to aid Spalding in publishing the *Georgia Republican*, Bryant began a journey that for two years shuttled him between Washington, Philadelphia, New York, and Providence. He made certain on his tour that his friends in the North knew of the accusatory letter against him that had been sent to the president in 1877 and that they had a full explanation of its source. Everywhere he made speeches, asked for money for the cause, and justified his work in the South. Bryant was soon optimistic that his newspaper could "be supported as a business enterprise by subscriptions and advertisements. . . . With the blessing of God I am sure to get enough North for free circulation to meet all deficiency." He sounded relieved to write that "my work is therefore marked out—a legitimate business for life; one that gives full scope for the display of whatever talents God has given me. The work marked out is what the education of my life has best fitted me for, and as I have before written, what I feel God has called me to do."[75]

During this stay in Atlanta, Emma and Alice were probably living in the boardinghouse Alice later described as the Shermans', the same house in which she had been born. The house must have been some distance from the city itself, since Alice reported that "we walked a long distance through the woods to a street car. On Sunday we went for the day, eating our lunch in my father's [newspaper] office."[76]

Bryant continued to write encouraging letters to his struggling wife and to his friend. Spalding faithfully reassured him, "Push ahead and work out your plans at the North. There is no lack of courage at this end of the line, and the daylight you have let in upon us inspires us with new hopes, and a confidence that our struggle will, before long, be crowned with success." Bryant's ability to command such dedication cannot be taken lightly. The paper, however, required more money than Bryant sent to sustain it, for it appeared only spasmodically in 1878 and ceased altogether in 1879. The influence that Bryant had exerted through the paper and through his office as chairman of the state committee was also slipping away, as he continued to remain in the North for the majority of his time. Spalding warned him of "a growing uneasiness among Republicans in Ga. that nothing is being done at organization, and your continued absence from the state adds greatly to the feeling among your personal friends . . . [that] your own political prospects in the state are irreparably damaged."[77]

Spalding's own plight was no less dire. As he saw the paper going under, he despaired for his future and spoke of "looking for work." He pleaded with Bryant to send money to rescue the *Georgia Republican* and him, "if you have any regard for a friend who has stood by you, notwithstanding starvation has stared him in the face for the past two years." When Bryant did not send the funds, despite the plea, his loyal colleague wrote with finality, "The Paper is suspended."[78]

Emma Bryant, who had visited her ill father in Illinois at the beginning of 1879, after the paper's demise took Alice there again. Her departure marked the start of one of John and Emma's longest separations, lasting until 1881, when she returned to Atlanta.[79]

Meanwhile, it was becoming obvious to many observers that Hayes's policy had not produced the desired results for Republicanism in the South. The experiment was a failure, and the elections of 1878 only confirmed it. Throughout the region, Republican candidates for governor were defeated, while congressional seats held by the party were reduced in number. Republican votes in chiefly white counties and in predominantly black counties declined in comparison with those of 1876. "The new strategy had not only failed to gain a substantial number of white votes, but [it] had cut drastically into the usual Republican majorities in counties with a high percentage of Negroes." Even Hayes was forced to admit that the venture had not accomplished what he had wished. Free elections, he said, were impossible in the South.[80]

So it seemed in Georgia, but the decimated Republicans there still scrapped for crumbs. The two leading factions in the dissent in 1876 were, in Bryant's absence, moving toward an open conflict in the 1880s. Norcross and those Republicans favoring a move to broaden the party's base by excluding blacks were becoming more active. Throughout the 1870s, they attempted to cooperate with the Independent Democrats of the state against Bourbon rule. Bryant contemplated this strategy but never fully accepted it; in at least one case, he deliberately campaigned for a Republican against an Independent. The Independent movement's greatest success continued to be Dr. William L. Felton, who was elected three times from the seventh district—in 1874, 1876, and 1878. Such victories were numbered, however. The taint of radical politics still associated with the Republicans proved no asset to Independents, and the Independent label did not measurably help Republicans. Furthermore, Farrow's long-held scheme to join the two by the popularity of Alexander Stephens came to naught when Stephens refused the fusion ticket's nomination for governor and instead, at Brown's urging, ran on the Bourbon ticket in 1882. Stephens, used to defeat the Republican/Independent coalition, died in office a few months later.[81]

Not to be forgotten among Republicans was the growing antagonism of the party's black membership. William Pledger and his faction were more interested in nurturing blacks who might replace the faltering white leadership than they were in Independentism. Had white Republican leaders read the pages of Pledger's *Athens Blade* in the early spring of 1880, they could not have been surprised by the demand to increase black power at the state convention in April that year. Continuing to stress the paucity of federal positions that blacks had held, Pledger in February scoffed at President Hayes's promise to appoint one black collector of revenue in the state. "The man to whom it is tendered ought to hurl it back into the face of the administration, that it may grow to a larger size. But a thousand dollars [the position's salary] is big sugar to a 'nigger.'" Blacks such as Pledger, among Georgia's Republicans, realized that they held the numerical balance of power in the party. Traveling columnist Jim Dudley anticipated the state convention with his advice to black readers, "We must know that the man, who wants our support, will give us a deal before we support him." Pledger took the idea a step further and resolved that blacks would "take a part in the assembling of the next State convention to select Generals from our ranks to a considerable extent." On another day he continued, "The colored men of Georgia mean to reorganize the party, to purge it of elements which have used it and abused it for their own selfish ends, and to place in the forefront men of ability, of principle, of character."[82]

By the time the convention had been called to order on April 21, 1880, the issue of black participation had been clearly drawn. Somewhat chaotic local ward meetings had produced a majority of black delegates, but also a good number of challenges, which, when presented, added to the confusion of the opening session. Bryant, on hand as chairman of the state central committee, tried to conciliate and reduce the rivalry between factions. The first day brought some public bickering beween Bryant and Pledger over the organization of the convention and a charge at the end by the Democratic press that they had conspired through the effort to put Pledger's name before the assembly. Both denied any collusion. On the second day, sensing the militant mood of the black delegates, Bryant spoke for an equal distribution of patronage in the state between black and white party members. The motion quickly followed that three-fourths of the state central committee be blacks and then the motion that three-fourths of the delegates to the national convention be blacks. The majority clearly approved the move to black power. Delegates elected to the national convention included fourteen blacks and eight whites, with eleven blacks and eleven whites as alternates. The boldest stroke of all came on the third day with the election of a new state party chairman. A popular black minister, W. J. White, was nominated, followed by the nomination of Bryant, "who had many warm supporters." After some discussion of these two, William A. Pledger's name was offered. Again sensing the spirit of the meeting, Bryant and White withdrew in favor of Pledger, who was "elected amidst great applause, by acclamation." A black man stood as the elected head of the Republican party in Georgia.[83]

Bryant, shut out, was not even selected as a delegate to the national convention. Elected four years before on the strength of black expectations, he had, for whatever reasons, brought about few changes for that constituency. This time the black Georgians would not look to white leadership—and certainly not to an absentee. Still, some mourned the shift against the carpetbagger. In the *Athens Blade,* one writer viewed the boycott against Bryant with mixed feelings: "One thing they did, however, they did not intend doing, in killing J. E. Bryant they killed themselves. We would not have it understood that we admire J. E. Bryant or advocate his cause, we admire his pluck and not the man, but we have long come to the conclusion that a white man is a white man North, East, South, and West, with but a few exceptions. . . . [Nevertheless,] the white men who are fighting J. E. Bryant are, in our opinion, meaner than he ever dared to be, and are not as timely republican."[84]

Pledger had also held that, among white men, Bryant at least had the interest of blacks at heart. In light of the friendly relations between the former and the present state chairmen, there is little reason to believe that Bryant was offended by the outcome of the convention. E. Q. Fuller, editor of the *Atlanta Methodist Advocate* and supporter of Bryant's educational interests, congratulated Bryant "on the results of the State Republican Convention. . . . I am glad to know that you are in hearty accord with Mr. Pledger the present chairman. . . . I trust white and colored will cooperate. . . . But the position assumed by the colored man in calling for leaders of their own race makes your declination both wise and honorable, especially in view of the fact that it was clearly evident that you would have been elected had you allowed your name to be used."[85]

On the surface, it might appear that finally, after long years of frustration, the black people of Georgia had some amount of power and prestige in state politics. Unfortunately, however, the wave of the future for Georgia Republicans was with the lily-whites. Pledger's election was considered by many as an aberration, and white party leaders declined either to support him or to lend him the aid essential for him to become an effective leader. Bryant himself was warned by well-meaning friends to stay away from the state and to dissociate himself from the black leadership in order to escape "the disgrace that will inevitably come upon them for their ignorance and want of integrity. . . . Let our colored friends run the party and be responsible for [the] results."[86]

Whether following this advice or merely continuing his own course, Bryant seemed unperplexed by the turn of events and his own loss of a leadership role. With his family in Illinois but no better off financially than they had been in Georgia, Bryant was now deeply involved in the great "Cause" to restructure the South through education and obviously relished his travels and freedom. He claimed that he had been uncertain even before the convention that he should seek to retain the chairmanship. In February, before the showdown in April, he had written to his wife, "Whether I can be again chosen chairman of the State committee or whether it is desirable that I should be are questions I am not prepared to settle. They are very important and let us make them the subject of earnest prayer. But important as these questions are the Cause which I advocate is *far very very* far above them."[87]

Having now assimilated and having made his peace with the Republican party's shift in strategy, the carpetbagger was prepared to devote his entire energies to a more indirect means of change. It had always been his dream to see the whole of Southern culture restructured; he would now redirect his own efforts in the attempt to implement the dream. Whether such a redirection would betray the reform impulse and his former commitment to equal rights for blacks was a question he left to history.

Six
The Closing Decades

Educate and elevate them and then will they assist in protecting, educating, and elevating the colored people.

The closing decades of the nineteenth century were a time of industrial expansion and social turmoil for the United States. Not until the last years of the century did the imperialism and blatant racism toward which the nation was moving become completely apparent. One legacy of the Civil War and Reconstruction had been a profound weariness with the race problem on the part of the great majority of whites; yet the question of the Negro's place in American society would not disappear, and it continued to command a prominent place in the national consciousness.

In earlier years the range of possible solutions to the problem had been variously suggested by the abolitionists, the Radical Republicans, and then the Southern Redeemers. With the strategic shift of the Republican party in the 1870s away from its former close identification with blacks and with the increasing emphasis of the Redeemers on the economic growth of the "New South," with its accompanying paternalism and discrimination against the Negro, the former abolitionists who remained active in public life were forced to rethink their earlier convictions. Historian James McPherson has concluded that many of the old antislavery advocates did not lose their concern for achieving equalitarian goals for blacks but redirected their methods of achieving them, primarily to education. Some, no doubt, were disillusioned with the fruits of Reconstruction and abandoned the hope of racial equality, and many may well have been at least partly influenced by the ideas of Social Darwinism that gripped America.¹

For John Emory Bryant the shift to educational goals did not conflict with his previous conviction, though he had opposed the retreat of Republicans when they had abandoned Radical policies and programs in the South. From his early years as a schoolteacher in Maine, he had maintained a firm belief that hard work and education would enable American society to achieve its full potential. Though gradualism and indifference replaced the immediatism of the reform impulse, faith in education remained intact for many Americans and surely for Bryant. The elective office he had sought in Georgia to fulfill his idealistic goals and material needs had eluded him, while the national party's strategy had undercut his political efforts. In the 1880s, therefore, and still keeping a close touch with state politics, the carpetbagger looked northward for the financial support he needed to justify his former work and to give new direction to his life. Thus, with new priorities, he turned from a sole concern for educating blacks to the need for reeducating whites, especially where their racial attitudes were involved.

Having invested so much of himself in championing black rights, Bryant perhaps experienced a certain amount of guilt in seeking a new emphasis, regardless of the necessity he saw for doing so. As the doors were closed in the field previously chosen, some new cause must be found that his conscience could approve.

From Illinois, Emma Spaulding Bryant's letters portrayed her musings about their future. How had the investment in Florida land worked out? John's answer did not inspire confidence. He apparently compared their life of several years back with that at the present. "Is it not possible, my darling, for you to answer me a plain question or two without going back into the past or dealing in generalities?" Emma wrote. You are thereby "increasing my anxiety and diminishing my faith in your ultimate success. What definite plans have you for making an immediate or very early *beginning* to paying your debts? . . . I know that it is only a general and large view which you take of it. . . . I am often troubled both for [Alice] and for you and for our future. God help us."²

Bryant seemed unable to allay Emma's fears but was seeking some reaffirmation of his work and perspective. He was deeply touched at this juncture by the writing of Albion W. Tourgée, probably the most famous of the carpetbaggers and certainly one of the most talented and literate.

Early in their careers in the South, the paths of JEB and Tourgée had crossed, and they had briefly contemplated publishing a Republican newspaper together. Much alike in temperament and outlook, they had gone separate ways, although Bryant found much in Tourgée's experience in North Carolina that matched his own in Georgia. Tourgée finally retreated from the South in 1879 after writing an account of his venture, which he entitled *A Fool's Errand*. In the book Tourgée described the folly of attempting to achieve an immediate change of attitudes concerning race, especially since those attitudes had been hardening for generations. "The social conditions of three hundred years," he wrote, "are not to be overthrown in a moment, and . . . differences which have ripened into war, are never healed by simple victory. . . . [But] fools . . . hoped that in some inscrutable way the laws of human nature would be suspended." Bryant clung to the fact that "Judge Tourgée . . . came to the same conclusion [that] I did." The judge also believed that the North and South were two civilizations, two distinct peoples, "two nations under one name. The intellectual, moral, and social life of each had been utterly distinct and separate from that of the other."[3]

Bryant found an audience for this assessment of "the Southern problem, its condition, its remedy" in the North, where he traveled in the 1880s as the representative of the Southern Advance Association. He himself had founded this society in 1877, the year after his second bitter failure to secure the congressional seat from Georgia's first district. The Southern strategy that President Hayes followed had been implemented the following spring. Afterward, Bryant apparently relinquished his hopes of ever securing an important political office in his adopted home.[4]

The Southern Advance had been born as the Atlanta Publishing Company, with its initial purpose that of financing the *Atlanta Republican,* the newspaper Bryant edited with W. L. Clark. After his split with Clark, the company backed the *Georgia Republican*; membership in the company was limited to those supporters of Bryant who underwrote the paper. The *Georgia Republican* never published more than scattered issues in 1878–1879, but in those issues and in his public speeches in Georgia and the North, Bryant expounded the need for reeducating the Southern masses to "national" or "American" ideas. By 1880, with the *Georgia Republican* played out and with Bryant's focus clearly on educational goals, the publishing company became the Southern Advance Association.

Bryant saw the association as a needed response to the Southern Historical Society, which was founded in 1873 by Southern leaders such as Wade Hampton of South Carolina and Alexander Stephens of Georgia. Bryant was incensed that these former Confederates blatantly sought to teach a "Southern view" of American history. He responded angrily to Hampton's claim in his first speech to the society that Southerners "were not subdued when Lee surrendered his starvelings at Appomattox." According to Hampton, the purpose of the Southern Historical Society was "to reflect the glory and maintain the principles involved in the late war . . . ; [and to] preserv[e] the honor of the South."[5]

Bryant was horrified to see this rhetoric shape history books published for Southern schoolchildren and written by such former rebels as Alexander Stephens himself and Joseph T. Derry of "Wesleyan Female College" in Macon, Georgia. The beliefs that Bryant recognized in these texts, "the heresies which made the rebellion possible," in his view, chiefly concerned states' rights, the just cause of the South, the good of slavery, and the superior chivalry of the Confederate soldiers during battle. Bryant explained that the Southern Advance Association, on the other hand, "had been organized to meet the Bourbons in the forum, and convince the people that the National or Union Cause, the cause of freedom, is right, and the Confederate or secession cause, the cause of slavery, wrong."[6]

While JEB had a high view of the Southern Advance Association and saw it as a corrective to the Southern Historical Society, his critics saw the association as a sham and a fraud. Henry Farrow, Bryant's old nemesis and a durable Southern Republican, challenged the carpetbagger in the pages of the *Providence* [Rhode Island] *Journal* in early 1881. In a series of letters to the editor, the two carried on the now familiar dispute over Bryant's methods and accomplishments. Farrow maintained that Bryant was misrepresenting the Southern Advance as a viable organization. Private correspondence reveals that Farrow had sought and could find only twelve or so persons in Georgia who acknowledged membership. (Bryant's records, however, show that some members were Georgia officeholders in Washington.) Farrow repeatedly and sarcastically ridiculed Bryant's claim that the association had "branches all over the state" of Georgia. As for Bryant's résumé of references to his good character that he carried with him in the North, Farrow dismissed these as the "tools of his trade" of chicanery. He argued that the "certificates of character" were themselves "evidence of his guilt."[7]

Farrow's primary charge was that Bryant was collecting "thousands" of dollars in donations from unsuspecting Northerners for a newspaper that was rarely published and was pocketing most of the money himself. These charges drove Bryant to publish in the paper a financial statement, one that Farrow promptly demolished with his own undocumented calculations.

Farrow found Bryant's self-imposed title of "political missionary" highly offensive and pleaded with Northerners to see "the utter folly and grievous wrong of making a political missionary field of our weary South, which is just beginning to show unmistakable signs of recovering from all the evil passions naturally attending the results of an unsuccessful rebellion." He ended with a plea that the readers ignore Bryant's causes and contribute, if they must, to the bona fide educational and religious institutions at work in the South, "for all the leading Denominations up North are, thank God! exerting themselves throughout the South with well directed efforts."[8]

The irony of Farrow's appeal was that Bryant himself had already turned to that channel. His experience of unfulfilled goals in Reconstruction, coupled with the Southern Historical Society's overt expression of Southern pride and antagonism toward the North, convinced JEB of the crucial need to inculcate whites in the South with "national ideas." He blamed the poverty and ignorance of lower-class Southern whites on the "slaveholder aristocracy" that did not believe in free labor and did not encourage public education. Poor whites should be taught, Bryant said, that "abolition freed them too. . . . Educate and elevate them and then will *they* assist in protecting, educating, and elevating the colored people." His strongest supporters included members of the Methodist Episcopal Church in Georgia. The very presence of this Northern church on Southern soil did little to endear its members to Southerners, especially members of the Methodist Episcopal Church, South. The "home missionary" efforts of the Northern Methodist Church had been impressive since the end of the war in establishing schools and providing aid to the freed slaves, but by the 1880s there was a general stir among the membership to involve the church in the work among the "destitute whites" of the South as well.[9]

Erasmus Q. Fuller, controversial editor of the *Atlanta Methodist Advocate,* was one denominational leader who assisted Bryant in working for that goal, Fuller being known as the "Christian soldier" and Bryant as the "political soldier" of the pair. The close relationship between the work of Bryant and Fuller was seen as early as 1879, when the Atlanta Republican

Publishing Company was struggling with the question of whether to drop the company's newspaper and bookstore. At that time the directors announced in the annual report: "As the *Methodist Advocate,* of Atlanta, the organ of the Methodist Episcopal Church in the South, is an advocate of free schools and the protection of the lives and rights of all citizens, it was decided to recommend to the friends of our cause in Georgia to subscribe for that paper until the Company is able to again issue the *Southern Advance and Georgia Republican,* which it will do as soon as possible."[10]

The *Methodist Advocate* had proclaimed in its early issues that "the paper is non-political and will remain so," but its Southern white readers were quick to discover the editor's predilection for Republican ideals. Fuller, on another occasion, more honestly admitted, "If piety be genuine and politics pure, why should they not agree? Our politics and religion agree admirably, and in harmony they lead to the elevation of all races." Bryant occasionally contributed to the paper, and while his tone was moderate in print, his views were undoubtedly well known. Albion Tourgée's columns also appeared in the paper. From time to time, stung as other Yankees were by Southern "ingratitude" for Northern missionary effort, the *Advocate* defended the motives and accomplishments of carpetbaggers. In one issue it reprinted the following comments from the *Atlanta Republican*: "Do not believe all 'strangers' are rogues . . . and enemies of the South. We have no shadow of doubt it can be shown that the 'carpetbagger' has been the greatest blessing to Georgia she has had in a couple of centuries."[11]

Fuller and Bryant were able to blend their energy and talent most successfully in educational work. The Methodist Episcopal church unashamedly proclaimed the necessity of "intellectual culture" as a preliminary to religion, for "the one prepares the way for the other. . . . The great mission of the church is to educate and [to] save—to educate that she may save." Because of the obvious and compelling educational plight of those released from slavery after the Civil War, the work of the church had been primarily among blacks. In 1875, however, at least one minister spoke out in the *Methodist Advocate* and urged that Methodist schools also be opened for whites. Through the Freedmen's Aid Society, he claimed, the church had given a great deal of money to black schools but little to white. He would not "deny the need of blacks, but why the strange neglect[?] Numerically, whites are twice as many; politically they are many fold more influential, and the same is true socially." The church's General Conference of 1880 reflected the same concern when it requested that the Society enlarge its work to include poor whites.[12]

There was enough support for this sentiment to inspire a "goodly number" to gather in April 1880 to discuss the opening of a "seminary" in Atlanta "for the accommodation of our white members and friends in this part of the state." A committee of seven, including Fuller and Bryant, was instructed by the group to "take steps toward the organization of a Board of Education by the Georgia Conference and toward the establishment of a Conference seminary in Atlanta, in cooperation with the one [one of the few for whites] already at Ellijay." Bryant made "the speech of the evening," and his address was reportedly "clear, strong, impressive and elegant, and in the broadest Christian charity."[13]

The committee appointed began at once to make its proposals concrete and practical, and by the next year a school had been opened under the patronage of the Southern Advance Association. The teacher employed, Miss M. H. Stokes, later remembered that "there were but fifteen or twenty children in attendance" on the first day; the number doubled in a month's time. She confided to Bryant:

> There is great need of just such a school as you and your friends have instituted. There is a large number of children in Atlanta for whom there is no room in the public schools and the class whom you are having taught are the very ones who either are too careless to try in time to get their children in, or, having done so, allow them to lose their places by irregular attendance. Unless you could see the parents, as I have done, you cannot appreciate the poverty, wretchedness and degradation of some of the families whose children we are attempting to raise from gross ignorance to a better life. It is sad to see how low down in the scale of humanity many of these people are; and just to think, they are Anglo-Saxons and Americans! It strikes me that we as citizens of the United States owe a duty to these poor white people. I, as well as you, believe in the education of the negro; but, while that is being done, the poor helpless white children should not be neglected. So far as I know, no other Church in this city is carrying on any such educational work for the poor, as yours is.

Earlier she had written, "If ever there was a mission needed, requiring money, laborers, and God's grace and blessing it is the mission you have started."[14]

The reputation of the school and the work of Miss Stokes contributed to the final success of the committee's endeavors in June 1883. At that time resolutions were passed by the conference meetings of the Marietta Street Methodist Episcopal Church, the Board of Directors of the Educational Society of the Georgia Conference of the Methodist Episcopal Church, and the Educational Convention of the Methodist Episcopal Church (representing the conferences of Holston, Virginia, Blue Ridge, Georgia, Alabama, Central Tennessee, Kentucky, and Arkansas). Similar in content, they each concluded: "Whereas there has been for the past two years a school taught . . . under the auspices of the Southern Advance Association, therefore, Resolved that this work . . . has a cordial approval and support of this . . . conference. . . . Resolved that we commend the Southern Advance Association to the favorable consideration of all benevolent people as in every way worthy of their confidence and support."[15]

The response of these conferences was gratifying to Bryant, but he was also aware of continued opposition to his work. One colleague carried on his "fight for right" against opponents in the church in Atlanta, while Bryant, in the meantime, continued to make his speeches throughout the North. There he met with some measure of success, but one report of a Methodist Episcopal missionary meeting in New York revealed that all was not well: "There are men going about the North trying to create a sentiment that they cannot sustain. The thing that our work needs is that the Bishops and the Secretaries shall give the benefit of their endorsement only to men who are worthy of it. We have had men traveling around from Conference to Conference to raise the paltry sum of $800 or less, & making their expenses out of the thing." The writer became more specific: "They have had a debate in the Preachers Meeting in Boston whether or not they shall endorse Col Bryant. I will simply say this, that if there were a proposition made to endorse him in this [New York] vicinity, my judgment is that it would not get five votes. (Gen. Fish—'I do not think it would get three.') I think that may be classed as privileged communication." Clearly the controversy revolved around Bryant. "Don't you see," the report continued, "the effect of a man of that kind going around where nobody believes in him? These are the things that damage our work. Let us cut loose all these barnacles, and let us put our money where we can live."[16]

Undeterred by such criticism, Bryant expanded the number of schools receiving aid from the Southern Advance and then approached the General Conference of the Methodist Episcopal Church for funds. After he was elected as a lay delegate to the general conference to be held in Philadelphia in May 1884, he prepared as for any political campaign. He outlined his objectives for the conference as (1) electing bishops sympathetic to "our white work" and (2) expanding the benevolent giving of the church to schools for whites in the South, placing "the white work of our church in the South in good shape."[17] Presumably JEB remained concerned about the education of blacks as well, but he was now consumed with gaining the church's support for his new work among whites.

In asking for support from the Methodist Episcopal Church, the Southern Advance Association entered a dispute of conscience of that body regarding its role in the South. In the 1870s Bishop Gilbert Haven, who supervised the work of the Northern Methodist Church in the lower and middle South, had worked to integrate congregations and conferences for black and white Methodists there. Ironically, Haven's work had greatly antagonized Southerners and had resulted only in furthering resistance to any "social mingling" of the races. Bryant's friend and coworker E. Q. Fuller was among those who had opposed Haven's stand and had insisted on equal but separate churches and schools for blacks.[18] Bryant and Fuller, working so closely together, probably agreed on this point; as a candidate Bryant had expressed the same view regarding schools at least.

Bryant's work was again at the center of a controversy. His developing concern for educational institutions to teach whites coincided with the rising antagonism within the Methodist Episcopal Church against preoccupation with black needs as well as against religious amalgamation between the two races. His requests would match the religious mood that in turn reflected the broader secular turn away from black concerns. As early as 1876, the Methodist Episcopal Church had skirted the touchy item of segregation by deciding to allow each congregation and conference to decide for itself how it would handle the issue.[19] At that time the matter still had strong adherents on both sides. Now, in 1884, the resistance was consolidated enough for a stand by the general conference, another indication of the mood of the 1880s.

Thus, at the general conference of 1884, at which JEB was a delegate, the church finally "condoned the policy of racial separation in the South." One bishop pointedly said, "The church has simply accepted the circumstances as she finds them, and . . . is trying to meet the needs of all." The same conference dealt with the question of benevolence directed toward educational work among white children, as represented by the petition of the Southern Advance Association. "We have had a *very hard* fight for our white work," Bryant reported from the conference. "It comes in two committees; one 'Freedmen's Aid and Southern Work,' the other [the] 'State of the Church.' I am a member of both committees. . . . We finished the fight . . . in the 'Freedmen's Aid' committee, and gained a victory, although we did not get all I wanted. . . . The fight in the 'State of the Church' committee will be ended I think today, and I believe in our favor."[20]

It is difficult to see any evidence of Bryant's expected success in the report made by the State of the Church Committee to the conference, unless it be in the simple wording of the injunction against discrimination: "No student shall be excluded from any and every school under the supervision of the Church, because of race, color, or previous condition of servitude," a statement, incidentally, that seemed to contradict the principle of segregation. The report of the Freedmen's Aid Society Committee, on the other hand, clearly reflected Bryant's influence. "The establishment of schools for the benefit of our white membership in the South," it began, "we believe to have been a wise and necessary measure. Their success has been gratifying. The beneficial results have not been confined to those immediately interested but their liberalizing effects upon public sentiment have greatly redounded to the advantage of our colored people." The amount of money accompanying this vote of confidence was not immediately specified but in the final resolve of the committee it pledged "such cooperation and assistance as we may be able to render." Nor did the committee turn its back on the black people of the South, for it resolved "to stand by and assist them in the further prosecution of this work, to the extent of our ability, and so far as possible, to the extent of their need in this direction [of education]." Some members criticized the committee's decision to give money only to "white education." Nevertheless, the mood of the majority went with Bryant's friend who believed in both causes, confessing that he did "still retain his boyhood abolitionist sentiments, but we cannot adopt the same policy that we could if the Millennium were just at hand."[21]

Bryant readily agreed and easily adapted his message to the need at hand, as he saw it. While his energies were being expended to a large extent on gaining the support of the Methodist church for educational work, however, he did not forget the concerns of the Republican party in Georgia. Since his election as state party chairman, William A. Pledger had struggled to be more than nominal head of the state's Republicans, though the white party members at both state and federal level were reluctant to give him the support he needed to be effective. By precedent Pledger should have held the office of chairman for a term of four years, 1880–1884, but his opponents were determined to force him to step down and to end black leadership.

The divisions within the party revolved around the personalities of a few men. Formerly unsuccessful candidate for governor, Jonathan Norcross, after Pledger's election in 1880, had moved quickly to form a splinter Republican group. In a series of newspaper articles, he advocated organizing a separate white party that, according to the sarcastic *Atlanta Constitution,* he believed would bring in the "mythical mass of men" just waiting to be in a Republican party without blacks. A small group, including W. L. Clark, editor of the *Atlanta Republican,* had met with Norcross in Atlanta in July 1880, to organize such a party.[22] But the splintering of the party had only highlighted its impotence in the fall elections, when no Republican or Independent candidate in Georgia was elected to national office and when the Democrats tightened their hold on state offices.

The faction led by Norcross was viewed as a somewhat "unprofessional" and emotional reaction to what others also perceived as the distasteful accident of black leadership. Party stalwarts such as Henry Farrow had received the call to support the "white Republicans," but had declined to attend Norcross's soiree.[23] The actual power in the party continued to reside neither in the black titular leaders nor in the lily-white faction but in the white patronage appointees and longtime Republicans like Farrow with connections among federal officeholders.

A new combination of these men, dubbed "the syndicate" by the press, emerged to meet the challenge of black leadership, while following the pattern of politics that had become familiar in Georgia during Reconstruction. The only new twist to the scenario was the previously latent and selective but now open and blanket antagonism between Northern-born and Southern Republicans. A fresh face in the Georgia mix was the controversial general of the Confederacy, James Longstreet. While Longstreet had the support of the syndicate, his accommodation to federal control during Reconstruction and even his support of Grant had done little to impress state party leaders such as Bryant, who probably resented his intrusion into Georgia Republicanism. When President Garfield appointed Longstreet to the post of United States marshal in Georgia in

1881, JEB wrote a letter of protest to James G. Blaine, senator from Maine and soon to become secretary of state, arguing that it was "cruel" and "unwise" to crush men who had labored so long for Republican principles and to give Longstreet such an important post. Better, Bryant went on, that men who have proven by hard work that their "interests are entirely in the South" be given the job. Northern-born men of ability and good character "are as popular and influential as Southern-born Republicans," Bryant concluded rather optimistically.[24]

Apart from Longstreet, the syndicate included Henry Farrow, James Atkins, William Felton, and John Conley. These men and others intended to build a "white Republican party" by taking control of the party organization and the delegation to the national convention, guaranteeing federal patronage positions for themselves and their allies, and trying once again to join Republican and Independent strength in the election of 1882.[25] From the initial meeting in December 1881, known as the "Markham House Conference," this group plotted its strategy.

Blacks were obviously excluded, as were carpetbaggers such as Bryant and A. E. Buck. Buck had gone to Georgia via Alabama after the war and had been slowly working his way into the higher echelons of Georgia Republicanism. He had served as one of three party referees on the committee that considered Atkins and Conley's charges against Bryant back in January 1877 after the 1876 election smear. In addition, he had earned a certain amount of respect in his appointed post as clerk of the circuit court in Atlanta. By the turn of the century, he was the most important leader in the state party. With Buck there were as many as five white Republicans in Georgia from Maine, among them C. H. Prince and John Emory Bryant. The hostility against this "Maine clique" by the syndicate and other Georgians rivaled that which had been endured by many Northern settlers in the South immediately after the Civil War. Farrow complained that "too many offices" in Georgia were filled with "Maine men."[26]

The move toward white control, then, was in essence a move to "redeem" the Republican party not only from identification with blacks but from Northern elements who held elective offices and/or patronage positions. This direction was paradoxical and ironic for the party of emancipation and equal rights—even if it did follow logically from Hayes's effort in 1877. Furthermore, for the time being it was virtually impossible to achieve these goals, since Northern-born and black Republicans could not be persuaded to renounce either their membership in the Republican party or their participation in politics—besides, the party needed them. Still, one Independent office seeker voiced a common sentiment when he complained that the Northerners were "not creditable representatives of any party." Another noted, "The struggle of Bryant and his crowd as the *Republican 'Bourbons'* to keep the Republican party in Ga. so small that there will be just engh. to fill the Federal offices, is desperate. They are now a greater hinderance to the growth of Republicanism than the 'Bourbon Democracy' in Ga."[27]

By 1882 open conflict between these party factions seemed inevitable. In August of that year, rival caucuses met in Atlanta, each claiming to represent the Republicans of Georgia. After the predictable verbal salvos and some pushing and shoving, the seemingly hopeless division was moved toward unity by the action of Pledger, who withdrew his name for reelection as chairman of the state central committee. A. E. Buck was then chosen to head the mostly black majority assembly. Though he was white, Buck was acceptable as a compromise to the black membership. In this way, the splinter group's immediate goal had been realized, namely, to rid the party of Pledger's leadership and to replace him with "a white man . . . (who) will give more respectability to the party and have more weight in the state and more weight at Washington." This group therefore agreed to the substitution of Buck and the party was reunited. As they prepared for the election, the syndicate publicly complained that the party's leadership had done no campaigning and organizational work for the past ten years, apparently forgetting that Farrow had been party chairman for four of those years. (Bryant gleefully reminded them of this fact!) As it was, the party had been reknit in time only for another resounding defeat by the Democrats in the fall of 1882, and when Alexander Stephens defected, the dream of a successful Independent-Republican coalition finally ended.[28]

Under Buck's chairmanship, Bryant became secretary of the state central committee once again, and in his travels in the North he found it a simple matter to combine the appeals of the Southern Advance Association and Georgia's Republican party. Some of Bryant's most enthusiastic audiences as he presented his twin appeal were the chapters of the Union League of America, where he frequently spoke. The league had fostered the initial work of the Republican party in Georgia after the Civil War, and Bryant and his adherents turned to the league as again the party struggled against

Democratic strength. In 1879 the directors of the Atlanta Republican Publishing Company had "decided that the Union League of America is the best organization to assist in the work we have undertaken, as [it] is a political missionary organization that has already accomplished very much for the Union cause and for American civilization." Bryant never seemed to tire of "delivering [his] address [at the meetings of the League] on the subject of the present condition of the South, showing that education and religion, the school and the Church, were the only remedies for existing evils in that section." Bryant became so involved with the Union League through his work for the party in Georgia that, by the end of the 1880s, he was a member of its executive committee, having risen first to the office of secretary and then to vice president of the national organization.[29]

Meantime, Republicans throughout the nation faced an unknown quantity in the person of Chester Arthur, who became president after the death of Garfield in 1881. Republican leaders from both factions of the party in Georgia were eager to expound to the new president their ideas for solving the party's ills. Farrow and Atkins, prime movers in the syndicate, made their bid early, and Bryant, likewise, in February 1882, sought a private audience with Arthur in order to give him an "inside view" of the situation in the state. Arthur was probably responsible for at least surface unanimity among party leaders in Georgia between 1882 and 1884, and A. E. Buck exerted a mediating influence by doggedly lobbying for patronage positions for divergent Republicans such as JEB and Farrow. The uneasy truce between the factions was short lived and was built on mutual mistrust and attempts to use each other. A friend warned Bryant against succumbing to the tactics of the syndicate:

> A few years ago, there was, or seemed to be, a combination among natives "to put none but Georgians on guard"; we thought that a grievous mistake: you fought faithfully against it, and it amounted to nothing; you now propose "to put none but ex-union soldiers on guard"; is that less of a mistake? . . . I ask you in all seriousness how can you hope to have any Republican success on the line you have marked out? and look at some of the men with whom you are to accomplish this end: Farrow, Jno. G. Clark, ex-confed soldiers, Atkins, conf deserter, Wilson—all of whom hate you with the bitterest hatred known to men, and who have entered your combination in the hope of using you (though I think they'll have to get up early to do it).
>
> Again I think the good of the Nation rests upon the success of Republican

principle, and I believe it to be the duty of every Republican to do all that lies in him in the interest of unity and harmony. . . . This can not be accomplished except by throwing wide open the doors . . . and inviting in all who are willing to cooperate for the accomplishment of this purpose."[30]

It did indeed seem that individuals in Georgia had lost perspective in the struggle for appointed office. Bryant's new drive for a place had begun in earnest in 1882. He wrote Emma that he hoped an office would "enable me to continue my work . . . [and] one that will enable me to provide for my family and pay something on my debts." As always he was able to command an impressive list of backers, such as former governor Joseph Brown, who claimed to admire his "conviction and courage," and C. H. Prince, carpetbagger and postmaster in Augusta, who knew Bryant to be a "man of marked ability . . . honest and able and . . . actuated by what he considers to be right." Bryant claimed that he badly needed a position with some monetary compensation, which seems understandable, for his only apparent income was from the contributions made to the Southern Advance. Moreover, the school sponsored by the association needed money, and Bryant's family was totally dependent on him. JEB's wife and daughter lived an indigent existence in Atlanta, where they had moved in early 1881. Emma Spaulding Bryant harbored grave thoughts about the future as she attempted to remain loyal to her husband's version of his idealistic goals. At the same time she had to provide for the essential needs of her daughter and herself. The potential patronage appointment of which John spoke so often became to Emma Bryant a ray of hope— "much hope I may say, that you may succeed in obtaining government office, . . . I am often troubled in regard to it. . . . I almost feel of late as if my life depends upon a different situation financially."[31]

To the strain of poverty, Bryant himself added the burden of conflict to his wife's load when he became obsessed with the idea that she should assist Miss Stokes with the teaching in the Fuller school. Emma Bryant refused, pleading her ill health (she had symptoms of coughing and jaundice) and her inability to deal with "children of any kind," and especially "such children." More realistically she chose to begin, through self-study and volunteer work in a school for black adults in Atlanta, to regain her previous skill in mathematics. This work required only three half-hours per week, at her option, and there she had the advantage of working with students "anxious to learn." An additional boon was that she was teaching, as she said, in a field "which I love myself." Ironically, this response infuriated Bryant, who interpreted the action as disapproval of his new focus on education for whites and accused his wife of "helping the colored" instead of him and the white children. Bryant clearly wanted her affirmation of his new emphasis. On at least one other occasion he had shown a similar vulnerability when he pleaded for support of his decision to bypass the immediate needs of blacks for educational work among white children, a move he hoped would not be interpreted as "any sacrifice of principle."[32]

Emma Bryant stood her ground, reminding her husband, "You do me grave injustice and fly off on a tangent when you reason that I am helping the colored *instead* of the white, Miss Packard [teacher of the school for blacks] *instead* of you. *I am doing nothing of the kind.*" With Alice's schooling to attend to, as well as the need to regain her own health, Mrs. Bryant felt the best plan was "reviewing math and learning the best methods for teaching it. . . . Otherwise [I] shall be utterly helpless to assist you, if the time comes when you start [another] seminary."[33]

Furthermore, Bryant had touched a sensitive nerve when he suggested, "Perhaps you will enjoy better health to have something to employ a part of your time out of the usual channel." His wife angrily sought "to have my husband remember that God has given me brains and judgment and a feeling of responsibility as well as to himself, and to cease to *distress* and *chafe* me by opposing every plan I make, and by attempting to think for me." Warming to the subject of women's capabilities and rights, she continued, "It is because I was born with a respect for the *inherent rights* of *every person,* for the right of each person to judge for him or herself what God requires of them, and do you suppose that I grant all this to you, as you know and the Father knows I have, and feel within me none of those rights?" She concluded somewhat disparagingly that proof of her sympathy for his work was her "willingness to help in it without any assured feeling of its success in your life time or mine."[34]

Emma depended on John's approval for most of her decisions, despite her brave words, but she was of necessity finding a new courage and independence. One consistent source of conflict between them concerned the place where she and her daughter lived, since Bryant's prolonged and frequent absence plus their lack of finances made housekeeping impractical. Usually forced to board, she resisted JEB's demand that she stay with the Fullers in order to help *them* through their similar monetary plight. The ruin of her health, she said, was a cost "too high" to pay in order to help them. Emma found the food offered by the Fullers distasteful, since it consisted predominantly of pork and starches.[35] The oppressive heat of Georgia summers and the unnutritious food were two factors of Southern living to which Emma Bryant never adjusted.

She was equally alarmed when her husband announced that he would attempt to pay Fuller a salary as president of the Southern Advance Association, of which Bryant remained secretary. "I am troubled," she wrote, "because I fully believe you are promising him what you cannot possibly do, . . . without crippling your missionary work and starving your own family."[36] Even after so many years of marriage, the priorities of the carpetbagger still baffled his wife.

The question of a change in her domicile had raised a deeper issue. In their letters, the husband and wife explored, in addition to his goals, the basic issue of control. "I have for many years believed that the germs of human nature, the essentials of it I may say, are the same everywhere, and all experience and observation confirms that view," wrote Emma Bryant, and "both sexes" have all these essential elements. Then, quoting a feminist axiom, she argued, "Admit that man's conscience should decide *woman's duties* and you admit that woman is not an accountable being. Man in attempting to define woman's sphere, steps out of his own sphere." She appealed next to her husband's legal background: if you were at the bar, "pleading for your own freedom (as I am), and had no lawyer, I would feel very generous, I think, if I were the opposing consul." And again to his benevolence: "I think that if you knew the added strength, moral, mental, and physical, that I should derive from it you would at least *ask* God to enlighten you [as to the wisdom of the move]."[37]

Since the Bryants saved only her letters on the matter, one must guess at his part in this exchange. From her perspective, after her careful attempts to win him over, she was appalled that his letters continued to prescribe what she "ought" to do. Determined but unaccustomed to making crucial decisions without his approval, she spoke of her freedom of choice and then persisted in asking his opinion, admitting that she would like the "benefit of his judgment," even if she chose not to follow his advice.

Finally, after much agonizing, Emma left the Fullers and found a small house outside Atlanta. She was convinced that she had made the right decision, both for herself and for her daughter. It was not the first house in which they had lived in Georgia, but it was a testimony to the changing atmosphere in the South that she was able to live there without the fear that soon after the war had required that she carry a loaded pistol to the door when her husband was not home or have a Negro guard sleep in the house to ensure the family's safety. She happily reported that she no longer worried about Alice's being ostracized at school, while she herself had found some measure of acceptance in several churches in Atlanta.[38]

Bryant's life as a speaker traveling the Northern circuit contrasts sharply with his wife's poverty in Georgia. Taking advantage of the years of travel and friendships in the North, Bryant apparently enjoyed his migratory existence and the hospitality afforded him among his associates. His detractors in New York and Georgia correctly pointed out that his expenses were usually subtracted first from the collections that were taken following his speeches in behalf of education in the South, though the donations sometimes went directly to specified schools. Also, he fully participated in the "social privileges" of the Union League in Philadelphia and New York. In one poignant exchange he described to his wife the marvelous view of the ocean that he enjoyed from his hotel window at Ocean Grove, New Jersey, a Methodist resort and retreat, where he was a guest of the Ocean Grove Association. In response, Emma recalled for him her poor, simple existence and her hope that someday they would have a few luxuries with which "to enrich Alice's life."[39]

In 1884 Bryant secured the patronage position he claimed to need and also received strong criticism for alleged mismanagement of funds, both coming in connection with election-year activities. As secretary of the state central committee in Georgia, Bryant sent letters to potential donors to the Republican party, requesting money for the presidential campaign. This circular explained that the Southern Advance Association had been "requested to raise and expend money for the state central committee . . . as the state central committee is in part composed of national officials and as the civil service law of congress prohibits such officials from receiving or expending money given by such persons for political purposes." Bryant promised that money received would "be disbursed by the executive committee under advice of the leading men of the party who can legally give such advice."[40]

The *Atlanta Constitution* gleefully reported the opposition that other factions in the Republican party had voiced upon receiving the letter. One critic, Thomas S. King, presumably a friend of Farrow's, published an open letter to Bryant in the leading Democratic paper in Atlanta that blasted him for his alleged misuse of funds that he had collected for the Southern Advance Association. They were "largely applied to your own benefit and to the benefit of those associated with you." He then listed a report with charges and figures matching those in Farrow's earlier attacks in the *Providence Journal,* showing that, from the assets of the association, Bryant had paid himself a salary of twelve thousand dollars, while the school in Atlanta had been given only six hundred dollars. "Being closely questioned you [Bryant] admitted receipts of the association have been 'something over twenty thousand dollars,'" but when asked how much of that amount had gone to education, could cite "having given and promised about $1,300 for education work." At the end of his statement, the writer called Bryant a "political traitor" for his actions during the legislatures of 1868–1870, presumably a reference to the attack Conley had made earlier, and concluded that he would contribute to the national party but "not one dollar for your disbursement."[41]

One may only marvel that Bryant blithely attempted such an arrangement. The accuracy of the accusation is questionable, of course, because it repeated charges that had already been answered, and Bryant's records nowhere indicate such wild personal spending at the expense of the educational work that he espoused so strongly. Nevertheless, it is difficult to see how he could have avoided mixing the political and educational monies at his disposal. Indeed, he saw no inconsistency in doing so; the education of poor white children was for the purpose of raising up a generation of white Southerners who believed in Republican principles, the same principles he allegedly worked for in political campaigns. The entire arrangement of combining personal aspirations with political causes goes back to the lean days of Reconstruction, when the radical ideas of black civil rights were joined with political goals for realizing change. How far the personal satisfactions by now outweighed the cause is not easy to measure, nor is the amount of good his speeches achieved by changing attitudes regarding racial equality. Like other politicos, Bryant tried to provide for his own future through speculative ventures as well, though he was not tremendously successful. He attempted with no luck to convert land in Florida into profit, and it will be remembered that he was paid in stock of the Western & Atlantic Railroad for effective lobbying efforts in Washington.[42] It is puzzling that none of this estate planning was ever visible in his or his family's life-style, except perhaps as enjoyed on his travels.

The patronage position, which JEB claimed to need, came to him through the usual route of party politics. He had lobbied for the post of United States marshal for northern Georgia for several years before the national convention was held in Chicago in 1884. There President Arthur's chief opposition was the perennial contender James G. Blaine from Maine, and Arthur needed every delegate he could muster. The *Atlanta Constitution* attributed the strength of the Arthur candidacy in the South to the fear among Southern Republicans of losing patronage jobs. "They do not care who may be the nominee," the *Constitution* contended, "if their office and influence is guaranteed."

The Georgia delegation, in fact, remained firm for Arthur to the end, and it was cited by the press for its diligent adherence to convention business. "The Georgia delegation," one reporter wrote, "be it said to their credit, that they are by all odds the strongest from the south, and are carefully attending to their duties in the convention. Wilson, Bryant, and Johnson are working hard. Pledger is heard in the hall, Devereaux on the national committee, and Buck is kept busy in counsel. A noticeable feature of the delegation is that they have not participated in the vilifying against the south, but nearly all have in all cases spoken well of their state."[43]

The solidarity of the Georgia delegation on the convention floor did not necessarily reflect accurately the party's factionalism back home. Before the convention, Norcross had again attempted to form a separate Republican party for whites only. This "Whig Republican" party had not proved a viable force against the regular party structure manned by Buck and Bryant, however, and while its representatives were not present in Chicago, Arthur's loss to Blaine at the convention proved a source of amusement to these Republicans back in Atlanta. The *Constitution* reported, "Buck and Bryant [had] held the delegates squarely to the 'boss' [Buck] and did not give a man of them a chance to stampede and fall on the winning side of the fence. This fact, it is claimed, settles their leadership in Georgia, and, in the event of Blaine's election, they would be sent to the rear to 'tote brush.' It is a square knock-down to the office holders' ring and all other republicans now feel emancipated from their arrogance and domination."[44]

Arthur did not forget the loyalty of the Georgia delegation. In that same summer of 1884, Arthur removed James Longstreet and appointed John Emory Bryant to be U.S. marshal for northern Georgia, a post that he had long sought. Anticipating vindictive action by Bryant, one Democratic reporter warned that, "having shown that he can collar and down the negro leaders, Bryant now proposes to make it warm not only for the democrats but for the white man's whig Republican party. Mr. Norcross will please keep an eye on his Skowhegan friend."[45]

The post reunited the family for a few months. Alice Bryant remembered the time when Bryant was marshal as one of her happiest. Despite his being, in her assessment, a "very strict disciplinarian," Alice loved her father "very greatly and was very happy when with him." During this period, when she was about thirteen, she "spent hours with him in his offices listening to the men talking politics." She also accompanied him to the barbershop and sat on the footrest of the chair while he was shaved. Alice was "deeply grieved" when JEB decided she was too old for such excursions, "as no girls or women went in those days."[46]

Bryant's term of office as marshal was short, since Arthur soon was a lame-duck president. While the inevitable charges against Bryant as an "obvious partisan" followed his resignation upon the election of a Democratic president, a scrupulous audit by a Democratic Treasury Department failed to reveal any debit against the marshal's office. In fact, after several years of haggling over closing the books from his term as marshal, JEB's accountant discovered that the Treasury Department ended up owing the marshal's office money, and he divided the surplus among the deputies who had served under Bryant.[47]

As important as the audit, perhaps, was the assessment of Bryant's term made by Independent Democrat Judge Emory Speer, native of Georgia and judge of district court: "In taking his leave of the late marshal the court feels it his duty to express the opinion that Col. Bryant has discharged the duties of the marshal's office with remarkable efficiency and skill, and with humanity and courtesy to all persons brought in contact with him." The judge went on to comment that "the office, within the knowledge of the court, has never been better conducted, and I am very sure that Col. Bryant retires from the discharge of his duties, not only with the good will of this court, but also of the judge of his district, now absent, and of the officers of the court." Then Judge Speer offered the recognition that Bryant had wanted so long. "I have the pleasure, by request of Colonel Bryant, who presents his commission as attorney and counselor at law, solicitor in chancery and proctor and advocate in the Circuit Court of the United States for the Southern District of Georgia, to direct that the clerk enter his name upon the rolls as a member of this bar.⁴⁸

If the judge's comments may be believed, Bryant realized his greatest acceptance in Georgia. Ironically, with it came his final departure from the South. With the loss of his highest patronage position and the fall of Arthur's administration, Bryant removed himself from the political situation in Georgia and instead worked exclusively with the national Union League. Emma Bryant also left Atlanta and found a new home base in Athens, Tennessee. There she taught at the East Tennessee Wesleyan University, while Alice enrolled as a student. Alice later attributed her mother's move to taking "up the burden of my education," while JEB was "struggling to succeed in business." The school was one of those that had been aided earlier by the Southern Advance Association, and Bryant had on occasion solicted funds for its program. Through some assistance from her brother, perhaps some from her husband, and her own effort, Emma Bryant at last found some relief from the poverty she knew in Georgia as she made good use of her former preparation for teaching. Clearly she relished the change in her situation. Her health improved, she discovered horseback riding, and she found occasion to enjoy some few extravagances such as ribbons and laces. Whether this separation was any different from the others is unknown, for there are only a few letters from this period, and most of those are between Alice and her father. While Alice loved and respected her mother, calling her "the stuff [of which] martyrs are made," she clearly adored her father, and her "picture" of him was "much brighter to me than that of my mother." With a touch reminiscent of John's earlier signature in letters to Emma, Alice signed hers Y[our] D[aughter].⁴⁹

Bryant, meantime, settled for a while in New York City and entered the business world of bonds and mortgages. Successful in that venture more than he had been previously, and claiming that "God seems to be leading me to large success," he felt no further need to petition for any federal office or patronage. He therefore assumed the role of political sage and freely shared his experience and advice on the Southern situation. The problem of blacks in American society became a favorite subject of his, and in his speeches on the topic he endorsed such orators as George Washington Cable in proclaiming the solution for racial troubles. On one occasion he reported that "Mr. George W. Cable, the well known Southern writer in an oration at Pittsfield, Mass. on Decoration day May 30, 1886, is reported to have said that the rebellion grew out of the conflict of two controlling ideas which were held in the two sections. The North believed that liberty meant the inalienable right of all men to freedom and to a government in which all consented to the rule of the majority for the time being." The contrast was clear, for Cable had continued, "The South believed that liberty was the privilege of the few and that the safety of society demanded that the privileged class should rule and that the under class should be kept under. . . . That idea is still prevalent and controlling; . . . they [Southerners] are not yet persuaded. . . . When they are, the race issue will disappear and not till then."[50]

Bryant agreed, for Cable's argument followed the old idea of "two civilizations" that Bryant had preached for years. He continued, "For the reasons stated by Mr. Cable the great mass of the white people at the South are opposed to the education and elevation of the colored race; and my judgement is from the best information I can obtain that the opposition has been gaining strength for more than five years. . . . When all Christians at the South favor the education and elevation of the colored people, as Northern Christians do, they will control public opinion upon that question, and they will unite with the people of the North in doing justice to that long oppressed race."[51]

Bryant was obviously addressing a Methodist gathering when he made that speech. The message nevertheless carried the remarkable interweaving of themes that had characterized his convictions throughout his entire life: the belief that the North was free of prejudice and founded on freedom and democracy; the place of education in "elevating" the Negro; the role of morality in improving society. In reflecting on his own business success, Bryant expressed the theology of the Gilded Age as he affirmed that God had "wondrously provided" for his needs over the years. His final good fortune was the result of "God's leading," and he saw God as a father "who lets you succeed."[52]

Emma Spaulding Bryant had some difficulty with both the theology and this interpretation of the hard years after the war; she challenged him to show her where the New Testament said that "a child of God would have riches." He answered with such verses as Matt. 6:33 ("and all these things shall be yours as well") and Phil. 4:6, 19 ("let your requests be made known"; "God shall supply your every need"). These passages "clearly refer to temporal affairs," he concluded and promised that he could explain to her the way he understood God's purpose for his life. He was "as certain of God's leading" as he was "of the $20.00" he enclosed in the letter.[53]

Bryant's attempt to justify his actions and successes over a lifetime illustrates the tendency of nineteenth-century political figures to describe their careers in religious terms. Bryant had come from the tradition of evangelical reform. Throughout his life he used the language of God's providence, God's task, and God's will to explain his causes and to sanctify his motives. It was not uncharacteristic that in looking back he sought some semblance of design. In one revealing letter, John noted three significant times that he saw as crucial turning points in his life: "The experience of 1868, which I shall call conversion, and that of 1875, and of 1888, were not alike in their manifestations, but it was the same Spirit."[54]

These three events cannot be identified with certainty. The occurrence of 1868, which Bryant called "conversion," was perhaps the jarring realization that Bullock and Blodgett would "betray" him—or perhaps it was the decision to fight them. By the experience of 1875, Bryant may have meant his attempt to run again for a congressional seat. Also about this time he began to call the Republican mission "a glorious Cause," perhaps to soften the recognition of its inglorious failure. The turning point in 1888 was probably the determination to leave Georgia permanently.

To interpret these critical points in political terms is only to hazard a guess. Bryant's daughter clearly states in her autobiography that her father experienced a religious conversion during Reconstruction. No extant letters have confirmed this event, but the turning points related by Bryant here may refer to it. Still, in JEB's life one might expect any revelation to have been closely related to some political crisis. In any case, his present intent was to woo back his independent and genuinely pietistic wife. We should, he urged, "leave . . . behind us" our disagreements and move toward "a happy future."[55]

Apparently they were able to smooth over their differences. In their final move, the Bryants together settled in Mount Vernon, New York, where John practiced law, worked in a real estate business, and edited for a short time yet another newspaper that voiced Republican principles. In her twenties now, Alice lived in Mount Vernon with her parents, where they exercised a good deal of supervision over her activities until she married. Emma Bryant was then free to aid her husband in operating a Methodist mission, one that featured teaching on the evils of alcohol as well as preaching, singing, some education, and food and clothing for unfortunates, both whites and blacks. To the end of his life, Bryant continued to participate in Republican politics and served as a delegate to county and state conventions in New York.[56]

In Bryant's later years he displayed the consistency that had marked his entire life. He apparently never lost his convictions nor the strength to act on what he considered to be right and advantageous to his goals. Though he never gained the elective office he sought so often in Georgia, he did not relinquish his interest in social issues or lose his zest for engaging in political give-and-take. At the Methodist mission in Mount Vernon, he returned to a simpler scheme for changing society—aiding individuals, not unlike his previous efforts. Only at the last did Bryant lose some of the physical energy and stamina that had marked his career. In those years he spoke more frequently of being tired and of feeling the need for rest. During her husband's fight against cancer in a New York hospital, Emma was allowed—against regulations—to have a cot in his room at night. Alice quoted her father as having persuaded the doctors, by saying, "She stood loyally by me all those dark days in the South, let her stay with me now." It was probably cancer that caused his death on February 27, 1900, at the age of sixty-three.[57]

At the time of his death, the investments on which Bryant prided himself had perhaps been eroded by the depression of the 1890s. In contrast to his assessment in 1889 of "financial success," his estate in 1900 amounted to only two thousand dollars—inadequate to pay even the debts he left behind. Emma Spaulding Bryant died the following year, in 1901, and their daughter filed suit for money supposedly owed Bryant by business associates. This action brought a countersuit charging that, in fact, Bryant owed several thousand dollars. Alice, also the beneficiary of her father's life insurance policy, accepted the court settlement for five hundred dollars.[58] Controversy concerning his affairs, a prominent feature of his life, had not ended even with the carpetbagger's death.

Conclusion: John Emory Bryant in Retrospect

Surveying the totality of John Emory Bryant's life, one sees a provocative and talented individual who aroused strong emotions, both positive and negative. From the time when, as a young temperance zealot, he was determined to go "forward . . . regardless of the consequences," Bryant proved to be an aggressive personality, yet one with deeply-held tenets of morality and reform. He was repeatedly involved in confrontations that required a review of his actions, including the army court-martial, the grand jury investigation in Augusta, and the review by the state central committee in Atlanta. In each case he met the charges, was usually exonerated, and left his enemies confounded. He himself welcomed the inquiries. But did he, as Farrow believed, prove his dishonesty by his character references? Was he simply a slippery character, or was there reason to believe in his virtue, to maintain that he was a carpetbagger of conscience?

The relentless and sometimes ruthless way Bryant attempted to further his own career, for example in the quest for Belcher's position, was reprehensible. Yet Turner could testify that Bryant had never acted against the best interests of blacks. His adherence to principle in the goals of the GERA and in the Georgia Constitutional Convention and his appointments while postmaster all indicate that this man took his causes seriously.

John D. Long, secretary of the navy under President William McKinley, commented that John Emory Bryant through his career had "almost achieved greatness."[1] Perhaps so, if greatness may be defined simply as durability and single-minded devotion to a cause, which by most standards it is not. Bryant managed to endure, if not flourish, as a politician in an incredibly perplexing period in the nation's history. The question of greatness aside, it is extremely difficult to assess and evaluate the life of someone who precipitated and then outlasted so much controversy. Any such an attempt must end by sympathizing with the ambiguity that nineteenth-century Georgians felt toward the tall and handsome, egotistical, idealistic, ambitious, talented, likable yet irritating, enthusiastic, indefatigable, self-righteous, and yet somehow suspicious "Big Skowheganite." By what measures may the man realistically be judged?

The first valid measure could be that of his critics and friends, as suggested above. Defeated Southerners found the institutions with which he was identified, such as the Freedmen's Bureau and the Republican party, conspicuously repugnant. And even within those institutions, divisions arose, so that Tillson's condemnation of the carpetbagger, for example, was not surprising. Tillson's view of how to restore order to the South was far different from Bryant's. When Southern Republicans such as Henry Farrow and James Atkins turned on the Northerners, their goals for the party in Georgia did not include the Yankees. Perhaps more revealing were JEB's supporters and their integrity, men such as Mansfield French, Rufus Saxton, Charles Stearns, John Caldwell, William Pledger, Henry M. Turner, and Erasmus Q. Fuller. It is hard to see how so many of them could have been deceived.

A second measure of the man was the causes to which he devoted his time and the ideology that informed them. Here one's attention is immediately drawn to concepts such as equal rights and education. Bryant was seemingly on the cutting edge of Radicalism; clearly he was ahead of most Republicans in Washington on the issues of equality. In one speech he even went so far as to say that blacks were socially equal, a claim he himself denied on other occasions. His commitment to civil rights, free labor, and free schools was unwavering (though it seems that he did not endorse integrated schools). Bryant's concern with his own well-being and his mild success as a businessman at the end of his life do not negate his toil and commitment to idealistic hopes of changing Southern racial prejudice and of educating both blacks and whites to ensure such change. Nor do they erase the years of struggle for these goals, when not only solvency but mere survival was at stake.

The mention of survival brings to mind the family with which John Bryant did not spend much time. The contribution made to Reconstruction by the wives of the carpetbaggers such as Emma Spaulding Bryant is easily overlooked. Yet her devotion and moral support enabled Bryant to pursue his goals. The assistance she gave in publishing the various newspapers was a tangible contribution to his work. Had he allowed her to do more and to establish the stable home that she desired, she might have helped to alter his negative image among Southerners.

His willingness to sacrifice her welfare for political causes raises a certain dilemma. Subsidies to Yulee, Clark, Fuller, and Cooper are probably only the beginning of ways he used his money, incurred debts, and thereby diminished the funds available to his own wife. But Emma was prepared to sacrifice for the cause. If JEB did in fact spend his limited money on education and Republicanism, she was his partner in the effort. Emma Bryant nevertheless saw the bankruptcy of the social system that made her rely on one so unreliable. Throughout her life she raised the subject of working and eventually realized that she must support herself if she would leave the bondage of dependency. With great inner strength Emma Bryant met the poverty, grew in self-confidence, and achieved a measure of financial independence and equality in the relationship with her husband.

The nagging suspicion remains that Bryant simply disregarded Emma, did not see her needs as a priority, refused to consider any substantial contribution she might make to his effort, and did not want her to change the traditional female role. In this respect, the treatment of his wife was symptomatic of the deeply rooted chauvinism, more than merely sexual or racial, of the white Northern Republicans. The evils of elitism, racism, and sexism, the first two of which the Yankees so readily recognized in Southerners, were all present in their own culture and in themselves as well. It is a measure of their presumption that the image of the society to which they would conform the South was so far from true equality.

This study shows again that the categories of caste, gender, and race are intertwined in ways that have not been fully explored. The blindness of the Radicals to the ramifications of equality for personal relationships calls for a new evaluation of their ideology. Perceptive Southern critics of the abolitionists had, before the war, confronted them with the implications of destroying the slave society, a society that had as its cornerstone paternalism, that is, a belief in male superiority and control.[2] An unwillingness to hear and see the inconsistencies in their own credo was one reflection of their arrogance.

The role of the carpetbaggers during Reconstruction has remained ambiguous. Their Southern contemporaries hated and misunderstood their purpose and achievements. Historians have tended to make either heroes or villains out of them and their Radical Republican supporters. John Emory Bryant's story is significant because he stood at neither extreme and was probably close to being a typical carpetbagger. To grasp the inconsistency of his "glorious Cause," coupled with his obvious shortcomings, is further to understand the motivations and actions of this group. Surely his career refutes the idea that simple vindictiveness or opportunism motivated all carpetbaggers. Bryant's career instead suggests the complexity of factors that shape a single life and compels at least a grudging respect for his convictions and purposes. Bryant was a complicated mixture of idealistic reform zeal on the one hand and a certain selfish realism on the other. In this respect he embodied or exemplified the fatal flaw of Radical Reconstruction itself. Never totally convinced that racial equality was either desirable or possible, the Republican party lost whatever moral imperative it had claimed and settled instead for the attempt at political survival. Individuals such as Bryant eventually yielded to the inevitable.

But the carpetbaggers cannot be brought into focus without again acknowledging the impossibility of their best intentions. They had honestly believed they could persuade Southerners to adopt their values. The idealistic and somewhat naive young man who expected to debate the "new age" of black rights on the basis of the Constitution and the Declaration of Independence failed to comprehend that his political rivals intended not to compete or debate but to destroy Republicanism.[3] The violence of Reconstruction grotesquely distorted the attempt at politics as usual.

Bryant was a man of the nineteenth century and unable to achieve his goals for himself, his party, the South, or the nation. Still, JEB's best aspirations represented the wave of the future in the dreams of other idealistic Americans. Though at the time of the carpetbagger's death the nation had again postponed its just settlement with blacks and clearly denied equality for all, the new century would ultimately see the vindication and enhancement of the germinal ideas championed by John Emory Bryant and his Radical Republican allies.

Notes

ONE. MAINE BACKGROUND

1 Journal of John Emory Bryant, October 18, 1853, in John Emory Bryant Papers, Manuscript Department, Perkins Library, Duke University, Durham, N.C. (hereinafter cited as JEB Papers). Bryant's journal covers the years 1853–1859. Unfortunately, the original is not extant. The JEB papers include notes transcribed from the journal by R. B. Zeller, a descendant of Bryant's. Veracity must be assumed.

2 John Langdon Sibley, *History of the Town of Union in the County of Lincoln, Maine* (Boston: Mussey, 1851), 96, 220; U.S. Census, Schedule I, Population, Microcopy M-432, Roll 259.

3 Bryant Journal, March 27, May 6, February 26, April 17, July 2, 1853; Sept 13, 1858, JEB Papers.

4 Bryant Journal, March 3, August 1, 1853; June 20, November 27, December 1, 4, 14, 31, 1854; January 8, 11, February 9, May 29, 1855; June 30, 1853, JEB Papers.

5 Bryant Journal, November 15, 1858; March 20, 1859; November 8, 1854; D. Spaulding to Bryant, February 12, 1860, JEB Papers; Carl N. Degler, *Out of Our Past: The Forces That Shaped Modern America* (New York: Harper & Row, 1959), 158; Walter Herbert Small, *Early New England Schools* (Boston: Ginn, 1914), 148, 187–89.

6 D. N. Peichel[?] to Bryant, January 10, 1851; beginning of Bryant Journal, vol. 5, 1858, JEB Papers.

7 Bryant Journal, February 1–21, 1853, JEB Papers.

8 S. M. Jennings to Bryant, October 16, 1859; Bryant Journal, March 1859, JEB Papers.

9 Bryant Journal, March 1859, JEB Papers.

10 D. H. Chandler to Bryant, December 20, 1859; Bryant Journal, March 1859, recalling incident in December 1858; T. B. Reed to Bryant, December 30, 1858, JEB Papers.

11 Bryant Journal, May 7, 1859; Composition paper, 1853; Bryant Journal, September 13, 1858; March 1859; S. M. Jennings to Bryant, February 12, 1860, JEB Papers.

12 Bryant Journal, March 22, 1853; May 24, 1854; June 30, 1853; May 6, 1855; May 25–29, 1858, JEB Papers.
13 Bryant Journal, June 9–13, 1858, JEB Papers.
14 H. P. Torsey to Bryant, April 20, 1857, JEB Papers.
15 Bryant Journal, August 27, May 2–June 4, 1853; February 3, 1855, JEB Papers; Alexander Pope, "An Essay on Man," in *English Poetry*, 3 vols., The Harvard Classics, vol. 1, *From Chaucer to Gray*, ed. Charles W. Eliot (New York: Collier, 1937), 439–40.
16 Louis Filler, *The Crusade Against Slavery, 1830–1860* (New York: Harper & Row, 1960), 28; William Warren Sweet, "The Church as Moral Courts on the Frontier," *Church History* 2 (1933): 14; Bryant to Emma Spaulding, March 13, 1864, JEB Papers.
17 Bryant Journal, February 27, March 20, 1853; March 19, 1854; August 31, June 12, April 24, July 17, 1853; May 26, 1854, JEB Papers. It is not clear to what group of "Millerites" Bryant refers, as the date William Miller set for the end of the world was March 21, 1844. By 1854, when Bryant wrote, the movement was largely defunct, though descendants of it continued in such sects as the Seventh Day Adventists. See Winthrop S. Hudson, *Religion in America* (New York: Scribner, 1965), 194–96; Alice Felt Tyler, *Freedom's Ferment: Phases of American Social History to 1860* (Minneapolis: University of Minnesota Press, 1944), 74–78. It is possible that local groups of persistent Millerites continued to set dates for the second coming of Christ.
18 Bryant to Emma Spaulding, December 25, 27, 1862, JEB Papers.
19 Bryant to Emma Spaulding, December 25, 1862; Autobiography of Alice Bryant Zeller, n.d., JEB Papers. Bryant "read law" in Maine before the war and he was admitted to the bar in 1866.
20 Filler, *Crusade Against Slavery*, 31.
21 Filler, *Crusade Against Slavery*, 41; Degler, *Out of Our Past*, 157–60.
22 Bryant Journal, June 13, 1854, JEB Papers.
23 Tyler, *Freedom's Ferment*, 262–64; Bryant Journal, August 20, 1853, JEB Papers; Emit Duncan Grizzell, *Origin and Development of the High School in New England Before 1865* (New York: Macmillan, 1923), 342; Bryant Journal, November 19, 1854; Mattie C. Bryan [Bryant?] to Bryant, December 23, 1855, JEB Papers.
24 Bryant Journal, March 22, 1855; September 2, 1853; December 8, 1854; April 25, June 8, 1855, JEB Papers.
25 Bryant Journal, June 30, July 26, 1854; Debating paper, April 1858; E. C. Doane to Bryant, June 4, 1855, JEB Papers.
26 C. Vann Woodward, *American Counterpoint: Slavery and Racism in the North-South Dialogue* (Boston: Little, Brown, 1971), 154; Eric Foner, *Free Soil, Free Labor, Free Men: The Ideology of the Republican Party Before the Civil War* (New York: Oxford University Press, 1970), 266; Eric Foner, *Politics and Ideology in the Age of the Civil War* (New York: Oxford University Press, 1980), 77–78; Bryant Journal, October 22, 1854, JEB Papers.
27 George M. Frederickson, *The Black Image in the White Mind: The Debate*

on *Afro-American Character and Destiny, 1817–1914* (New York: Harper & Row, 1971), 107–17.

28 John Bryant to Emma Bryant, 1880s correspondence, JEB Papers; David M. Potter, *The Impending Crisis, 1848–1861* (New York: Harper & Row, 1976), 459.

29 Bryant Journal, September 30, 1853; October 6, 1854; May 18, 1855; E. C. Doane to Bryant, June 4, 1855, JEB Papers. Doane was responding to Bryant's letter and quoted him on the subject. Differing from JEB, he expected that the Know-Nothings would prove "ineffectual."

30 An exposition was the equivalent of a graduation exercise. Friends and family attended the ceremony at the end of a term and heard the oratory of selected students. At one time Bryant had two pieces accepted for such an occasion. Bryant also held expositions at the end of the schools that he conducted. Bryant Journal, June 1, 5, 14, 1855, JEB Papers. See also Grizzell, *High School in New England*, 333–34. Bryant Journal, January 23, 1855; Foner, *Free Soil, Free Labor, Free Men*, 228, 230 (quoted).

31 E. C. Doane to Bryant, June 4, 1855, JEB Papers; Foner, *Free Soil, Free Labor, Free Men*, 260.

32 Bryant Journal, June 25, 1853, JEB Papers; Foner, *Free Soil, Free Labor, Free Men*, 227–28.

33 John L. Thomas, "Romantic Reform in America, 1815–1865," *American Quarterly* 17 (Winter 1965): 659; John L. Thomas, "Antislavery and Utopia," in *The Antislavery Vanguard: New Essays on the Abolitionists*, ed. Martin Duberman (Princeton: Princeton University Press, 1965), 240–69; Filler, *Crusade Against Slavery*, 40.

34 Foner, *Free Soil, Free Labor, Free Men*, 236, 241–42.

35 Frederickson, *Black Image in the White Mind*, 130–45; Foner, *Free Soil, Free Labor, Free Men*, 60.

36 Foner, *Free Soil, Free Labor, Free Men*, 261–66; Richard Hofstadter, *American Political Tradition and the Men Who Made It* (New York: Vintage, 1948), 119; Henry Wilson, *History of the Rise and Fall of the Slave Power in America*, in *Causes of the Civil War*, Kenneth Stampp, ed. (Englewood Cliffs, N.J.: Prentice-Hall, 1965), 12; C. Vann Woodward, *The Burden of Southern History*, rev. ed. (New York: Mentor, 1960), 58–70; Foner, *Politics and Ideology*, 73–74; E. C. Doane to Bryant, June 4, 1855, JEB Papers. Phillip S. Paludan underlines Doane's statement in "The American Civil War Considered as a Crisis in Law and Order," *American Historical Review* 77, no. 4 (October 1972), 1013–34.

37 Bryant Journal, July 4, July 30–August 1, September 14, October 1, 1854; March 31, 1855, JEB Papers.

38 R. Elder to Bryant, March 24, 1857; O. H. Heen to Bryant, December 22, 1857; Hattie Howe to Bryant, November 11, 1858, JEB Papers. "Black Republican" was a pejorative epithet used by the enemies of the Republican cause in its early development. S. C. Tuck to Bryant, December 30, 1859; January 21, April 16, 1860, JEB Papers.

39 H. H. Morrill to Quentin Smith, Worthy Patriarch of Wayne, April 30,

1859; D. H. Chandler to Bryant, April 18, 1860; Bryant to D. H. Chandler, March 31, 1860, JEB Papers.
40 Bryant to D. H. Chandler, March 31, 1860, JEB Papers.
41 Hofstadter, *American Political Tradition*, 125–26.

TWO. BRYANT IN THE CIVIL WAR

1 Willie Lee Rose, *Rehearsal for Reconstruction: The Port Royal Experiment* (New York: Vintage, 1964).
2 Bryant to Emma Spaulding, September 1, 1861, JEB Papers; William E. S. Whitman and Charles H. True, *Maine in the War for the Union* (Lewiston, Maine: Dingley, 1865), 192. Although Whitman does not so indicate, there is little doubt that Bryant himself wrote the chapter in this book on the Eighth Maine. Eyewitness accounts of events in which he participated, views sympathetic to Bryant's positions, plus his own heroism spotlighted throughout all lead to this conclusion.
3 Bryant to Emma Spaulding, September 29, October 6, 1861, JEB Papers.
4 Whitman, *Maine in the War*, 193; Dudley Taylor Cornish, *The Sable Arm* (New York: Longmans, Green, 1956), 18; Benjamin Quarles, *The Negro in the Civil War* (New York: Russell & Russell, 1968), 70.
5 Rose, *Rehearsal*, 11; Whitman, *Maine in the War*, 194; Rose, *Rehearsal*, 11.
6 Rose, *Rehearsal*, 106–7; Bryant to Emma Spaulding, December 4, 1861; Union Army Scrapbook, December 15, 1861, JEB Papers.
7 Orders issued December 17, 1861, signed T. W. Sherman, Union Army Scrapbook; Bryant to Emma Spaulding, January 1, 1861 [1862]; September 29, 1861, JEB Papers.
8 Bryant to Emma Spaulding, January 1, 1861 [1862]; January 19, 1862, JEB Papers; John L. Stephens to Governor Washburn, December 25, 1861, Maine State Archives, Augusta, Maine. JEB made another try for promotion in April–May 1862 through a rash of letters to the governor from various men in his company.
9 Bryant to Emma Spaulding, January 1, 1861 [1862]; February 8, March 14, 1862, JEB Papers.
10 Bryant to Emma Spaulding, April 18, 1862, JEB Papers.
11 Special Order, granting sixty-day leave to Capt. John E. Bryant, through Col. J. D. Rust, June 21, 1862, Union Army Scrapbook; Bryant to Emma Spaulding, June 29, July 28, 1862, JEB Papers.
12 Bryant to Emma Spaulding, February 8, 1862; General Orders 9, issued March 5, 1862, by order of Brig. Gen. E. L. Viele, Union Army Scrapbook, JEB Papers.
13 Cornish, *Sable Arm*, 24.
14 Lincoln to Greeley, August 22, 1862, *War of the Rebellion, Official Records of the Union and Confederate Armies* (Washington, D.C., 1894–1900), 3d ser., 2:433–34 (hereinafter cited as *O.R.*). The critic is quoted in Tilden G. Edel-

stein, *Strange Enthusiasm: A Life of Thomas Wentworth Higginson* (New Haven: Yale University Press, 1968), 263.

15 James M. McPherson, *The Negro's Civil War* (New York: Vintage, 1967), 41; see Lawanda Cox, *Lincoln and Black Freedom: A Study in Presidential Leadership* (Columbia: University of South Carolina Press, 1981), 7–35, for defense of Lincoln's actions and antislavery sentiments.

16 *New York Times*, August 6, 21, 1862; February 10, 16, 1863.

17 McPherson, *Negro's Civil War*, 46; Rose, *Rehearsal*, 146–47; Cornish, *Sable Arm*, 38; Pierce to Hunter, May 11, 1862; Pierce to Chase, May 12, 1862, O.R., 3d ser., 2:51–53.

18 Cornish, *Sable Arm*, 49.

19 Hunter to Stanton, June 23, 1862, O.R., 3d ser., 2:196–98; Hunter to Stanton, August 10, 1862, O.R., 3d ser., 2:346.

20. *U.S. Statutes at Large*, 12:589–92; McPherson, *Negro's Civil War*, 165; Mary Frances Berry, *Military Necessity and Civil Rights Policy: Black Citizenship and the Constitution, 1861–1868* (Port Washington, N.Y.: Kennikat Press, 1977), 41–43.

21 Rose, *Rehearsal*, 152–53; Stanton to Saxton, August 25, 1862, O.R., 1st ser., 14:377.

22 Edelstein, *Strange Enthusiasm*, 261; Quarles, *Negro in Civil War*, 124; Rose, *Rehearsal*, 26–27.

23 Henry M. Crydenwise to his parents, January 26, 1862, Crydenwise Papers, Manuscript Department, Perkins Library, Duke University, Durham, N.C.; Bryant to Emma Spaulding, September 30, 1862, JEB Papers; Rose, *Rehearsal*, 197.

24 Bryant to Emma Spaulding, October 23, 1862, JEB Papers.

25 Bryant to Emma Spaulding, October 23, September 13, 1862, JEB Papers.

26 Henry M. Crydenwise to his parents, January 26, 1862, Crydenwise Papers; Bryant to Emma Spaulding, September 8, 1862, JEB Papers.

27 Bryant to Emma Spaulding, September 8, 1862, JEB Papers.

28 Bryant to Emma Spaulding, September 15, 1862, JEB Papers.

29 Whitman, *Maine in the War*, 194; Bryant to Emma Spaulding, December 27, 1862; Col. John D. Rust to Bryant, July 14, 1862; Bryant to Emma Spaulding, October 23, 1862, JEB Papers.

30 Bryant to Emma Spaulding, December 25, 1862, JEB Papers.

31 General Court-Martial, [Proceedings in the case of] Capt. John E. Bryant, Co. C, 8th Maine Vols., Headquarters, U.S. Forces, Port Royal Island, Beaufort, S.C., January 23, 1863, National Archives, Washington, D.C.

32 Bryant Court-Martial Proceedings; Special Order 3, issued February 11, 1863, by command of Col. John D. Rust, Union Army Scrapbook, JEB Papers.

33 Saxton to Stanton, October 13, 1862, O.R., 3d ser., 2:663–64.

34 Cornish, *Sable Arm*, 83; Thomas Wentworth Higginson, *Army Life in a Black Regiment* (Boston: Fields, Osgood, 1870; reprint, East Lansing: Michigan State University Press, 1960), 214.

35 Whitman, *Maine in the War*, 197; Rose, *Rehearsal*, 193; Higginson, *Army*

Life, 1–2; Edelstein, *Strange Enthusiasm*, 253–55, 165–74, 257, 264; Cornish, *Sable Arm*, 142–43; *New York Times*, February 10, June 11, 1863.

36 Bryant to Emma Spaulding, March 8, 9, 20, 28, 1863; Proceedings from the Board of Examination, Union Army, John Emory Bryant case, April 17, 1863, Union Army Scrapbook, JEB Papers; "Extract from Proceedings of a Board of Examination in the Case of Captain John E. Bryant, 8th Maine Vols.," April 17, 1863, Maine State Archives.

37 Edelstein, *Strange Enthusiasm*, 270–76.

38 Higginson, *Army Life*, 96–97; Cornish, *Sable Arm*, 140–41; "Report of Col. John D. Rust, Eighth Maine Infantry," April 2, 1863, O.R., 1st ser., 14:233.

39 Unidentified newspaper article [*New York Tribune?*], April 1863, JEB Papers; Higginson, *Army Life*, 91.

40 Whitman, *Maine in the War*, 197; Bryant to editor, *New York Tribune*, May 11, 1863; J. F. Twitchell, Lt. Col., and J. D. Mitchell, Surgeon, to editor, *New York Tribune*, April 30, 1863, clipping in JEB Papers.

41 Cornish, *Sable Arm*, 104.

42 Bryant to Emma Spaulding, June 3, 1863, JEB Papers.

43 Cornish, *Sable Arm*, 143, 146–47; McPherson, *Negro's Civil War*, 187–92; Bryant to Emma Spaulding, June 3, 1863, JEB Papers; comment made in April 1863, quoted in Cornish, *Sable Arm*, 93.

44 Rose, *Rehearsal*, 196; McPherson, *Negro's Civil War*, 63–64; Bryant to Emma Spaulding, January 1, 1864, JEB Papers.

45 W. C. Morrison, 2d S.C. Vols., Colored, "Coosaw Island," Union Army Scrapbook, JEB Papers; see Berry, *Military Necessity*, on linking citizenship to military service.

46 Bryant to Emma Spaulding, January 4, March 6, 8, January 27, 1863, JEB Papers.

47 Bryant to Emma Spaulding, March 8, 1863; Special Order granting twenty-day leave to Capt. John E. Bryant, June 14, 1863, Union Army Scrapbook; Bryant to Emma Spaulding, July 19, 1863, JEB Papers.

48 Bryant to Emma Spaulding, July 12, November 1, 1863, JEB Papers; Higginson, *Army Life*, 179.

49 Higginson, *Army Life*, 104–5.

50 Whitman, *Maine in the War*, 199; undated, unidentified newspaper clippings, JEB Papers.

51 Bryant to Emma Spaulding, November 12, 1863; Mansfield French to Bryant, October 9, 1863, JEB Papers.

52 Higginson, *Army Life*, 179; Bryant to Higginson, Report from Picket Station Headquarters, Barnwell Island, S.C., November 27, 1863, JEB Papers; Report of Gen. Rufus Saxton, November 30, 1863, O.R., 1st ser., 28, pt. 1, 745–46.

53 Beaufort, S.C., correspondent of the *Boston Traveller*, November 28, 1863; newspaper clipping, Port Royal, S.C., the *Free South*, November 28, 1863; Bryant to Emma Spaulding, November 1, 30, 1863, JEB Papers. But an Adj. E. H. Reynolds, probably the same man, as late as February 1864 was keeping Rust informed of Bryant's activities. See n. 56 below.

54   L. Alford to Bryant, February 20, 1864; Bryant to Emma Spaulding, March 8, 1863, JEB Papers.

55   Bryant to Emma Spaulding, January 1, February 15, 23, 1864, JEB Papers (Bryant says lieutenant, but surely he meant lieutenant colonel, since he was already a captain); Gen. Rufus Saxton to Gov. Samuel Coney, February 23, 1864; Mansfield French to _____ [Governor Coney?], February 23, 1864, Union Army Scrapbook, JEB Papers and Maine State Archives; Bryant to Emma Spaulding, March 13, 1864, JEB Papers.

56   E. H. Reynolds to Col. John D. Rust, February 20, 1864, Maine State Archives; Bryant to Emma Spaulding, November 12, 1863; May 12, 1864, JEB Papers.

57   Special Order granting a thirty-day leave to Capt. John E. Bryant, May 29, 1864, Union Army Scrapbook; Bryant to Emma Spaulding (Bryant), October 6, December 4, 1861; May 20, October 21, November 3, 1863; January 18, June 28, 1864, JEB Papers. I assume that JEB did attend the exposition as he planned. No physical description of Emma was found.

58   Bryant to Emma Spaulding, March 8, 28, November 12, 1863, JEB Papers.

59   Special Order 35, U.S. Forces, Port Royal Island, Headquarters, Beaufort, S.C., February 15, 1864, issued by order of Brig. Gen. R. Saxton, signed by Stuart M. Taylor; Special Order 140, U.S. Forces, District of Beaufort, Headquarters, Beaufort, S.C., July 12, 1864, issued by order of Brig. Gen. R. Saxton, signed by Stuart M. Taylor, Assistant Adjutant General, Union Army Scrapbook, JEB Papers.

60   Special Order 275, Washington, Department of War, Adjutant General's Office, August 19, 1864, Union Army Scrapbook; John Bryant to Emma Bryant, July 29, 1864, JEB Papers.

61   John Bryant to Emma Bryant, August 24, 1864, JEB Papers.

62   Whitman, *Maine in the War*, 204; see James C. Mohr, ed., and Richard E. Winslow III, assoc. ed., *The Cormany Diaries: A Northern Family in the Civil War* (Pittsburgh: University of Pittsburgh Press, 1982), 462–74, for another eyewitness account of the battle of Petersburg.

63   John Bryant to Emma Bryant, August 12, 29, 1864; Special Order 125, Headquarters 18th Army Corps in the Field, Virginia, September 3, 1864, issued by command of Maj. Gen. E. E. C. Ord, Theodore Reed, Assistant Adjutant General, Union Army Scrapbook; Whitman, *Maine in the War*, 205, 207; Special Order 244, Headquarters, Department of Virginia and North Carolina, in the Field, Virginia, September 5, 1864, issued by command of Major General Butler, signed by R. Davis, Assistant Adjutant General, Union Army Scrapbook, JEB Papers.

THREE. PRESIDENTIAL RECONSTRUCTION

1   Michael Perman, *Reunion Without Compromise: The South and Reconstruction, 1865–1868* (Cambridge: Cambridge University Press, 1973),

11–12; Eric L. McKitrick, *Andrew Johnson and Reconstruction* (Chicago: University of Chicago Press, 1960), 15–41; for the specifics of the Southern effort, see Dan T. Carter, *When the War Was Over: The Failure of Self-Reconstruction in the South, 1865–1867* (Baton Rouge: Louisiana State University Press, 1985).

2 Bryant to Emma Spaulding, July 12, 19, 1863; April 24, 1864, JEB Papers.

3 Jacqueline Jones, *Soldiers of Light and Love: Northern Teachers and Georgia Blacks, 1865–1873* (Chapel Hill: University of North Carolina Press, 1980), 14–48; *New York Times,* October 24, November 2, 1865; Lawrence N. Powell, *New Masters: Northern Planters in the Civil War and Reconstruction* (New Haven: Yale University Press, 1980), 30–31.

4 Richard N. Current, "Carpetbaggers Reconsidered," in *A Festschrift for Frederick B. Artz,* ed. David H. Pinkney and Theodore Ropp (Durham, N.C.: Duke University Press, 1969), 144.

5 For the old view of carpetbaggers, see Clara Mildred Thompson, *Reconstruction in Georgia: Economic, Social, and Political, 1865–1872* (New York: Columbia University Press, 1915), 217. Thompson describes a carpetbagger as "a Republican adventurer who came South after the war and won political office by controlling the negro vote." See Avery Craven, *Reconstruction: The Ending of the Civil War* (New York: Holt, Rinehart & Winston, 1969), 230–31, for a more recent statement of the same viewpoint; Lawrence N. Powell, "The Politics of Livelihood: Carpetbaggers in the Deep South," in *Race, Region, and Reconstruction: Essays in Honor of C. Vann Woodward,* ed. J. Morgan Kousser and James M. McPherson (New York: Oxford University Press, 1982), 315–47.

6 Horace Greeley to Bryant, February 5, 1867; unidentified clipping, 1866, JEB Papers. Greeley's letter read: "You [unintelligible] against those who aim to make a living out of the blacks, whether as slaveholders or otherwise. It seems to me that no one can help them who has to live out of them and their friends. I will assume that you mean well; but I wish you would get to earning your living by some honest industry and leave the blacks to the good providence by which they have been *emancipated.* Yours, Horace Greeley." Bryant seemed to believe in helping providence a bit.

7 Powell, *New Masters,* 55–72; Jones, *Soldiers of Light and Love,* 81–84. Again the political arena, including the question of black education, evoked the ostracism. Powell has shown that Yankees who came and remained as planters got along well with their Southern neighbors when they stuck to farming (pp. 71–72). Political winds, however, sometimes changed that accommodation.

8 Herman Belz, *A New Birth of Freedom: The Republican Party and Freedmen's Rights, 1861–1866* (Westport, Conn.: Greenwood Press, 1976), 177. In his discussion of Republican motives and the party's limited concept of equality before the law, Belz suggests that the real significance of such a concept should not be belittled by the twentieth-century judgment that real equality involves more. Bryant to the Reverend Geo. Whipple, August 6, 1867, American Missionary Association Archives, Amistad Research Center, New Orleans, Louisiana (hereinafter cited as AMA Archives).

9 Richard N. Current, *Northernizing the South* (Athens: University of Georgia Press, 1983), 50–82.

10   U.S. Statutes at Large, 13:507–9. Herman Belz emphasizes that the bill was designed to aid black and white refugees equally and that the government's help was understood to be temporary. He argues that critics of the bureau bill insisted on minimal governmental jurisdiction and on no reverse discrimination against whites. See his *New Birth of Freedom*, 92–108, as well as his "Freedmen's Bureau Act of 1865 and the Principle of No Discrimination According to Color," *Civil War History* 21 (September 1975): 197–217.

11   George R. Bentley, *A History of the Freedmen's Bureau* (Philadelphia: University of Pennsylvania Press, 1955), 46, 51–52; William S. McFeely, *Yankee Stepfather: General O. O. Howard and the Freedmen* (New Haven: Yale University Press, 1968), 7–8; Woodward, *American Counterpoint*, 161.

12   James M. McPherson, *The Struggle for Equality: Abolitionists and the Negro in the Civil War and Reconstruction* (Princeton: Princeton University Press, 1964), 251–55; McFeely, *Yankee Stepfather*, 61.

13   McPherson, *Struggle for Equality*, 256; Henry Ward Beecher, William Patton, George Whipple, and J. A. Eldridge, committee for the American Missionary Association, to president of the United States Andrew Johnson, n.d., Bureau of Refugees, Freedmen, and Abandoned Lands, Microcopy 752 (hereinafter cited as BRFAL, M 752), Reel 19, National Archives, Washington, D.C.

14   McPherson, *Struggle for Equality*, 251; Henry Ward Beecher et al., committee for AMA to Andrew Johnson, n.d., BRFAL, M 752, Reel 19. I read the account of this visit somewhat differently from Ronald Butchart, who states that the AMA "did not question" the land decision (*Northern Schools, Southern Blacks, and Reconstruction: Freedmen's Education, 1862–1875* [Westport, Conn.: Greenwood Press, 1980], 72).

15   Bvt. Brig. Gen. F. D. Sewall, inspector general, Bureau of Refugees, Freedmen, and Abandoned Lands, to Gen. O. O. Howard, December 15, 1866, BRFAL, M 752, Reel 39; Warren Hoffnagle, "The Southern Homestead Act: Its Origins and Operation," *Historian* 32, no. 4 (August 1970), 612–29; Claude F. Oubre, *Forty Acres and a Mule: The Freedmen's Bureau and Black Land Ownership* (Baton Rouge: Louisiana State University Press, 1978), 185–88. Oubre reported a flurry of homesteading activity in Florida, but there, as elsewhere, it had little lasting success (pp. 135–57). The greatest successes for blacks under the homesteading promise occurred in 1879–1880 as thousands of blacks migrated to Kansas, seeking escape from post-Reconstruction "Redeemer" rule in Louisiana and Mississippi. See Nell Irvin Painter, *The Exodusters: Black Migration to Kansas After Reconstruction* (New York: Knopf, 1977).

16   Robert Habersham, chairman, to O. O. Howard, Report of the meeting of planters, Savannah, Georgia, June 6, 1865, BRFAL, M 752, Reel 74. Planters as a group were utterly unprepared for change, as James Roark has demonstrated in *Masters Without Slaves: Southern Planters in the Civil War and Reconstruction* (New York: Norton, 1977). See also James Oakes, *The Ruling Class: A History of American Slaveholders* (New York: Knopf, 1982), 225–42.

17   Quoted in McFeely, *Yankee Stepfather*, 84–85. Belz insists that the Freedmen's Bureau was designed narrowly to meet humanitarian needs, avoiding the guise of governmental apprenticeship of blacks, to satisfy laissez-faire critics of any

government intervention at all (*New Birth of Freedom,* 92–108); Dispatch from General Saxton to Bryant, August 15, 1865, Bryant Letterbook, JEB Papers.

18 Bentley, *History of the Freedmen's Bureau,* 230, n. 65. The hierarchy of officials under O. O. Howard differed from state to state. Howard suggested on February 12, 1867, that the titles be standardized as commissioner (head of the bureau), assistant commissioner (a state head), sub-assistant commissioner (over a district within a state, with local agents responsible to him), and agent (over the smallest, local bureau area, as a county or city). Frequently used instead of sub-assistant commissioner was superintendent, as was true in Bryant's case. Bryant's districts were Barnwell and Edgefield, covering some of South Carolina as well as some of Georgia. McFeely, *Yankee Stepfather,* 10; Martin Abbott, *The Freedmen's Bureau in South Carolina, 1865–1872* (Chapel Hill: University of North Carolina Press, 1967), 12–13.

19 Eugene D. Genovese, *The Political Economy of Slavery: Studies in the Economy and Society of the Slave South* (New York: Vintage, 1965), 28; Oakes, *The Ruling Class,* xi–xii, 192–224; Woodward, *American Counterpoint,* 162.

20 Bryant to Emma Spaulding, January 27, 1863; September 1, 1862; May 20, 1863, JEB Papers.

21 John Bryant to Emma Bryant, May 29, 1865, JEB Papers.

22 Leon F. Litwack, *Been in the Storm So Long: The Aftermath of Slavery* (New York: Knopf, 1979). Litwack's account of blacks after the war is unforgettable. On mobility see chapter 6, especially pp. 305–9. Blacks traveled around mostly for specific reasons, such as seeking family members from whom they had been separated by slavery. The extent of mindless wandering after freedom has been greatly exaggerated. See also McFeely, *Yankee Stepfather,* 155; Roger L. Ransom and Richard Sutch, *One Kind of Freedom: The Economic Consequences of Emancipation* (New York: Cambridge University Press, 1977), 61–64; Joel Williamson, *After Slavery: The Negro in South Carolina During Reconstruction, 1861–1877* (Chapel Hill: University of North Carolina Press, 1965), 33. For a more detailed study of the bureau in Georgia, see Paul Cimbala, "The Terms of Freedom: The Freedmen's Bureau and Reconstruction in Georgia, 1865–1870" (Ph.D. diss., Emory University, 1983). Cimbala calls the first months "the uncertain summer of 1865" (pp. 11–70); Robert Cruden, *The Negro in Reconstruction* (Englewood Cliffs, N.J.: Prentice-Hall, 1969), 20.

23 Saxton's written orders, May 15, 1865, Bryant's Letterbook, JEB Papers; McPherson, *Struggle for Equality,* 257. See also Edmund L. Drago, *Black Politicians and Reconstruction in Georgia: A Splendid Failure* (Baton Rouge: Louisiana State University Press, 1982), 14. Drago suggests that the order was a response to the urging of black leaders in Georgia. Belz notes that blacks were effectively segregated by the order. Blacks, in the *New Orleans Tribune,* denounced the order as "internal colonization," reminiscent of Indian reservations. See Belz, *New Birth of Freedom,* 150–51; J. W. Alvord to O. O. Howard, September 1, 1865, BRFAL, M 752, Reel 74.

24 Bryant's efforts predated the bureau's more organized attempts at health care for blacks, but his troubles were a harbinger of things to come. Todd Savitt has

spotlighted these difficulties in his "Politics in Medicine: The Georgia Freedmen's Bureau and the Organization of Health Care, 1865–1866," *Civil War History* 28, no. 1 (March 1982): 45–64. Quotations are from dispatches between General Saxton and Bryant, summer 1865, Bryant Letterbook, JEB Papers.

25 General Tillson to O. O. Howard, September 24, 1866, BRFAL, M 752, Reel 37; Abbott, *The Freedmen's Bureau in South Carolina*, 12; General Saxton to Gen. O. O. Howard, General Order 21, December 8, 1865, Headquarters Assistant Commissioner, Charleston, BRFAL, M 752, Reel 19.

26 *Macon Daily Telegraph*, June 16, 24, 1865. On the 24th, Bryant published a notice that the regulations outlined on the 16th had been approved and were in effect. For a detailed examination of the contracts approved by Bryant and others, see Cimbala, "Terms of Freedom," 39–53.

27 Diary of Ella Thomas, July 22, 1865, Ella Thomas Papers, Manuscript Department, Perkins Library, Duke University, Durham, N.C.; T. J. Macquire to O. O. Howard, July 20, 1865, BRFAL, M 752, Reel 3; Thomas Diary, October 9, 1865, Thomas Papers.

28 Charles Stearns, *The Black Man of the South and the Rebels* (New York: American News, 1872), 106–7.

29 Bentley, *History of the Freedmen's Bureau*, 152; Circular 4, Bureau of Refugees, Freedmen, and Abandoned Lands, Augusta, Ga., November 15, 1865, Georgia State Archives, Atlanta, Ga.; Bryant to Saxton, September 6, 1865, JEB Papers.

30 John W. Sullivan to Edward W. Kinsley, August 2, 1865, quoting a letter from Gen. Edward Wild to his wife, Edward W. Kinsley Papers, Manuscript Department, Perkins Library, Duke University, Durham, N.C.; see General Order 4, District of Savannah, 1st Division, Department of Georgia, July 22, 1865. See BRFAL, M 752, Reel 74, for an example of the red tape necessary for agents of the bureau to receive aid from the military.

31 J. S. Fullerton to O. O. Howard, July 21, 1865, BRFAL, M 752, Reel 14. Cimbala flatly dismisses Saxton as an inept administrator ("Terms of Freedom," 57, 72).

32 F. D. Sewall to O. O. Howard, December 15, 1866, BRFAL, M 752, Reel 39; McFeely, *Yankee Stepfather*, 71–72. Oubre is less generous with Saxton's last stand and credits Saxton with privately requesting a return to quartermaster duties, since he "could not afford" resignation. Saxton did serve in that capacity until 1888 in Atlanta, where he also continued his mission to blacks by teaching there. See Oubre, *Forty Acres and a Mule*, 59, n. 23; Saxton to O. O. Howard, January 14, 1866, BRFAL, M 752, Reel 74.

33 J. S. Fullerton to O. O. Howard, August 11, 1865, BRFAL, M 752, Reel 74; Davis Tillson to O. O. Howard, July 17, 25, 1865, O. O. Howard Papers, Special Collections, Bowdoin College Library, Brunswick, Maine.

34 O. O. Howard to Tillson, summary of letter of December 21, 1865, in Register, BRFAL, M 752, Reel 3; Tillson to O. O. Howard, January 6, 1866, BRFAL, M 752, Reel 20. Cimbala's recent attempt to rehabilitate Tillson's reputation is impressive, but he himself recognizes Tillson's basic conservatism and his

fear "that slavery had hampered the freedmen's moral development"; he saw mostly "their dense ignorance." See Cimbala's "Terms of Freedom," 134, and his "Talisman Power: Davis Tillson, the Freedmen's Bureau, and Free Labor in Reconstruction Georgia, 1865–1866," *Civil War History* 28, no. 2 (June 1982), 153–71. Tillson may well have been motivated in his policies by a belief in free labor, but his failure to see blacks as individuals and his efforts to coerce them to fit his definition of their proper role was a form of the paternalism destined to prevent their real freedom. *Augusta Daily Chronicle and Sentinel,* January 10, 1866. Clyde Oubre points out that the Freedmen's Bureau policy of requiring contracts worked against blacks' hope for land ownership. In his judgment, the deadline should have been extended another year (*Forty Acres and a Mule,* 186).

35 Alan Conway, *The Reconstruction of Georgia* (Minneapolis: University of Minnesota Press, 1966), 118–19; Charles Devens to W. L. M. Burger, Asst. Adj. Gen., Department of Georgia, December 28, 1865, BRFAL, M 752, Reel 19; Thompson, *Reconstruction in Georgia,* 50–51; Dan T. Carter, "The Anatomy of Fear: The Christmas Day Insurrection Scare of 1865," *Journal of Southern History* 42 (August 1976): 360; see also Carter, *When the War Was Over,* 192–202.

36 Bryant to Saxton, January 5, 1866, JEB Papers.

37 Bentley, *History of the Freedmen's Bureau,* 186; Elizabeth Studley Nathans, *Losing the Peace: Georgia Republicans and Reconstruction, 1865–1871* (Baton Rouge: Louisiana State University Press, 1968), 19; Belz, *New Birth of Freedom,* 69.

38 Broadside announcing the meeting, January 1866; Proceedings of the Freedmen's Convention, Augusta, January 10, 1866; Proceedings of the Council of the Georgia Equal Rights Association, April 1866, JEB Papers. Drago's study of Georgia blacks during Reconstruction links this meeting to the movement for black education originating with black leaders (*Black Politicians,* 27). The broadside invites a much wider convention, however, than the forty delegates Drago recognizes. Drago seems to think it was a surprise that the work of the convention was political, as announced. Drago errs in calling the association the Georgia Equal Rights and Educational Association here. This name change did not occur until October 1866, as will be seen. The error was conceivably made because Bryant wrote an article, the manuscript of which exists in the AMA files and at Duke University, which Bryant titled first "The Georgia Educational Movement" and then changed to the "Georgia Education Association." In letters Bryant used the terminology of "The Association," which was used for the GERA as well. Bryant's manuscript was also quoted by Robert Morris in his *Reading, 'Riting, and Reconstruction: The Education of Freedmen in the South, 1861–1870* (Chicago: University of Chicago Press, 1981), 125–26. Allen Chandler Smith claims that five thousand blacks attended the Augusta convention, surely an inflated figure ("The Republican Party in Georgia, 1867–1871" [M.A. thesis, Duke University, 1937], 21). In focusing on black leadership, Drago implies that blacks used Bryant, instead of the other way around, a neat—though not necessarily accurate—twist to the traditional treatment of such coalitions between blacks and radical Republicans (*Black Politicians,* 29). My sense is that a little of both was probably true. Bryant

agreed with black leaders on the importance of both education and political equality for blacks.

39 Clipping from the *Loyal Georgian,* January 20, 1866. The phrase quoted, undoubtedly written by Bryant, was also used in the concluding paragraph of the proceedings. Proceedings of the Freedmen's Convention, Augusta, January 10, 1866, 8–12.

40 Proceedings of the Freedmen's Convention, 15–19.

41 Proceedings of the Freedmen's Convention, 17–21.

42 Proceedings of the Freedmen's Convention, 22–28. Foner quotes Bryant's speech to illustrate the Northern commitment to free labor (*Politics and Ideology,* 102).

43 Proceedings of the Freedmen's Convention, 28–31.

44 Proceedings of the Council of Georgia Equal Rights Association, April 1866, JEB Papers; Edwin S. Redkey, "Bishop Turner's African Dream," *Journal of American History* 54 (September 1967): 271–90.

45 H. M. Turner to Bryant, April 6, 12, 13, 1866, JEB Papers.

46 Bentley, *History of the Freedmen's Bureau,* 186; George M. Frederickson, *The Inner Civil War: Northern Intellectuals and the Crisis of the Union* (New York: Harper & Row, 1965), 131; Susie Lee Owens, *The Union League of America: Political Activities in Tennessee, the Carolinas, and Virginia, 1865–1870* (New York: New York University, 1947), an abridgement of her dissertation, completed in 1943 at New York University. Owens criticizes severely the Radicals as a group, whom she sees as manipulators of the freed slaves. See also Roberta F. Cason, "The Loyal League in Georgia," *Georgia Historical Quarterly* 20 (June 1936): 125–53; and Walter Lynwood Fleming, *The Sequel of Appomattox: A Chronicle of the Reunion of the States* (New Haven: Yale University Press, 1920), 174–95, for a brief description of the league's formation and activity, elaborate and secret ritual, and catechisms for instructing blacks in Radical Republicanism. I find both Fleming and Cason to be blatantly biased.

47 Bryant to J. M. Edmunds, April 27, 1871; Commission to John Emory Bryant from the Union League of America, September 16, 1868, JEB Papers. The Farrow Papers are disappointingly slim during these years and neither confirm nor deny early conflicts between these groups.

48 Proceedings of the Council of the Georgia Equal Rights Association, April 4, 1866, JEB Papers; Proceedings of the Convention of the Equal Rights and Educational Association of Georgia, Macon, October 29, 1866, JEB Papers.

49 J. W. Alvord to O. O. Howard, September 1, 1865; also printed report on "Schools and Finances of the Freedmen," by J. W. Alvord, agent, Freedmen's Bureau, BRFAL, M 752, Reel 74; Bentley, *History of the Freedmen's Bureau,* 171–72; J. W. Alvord to O. O. Howard, September 1, 1865, BRFAL, M 752, Reel 74; Jones, *Soldiers of Light and Love,* 73–76.

50 Manuscript copy of article written by Bryant for the *New York Independent,* January 1866, JEB Papers. Bryant to the Reverend E. P. Smith, July 9, 1867. Manuscript copy of "The Georgia Educational Movement," written by Bryant, n.d. [1867?], AMA Archives; Report of J. W. Alvord, 1866, BRFAL, M 752, Reel

74; Clipping from the *Loyal Georgian,* January 27, 1866, JEB Papers. Despite the efforts of Bryant and others, white teachers continued to outnumber blacks. See Morris, *Reading, 'Riting, and Reconstruction,* 126, for statistics.

51 Bryant to the Reverend E. P. Smith, July 9, 1867, AMA Archives; Letters of endorsement, 1866–1867, from O. O. Howard, Henry Ward Beecher, and others, JEB Papers. See also Bentley, *History of the Freedmen's Bureau,* 181; Cimbala, "Terms of Freedom," 411–12.

52 Butchart, *Northern Schools,* 31, 55, 74, 113–14, 135–53. Though more charitable in his assessment, Robert Morris essentially agrees with Butchart in his evaluation that education for the freed slaves became an accommodation to racism (*Reading, 'Riting, and Reconstruction,* x–xi, 212–16, 248). See Carter, *When the War Was Over,* 186, to contrast the view of Southern whites on education for blacks.

53 Morris, *Reading, 'Riting, and Reconstruction,* 126; Bryant to the Reverend E. P. Smith, July 9, 1867, AMA Archives; Cimbala, "Terms of Freedom," 436. Cimbala, who frequently dismisses Bryant as merely "political" (rather odd, since he describes in detail the political maneuvering of other agents of the bureau without comment), is forced to agree with Bryant's judgment of Eberhart.

54 Cimbala, "Terms of Freedom," 400; Bryant to the Reverend E. P. Smith, July 9, 1867, AMA Archives.

55 Proceedings of the Equal Rights and Educational Association of Georgia, Macon, October 29, 1866 (quoted); Proceedings of the Council of the Georgia Equal Rights Association, April 4, 1866, JEB Papers; Nathans, *Losing the Peace,* 24–25.

56 H. M. Turner to Bryant, April 6, 12, 13, 1866, JEB Papers.

57 Manuscript copy of article written by Bryant for the *New York Independent,* January, 1866, JEB Papers; "The Georgia Educational Movement," AMA Archives; Bryant to Edgar Ketchum, January 4, 1866, AMA Archives. Drago agrees that the black churches in Georgia served political purposes (*Black Politicians,* 20).

58 Clipping from the *Loyal Georgian,* January 20, 1866, JEB Papers. Unfortunately, few copies of the *Loyal Georgian* have survived, though Bryant's file contains a number of clippings. The Library of Congress houses a Negro Newspapers file, filmed by the American Council of Learned Societies, which contains a few issues of the *Loyal Georgian.*

59 Belz, *New Birth of Freedom,* 157; *Augusta Loyal Georgian,* January 20, 1866; Proceedings of the Freedmen's Convention, Augusta, January 10, 1866, JEB Papers.

60 Letter of Mary R. Williams to H. M. Turner, quoted in letter from H. M. Turner to O. O. Howard, May 22, 1866, BRFAL, M 752, Reel 36. Williams wrote from South Carolina, where conditions were similar to those in Georgia; George C. Rable, *But There Was No Peace: The Role of Violence in the Politics of Reconstruction* (Athens: University of Georgia Press, 1984), 1–32.

61 Bentley, *History of the Freedmen's Bureau,* 179; Thompson, *Reconstruc-*

tion in Georgia, 128; Stearns, *The Black Man of the South*, 131–33; Henry Lee Swint, *The Northern Teacher in the South, 1862–1870* (New York: Octagon Books, 1967), 94–98; Jones, *Soldiers of Light and Love*, 81–84; Diary of Emma Bryant, April 28, 1866, JEB Papers; Davis Tillson to O. O. Howard, May 7, 1866, Howard Papers; Stearns, *The Black Man of the South*, 107.

62 Diary of Emma Bryant, April 30, June 20, 1866; Emma Bryant to John Bryant, October 21, December 30, 1866; "Jos." to "Cousin John" Bryant, June 23, 1866, JEB Papers. Bryant's daughter, Alice, in her autobiographical sketch, credits her father's longevity in the South to the distinction he drew between personal and public speech. He would say anything to support his principles in print or in a formal speech. He was careful, however, not to offend personally or to take offense at personal insults. The accuracy of her statement is questionable, but it points to an interesting distinction.

63 Tillson to O. O. Howard, May 12, 1866, BRFAL, M 752, Reel 27.

64 William E. Spong to O. O. Howard, March 25, 1866, BRFAL, M 752, Reel 29; Tillson to O. O. Howard, December 1, 1865, BRFAL, M 752, Reel 20.

65 Tillson to O. O. Howard, June 11, 1866, BRFAL, M 752, Reel 32; Tillson to O. O. Howard, May 7, 1866, Howard Papers; Bryant to Tillson, June 5, 1866, BRFAL, M 752, Reel 32; Tillson to O. O. Howard, June 15, 1866, Howard Papers.

66 Bryant to O. O. Howard, June 11, 1866; Tillson to O. O. Howard, June 11, 1866; Special Order 4, Headquarters, District of Georgia, June 7, 1866.

67 Special Order 4, Headquarters, District of Georgia, June 7, 1866; Tillson to O. O. Howard, June 16, 1866, BRFAL, M 752, Reel 32. Tillson apparently sent Howard some letters from others critical of Bryant. One report from agent John Deveaux claimed that the captain had overcharged a poor black woman and was "doing all in his power to create and foster a bad and unchristian feeling between the negroes and their white neighbors" (John Deveaux to Tillson, May 7, 1866); Bryant to Howard, June 16, 1866, Howard Papers.

68 McFeely, *Yankee Stepfather*, 107–29; Carter, *When the War Was Over*, 235–36.

69 Letters to O. O. Howard from agents J. E. Cornelius, July 1, 1866; S. C. Armstrong, May 25, 1866; A. Baird, July 4, 1866; John Deveaux, June 6, 1866, BRFAL, M 752, Reels 31 and 35.

70 Handwritten eyewitness report of the Macon meeting, presumably by Bryant, n.d. [Spring 1866], JEB Papers.

71 Bentley, *History of the Freedmen's Bureau*, 129, 126; McFeely, *Yankee Stepfather*, 249.

72 Tillson's Speech, October 27, 1865, BRFAL, M 752, Reel 20; Bentley, *History of the Freedmen's Bureau*, 129; Letter to editor, unidentified newspaper, Lexington, Ky., November 4, 1865, BRFAL, M 752, Reel 20. For a defense of Tillson's ruling, see Cimbala, "Terms of Freedom," 105–6; Tillson to Prov. Gov. James Johnson, copy to O. O. Howard, October 25, 1865, BRFAL, M 752, Reel 20. Tillson expressed frustration with the white Georgians he was supposedly

helping. Even he was not immune to derogatory remarks and insulting snubs by Southerners determined "to avoid touching a *dirty* Yankee" (Davis Tillson to O. O. Howard, June 15, 1866, Howard Papers).

73 The Reverend M. Harris to Bryant, July 5, 1866; H. M. Turner to Bryant, June 18, 1866, JEB Papers.

74 Proceedings of the Council of the Georgia Equal Rights Association, July 1866; Emma Bryant to John Bryant, August 25, 1866, JEB Papers. The Union League gathering followed the National Union Convention to that city two weeks later; J. H. Caldwell to General Fisk, forwarded to O. O. Howard, September 3, 1866, BRFAL, M 752, Reel 37.

75 Emma Bryant to John Bryant, August 25, September 23, October 2, 1866, JEB Papers.

76 Emma Bryant to John Bryant, October 26, 29, 1866; Pamphlet, "The Georgia Publishing Company," n.d. [November 1866?], JEB Papers. Another pamphlet lists members of the Loyal Georgian Publishing Company as a combination of blacks and Northern whites, including C. H. Prince, C. C. Richardson, T. G. Campbell, and Simeon Beaird.

77 Tillson to Gen. W. E. Whipple, October 9, 1866, BRFAL, M 752, Reel 37. Appropriately, Tillson himself became a planter in Georgia in 1867, though he quickly failed in the effort, as did many Northerners. See Powell, *New Masters*, 151–52; F. D. Sewall to O. O. Howard, December 6, 1866, BRFAL, M 752, Reel 39.

78 F. D. Sewall to O. O. Howard, December 15, 1866, BRFAL, M 752, Reel 39; William Cohen, "Black Immobility and Free Labor: The Freedmen's Bureau and the Relocation of Black Labor, 1865–1868" (Paper presented at the annual meeting of the Southern Historical Association, Charleston, S.C., November 1983).

79 Edward E. Howard to Bryant, January 26, 1867, JEB Papers; McFeely, *Yankee Stepfather*, 7.

80 Proceedings of the Equal Rights and Educational Association of Georgia, Macon, October 29, 1866, JEB Papers.

81 Lucy Bryant to Bryant, January 6, 1867, JEB Papers. It was not unusual for Northerners to gain admittance to the bar in their home states, rather than risk opposition in the South. Albion Tourgée, a judge in North Carolina during Reconstruction, was admitted to the Ohio bar in 1867 to practice law in North Carolina. Not until 1889 was Bryant enrolled as a member of the Georgia bar (see below, chapter 6); John Bryant to Emma Bryant, n.d. [October, 1866?], JEB Papers.

FOUR. CONGRESSIONAL RECONSTRUCTION

1 Michael Perman, *The Road to Redemption: Southern Politics, 1869–1879* (Chapel Hill: University of North Carolina Press, 1984), xii–xiii; C.

Vann Woodward, *Origins of the New South, 1877–1913* (Baton Rouge: Louisiana State University Press, 1967), 22.

2   William Gillette believes that the political goal was the only goal of Reconstruction (*Retreat from Reconstruction, 1865–1879* [Baton Rouge: Louisiana State University Press, 1979], xiii–xiv); but see Belz, *New Birth of Freedom*, 141–42, 157–58. The experience of carpetbaggers Stearns, Morgan, and even Bryant lends evidence to the point made here.

3   *House Miscellaneous Documents*, 40th Cong., 3d sess., no. 52, 13 (hereinafter cited as *House Misc. Doc.*); *Augusta Chronicle and Sentinel*, August 1867.

4   *Augusta Loyal Georgian*, May 9, 16, 1867.

5   Emma Bryant to John Bryant, January 11, April 27, 1867; Maria Eberhart to Emma Bryant, May 13, 1867; "Sister" to Emma Bryant, June 9, 1867, JEB Papers.

6   *Augusta Loyal Georgian*, August 10, 1867.

7   "Speech of Ex-Gov. Jos. E. Brown, Delivered at . . . Atlanta, Ga., . . . March 4th, 1867," 5, printed transcript in the DeRenne Collection, Special Collections, University of Georgia Library, Athens, Ga.; *Atlanta Constitution*, June 18, 1868. Brown continues to raise the ire of historians. See Carter, *When the War Was Over*, 265–66, for a scathing denunciation. Rable, *But There Was No Peace*, 65, is more generous and recognizes Brown's pragmatism.

8   Joseph Brown to Henry M. Turner, June 1867; *Atlanta Daily Era*, February 26, 1867; Brown to Rufus Bullock, December 3, 1868; Brown to William D. Kelly, March 18, 1867, Joseph Emerson Brown Papers, Felix Hargrett Collection, University of Georgia Library, Athens, Ga.

9   Statement of John A. Beck, n.d.; Circular for Grand Council Chamber of the Union League Association in Georgia, February 5, 1868, Henry P. Farrow Papers, Special Collections, University of Georgia Library, Athens, Ga.; Olive Hall Shadgett, *The Republican Party in Georgia from Reconstruction Through 1900* (Athens: University of Georgia Press, 1964), 5; *Atlanta Daily New Era*, March 5, 1867.

10   Emma Bryant to John Bryant, August 27, September 29, October 10, 1867.

11   Emma Bryant to John Bryant, December 13, 1867; letters from Sarah Jane Cooper to Bryant, January 13, May 17, 1868, imply that he may have been subsidizing a black student's education at Oberlin College during this time.

12   Historians have not agreed on either the number of delegates or their breakdown. See Nathans, *Losing the Peace*, 56–57, and Thompson, *Reconstruction in Georgia*, 189; Richard L. Hume, "The 'Black and Tan' Constitutional Conventions of 1867–1869 in Ten Former Confederate States: A Study of Their Membership" (Ph.D. diss., University of Washington, 1969), 1:207–10, 226–30.

13   See Perman, *Reunion Without Compromise*, 327–36, for a discussion of the Southern strategy.

14   A word is needed to clarify the sometimes misleading terms "moderate" and "radical" as they were used in Georgia politics during Reconstruction. At the

outset of congressional Reconstruction, radicals followed the leadership of the Augusta ring and moderates were willing to accept general Reconstruction policy but took a middle ground, attempting compromise. Later the term "radical" meant accepting Bullock's leadership, while "moderate" meant working for Republican principles but against the governor. These designations were not satisfactory, as seen later.

15 Joseph H. Parks, *Joseph E. Brown of Georgia* (Baton Rouge: Louisiana State University Press, 1977), 396, 401; "Speech of Governor Joseph E. Brown, Delivered at Marietta, Georgia, Wednesday, March 18, 1868," 6–7, printed transcript in the DeRenne Collection, Special Collections, University of Georgia Library, Athens, Ga. (hereinafter cited as Brown's Marietta speech); *Atlanta Daily New Era*, January 11, 1868.

16 Handwritten copy, "A Speech Delivered in McIntier Hall, Sav[annah], August 20th, 1874, by Hon. H. M. Turner in Reply to Charges Made Against the Hon. John E. Bryant by Hon. T. G. Campbell, Previous to His Nomination to Congress. Phonographically reported by Amey T. Adlington," JEB Papers ("phonographically reported," presumably to guarantee the fidelity of the transcript); *Atlanta Daily New Era*, February 28, 1868.

17 A study of women's property rights under the Radical Republicans shows that the Georgia Constitution also included for Republican political profit a married women's property provision, "packaged with homestead exemption." See Suzanne D. Lebsock, "Radical Reconstruction and the Property Rights of Southern Women," *Journal of Southern History* 43 (May 1977): 202–4; Brown's Marietta speech, 6–7.

18 *House Misc. Doc.*, no. 52, 18. Akerman became Grant's attorney general in 1870 and was an advocate of black rights. See William S. McFeely, *Grant: A Biography* (New York: Norton, 1981), 366–74; also McFeely, "Amos T. Akerman: The Lawyer and Racial Justice," in *Race, Region, and Reconstruction*, ed. Kousser and McPherson, 395–415. More on Akerman's relationship to John Emory Bryant will be seen below.

19 Hume, "Black and Tan Conventions," 238–41. The amounts of the reductions were from $2,500 to $1,000 for real estate and from $2,000 to $500 for personal property. As Hume has categorized the key votes, Bryant voted a consistent radical ticket, except in this case. See Hume, "Black and Tan Conventions," 237–41, and Nathans, *Losing the Peace*, 62–63. On the issue of debts, J. Mills Thornton III has pointed out the irony of the fact that a triumphant Confederacy would have been burdened "with a huge war-time debt, larger than the Reconstruction debt, the validity of which was later questioned" ("Fiscal Policy and the Failure of Radical Reconstruction in the Lower South," in *Race, Region, and Reconstruction*, ed. Kousser and McPherson, 349–94.

20 McFeely, "Amos T. Akerman," 403.

21 Bryant to [Amos Akerman?], May 17, 1871, JEB Papers; R. P. Lester et al. to Henry P. Farrow, November 10, 1867, Farrow Papers; copy of mail-out instruction, Atlanta, January 20, 1868, from E. M. Timoney, secretary of Union League of America of Georgia, to "Dear Sir," JEB Papers.

22 *Atlanta Daily New Era*, February 4–12, 1868. Bryant returned the body of C. C. Richardson to Maine for burial. He received a warm letter of appreciation from Richardson's family, who remembered Bryant's entrance to the bar in Maine and wished him well. "You are enjoined in a noble cause, and I hope you will be spared and have a reward of success" (E. B. Richardson to Bryant, March 14, 1868, JEB Papers). Ironically, Emma Bryant had said of Richardson not long before his death, "I shall be glad when you are well rid of Richardson, for I do not believe him to be a man of pure character or great abilities" (Emma Bryant to John Bryant, November 1, 1867, JEB Papers).

23 Notation in Bryant's handwriting on envelope of letter from office superintendent of Public Works, State of Georgia (letter missing, n.d.), JEB Papers; personal memo of Henry P. Farrow, dated August 16, 1883, Farrow Papers.

24 Contract signed by E. Hulbert, superintendent of Western & Atlantic Railroad, August 10, 1868; approved by Gov. Rufus Bullock, August 21, 1868, Farrow Papers.

25 *Augusta Loyal Georgian*, February 15, 1868; Rufus Bullock to John E. Bryant, April 29, 1868; Bryant to "My Colored Friends of Augusta," March 15, 1867, JEB Papers.

26 Brown to William D. Kelly, March 18, 1868, Brown Papers.

27 Nathans, *Losing the Peace*, 96–99; Charles G. Bloom, "The Georgia Election of April, 1868: A reexamination of the Politics of Georgia Reconstruction" (M.A. thesis, University of Chicago, 1963), 41–54, 86.

28 Allen W. Trelease, *White Terror: The Ku Klux Klan Conspiracy and Southern Reconstruction* (New York: Harper & Row, 1971), 74–78; Elizabeth Otto Daniell, "The Ashburn Murder Case in Georgia Reconstruction, 1868," *Georgia Historical Quarterly* 59 (Fall 1975): 296–312. Joe Brown served as chief prosecutor in the Ashburn murder trial. See Parks, *Brown*, 415, and Rable, *But There Was No Peace*, 71.

29 Charles Bloom has revised Mildred Thompson's analysis, which gave Republicans a narrow margin in the senate and Democrats control in the house. Bloom shows persuasively that Republicans captured both houses. Elizabeth Nathans and Bloom agree on the membership breakdown, derived from voting records on certain key issues. See Bloom, "The Georgia Election," 68–72; Nathans, *Losing the Peace*, 108.

30 Post Office Department to Henry Farrow, January 27, 1868, Farrow Papers; Bryant to Joshua Hill, May, 1871, JEB Papers; Bryant to [William Chandler?], October 5, 1868, William E. Chandler Papers, Library of Congress, Washington, D.C.; Bryant to [Amos Akerman?], May 17, 1871; Bryant to J. M. Edmunds, April 27, 1871, JEB Papers.

31 John H. Caldwell, *Reminiscences of the Reconstruction of Church and State in Georgia* (Wilmington, Del.: Thomas, 1895), 19; Morris, *Reading, 'Riting, and Reconstruction*, 145–46; Caldwell, *Reminiscences*, 20.

32 Bryant to [William Chandler?], October 5, 1868, Chandler Papers. Nathans, for example, assumes that Bryant and Caldwell were cut from patronage positions first and broke with Bullock afterward (*Losing the Peace*, 103).

33 Drago, *Black Politicians*, 45–62.
34 Bryant to Joseph Stevens, May 22, 1871, JEB Papers.
35 W. L. Clift to Bryant, May 15, 1868; Emma Bryant to John Bryant, n.d. [July 1868?]; July 6, 1868, JEB Papers.
36 Emma Bryant to Bryant, July 9, 1868, JEB Papers.
37 J. W. Clift to J. A. J. Creswell, June 10, 1869, JEB Papers; F. A. Kirby to Rufus Bullock, July 9, 1868, Governor Rufus Bullock Correspondence, Georgia Department of Archives and History, Atlanta, Ga. It is unclear why Kirby questioned Bryant's eligibility, for Bryant was thirty-one years of age, a citizen of the United States, a native-born American, and had maintained his residence in Georgia since 1866.
38 Bryant to [William Chandler?], October 5, 1868, Chandler Papers. Brown's biographer states that he "no doubt wished to be rewarded for his political service" but that he probably did not want the supreme court position. The pay was low, and it took Brown "out of active politics" (Parks, *Brown*, 424).
39 Bryant to [William Chandler?], October 5, 1868, Chandler Papers; *Augusta National Republican*, August 22, 1868. Blodgett remained the chairman of the Republican central committee. *Augusta National Republican*, August 4, 1868; Kenneth Coleman, ed., *A History of Georgia* (Athens: University of Georgia Press, 1977), 239; Thornton, "Fiscal Policy," 378–79, 389; Bryant later accepted segregated schools. Whether he was more radical at this time in his views toward integrated schools has not been confirmed.
40 *Augusta National Republican*, July 19, 1868; *Atlanta Constitution*, August 21, 1868.
41 *Atlanta Constitution*, September 15, 18, 1868; *Augusta Daily Press*, February 14, 1868; John H. Caldwell to W. E. Chandler, August 19, 1868; John H. Caldwell to William Chaflin, September 1, 1868, Chandler Papers.
42 J. W. Clift to J. A. J. Creswell, June 10, 1869, JEB Papers; *Augusta National Republican*, July 30, 1868. See Nathans, *Losing the Peace*, 114–26, for a detailed discussion of the summer legislation; Extract from the Report of Maj. Gen. George C. Meade, October 31, 1868, in "Have the Reconstruction Acts Been Fully Executed in Georgia?"; *Speech of Governor [Rufus] Bullock of Georgia* (Washington, D.C.: Chronicle Printing, 1868, in Felix Hargrett Collection, University of Georgia Library, Athens, Ga.; James E. Sefton, *The United States Army and Reconstruction, 1865–1877* (Baton Rouge: Louisiana State University Press, 1967), 199.
43 Brown's Marietta speech, 7; Georgia's third black senator, A. A. Bradley, had been expelled earlier in the summer, ostensibly for the reason that he was ineligible because of a felony charge in New York. Four mulatto representatives were allowed to keep their seats when they pleaded less than one-eighth Negro blood. H. M. Turner, who was also light skinned, scorned this denial of a black heritage, reproving and pleading with the four to remain silent, "Sit down; don't make yourself a jack to be galled by white people." See *Augusta National Republican*, August 29, 1868; *Atlanta Constitution*, August 28, 1868.
44 John H. Caldwell to William Chaflin, September 1, 1868, Chandler Papers; *Augusta National Republican*, September 4, 1868.

45 *Atlanta Constitution,* September 4, 1868.
46 Drago, *Black Politicians,* 53.
47 Nathans, *Losing the Peace,* 125. Nathans suggests that it "seems more than a mere coincidence" that so many Radicals abstained from voting, but Drago does not accept Bullock's culpability (*Black Politicians,* 53–54); *House Misc. Doc.,* no. 52, 2; John Caldwell to William Chaflin, September 1, 1868, Chandler Papers; Georgia was included in the Omnibus Bill of June 1868 and, upon ratifying the Fourteenth Amendment, had been readmitted to the Union. The same bill struck the relief clause from Georgia's constitution, even as Amos Akerman had warned. Former governor Brown's pleading with congressmen that the relief section be "left as ratified" to help maintain support for the Republican administration, "against the press, the politicians, and the property of the state," was to no avail (Brown to Schuyler Colfax, June 9, 1868, Brown Papers).
48 Rable, *But There Was No Peace,* 69–74; *House Misc. Doc.,* no. 52, 37 (quoted); Coleman, *History of Georgia,* 221.
49 *Athens Southern Banner,* December 17, 1869.
50 Otis A. Singletary, *Negro Militia and Reconstruction* (Austin: University of Texas Press, 1957), 9–11. The Republican governor in Mississippi, Adelbert Ames, was just as hesitant about sanctioning a black militia because he feared an all-out race war would result. See Blanche Butler Ames, comp., *Chronicles from the Nineteenth Century: Family Letters of Blanche Butler and Adelbert Ames,* 2 vols. (Clinton, Mass.: n.p., 1957), 1:157, 166–67. On Grant's policy and Ames's fear, see McFeely, *Grant,* 36, and Gillette, *Retreat from Reconstruction,* 34–36, 135; Letter to Governor Bullock, May 15, 1870, Governor Rufus Bullock Correspondence, Georgia Department of Archives and History, Atlanta, Ga.
51 John H. Caldwell to William Chaflin, August 19, 1868; Bryant to [William Chandler?], October 5, 1868, Chandler Papers; O. O. Howard to Bryant, October 5, 1868, JEB Papers. JEB's "commission" from the Union League, noted in chapter 3, was probably issued in anticipation of the election.
52 Emma Bryant to John Bryant, October 8, 1868, JEB Papers.
53 Nathans, *Losing the Peace,* 144; Stearns, *The Black Man of the South,* 252–57. From the beginning, Bryant had clashed with Bullock and had disapproved the poll tax. Too late, Bullock recognized the tax's threat to black voter participation and tried to suspend it. Democratic officials, however, refused to honor the governor's suspension order. But see Thornton, "Fiscal Policy," 377, for a fresh look at why the poll tax was important financially to Reconstruction governments; Trelease, *White Terror,* 119.
54 *House Misc. Doc.,* no. 52, 6, 10, 48–49.
55 Wallace Calvin Smith, "Rufus B. Bullock and the Third Reconstruction of Georgia, 1867–1871" (M.A. thesis, University of North Carolina, 1964), 59.
56 Brown to Bullock, December 3, 1868, Brown Papers. Brown's idea illustrates what Perman called the "Centrist" movement (*Road to Redemption,* 4–21); *House Misc. Doc.,* no. 52, 12–13.
57 *Augusta Daily Press,* January 30, February 7, 1869; *Athens Southern Banner,* September 10, 1869; Linton Stephens to Joseph Brown, July 26, 1871, Brown Papers. But Thornton states that Georgia's receipt/disbursement figures remained

stable during the Republican tenure, a situation not found in other lower Southern states ("Fiscal Policy," 389). Alice E. Reagan presents a new look at Kimball in her *H. I. Kimball, Entrepreneur* (Atlanta: Cherokee, 1983). Unfortunately, it sheds little light on his questionable ventures during Reconstruction but instead takes the long view, emphasizing how Kimball's enthusiasm and business deals benefited Atlanta's industrial recovery and growth. Reagan hints that Bullock was a victim of Kimball's propensity for moving ahead on business arrangements before needed capital was in the bank (p. 59). Bullock did not seem to hold this practice against Kimball but continued to work with him.

58 *Augusta Daily Press*, February 26, 1869; Drago, *Black Politicians*, 54.

59 *Augusta Daily Press*, February 9, 1869; Dr. Samuel Bard had come to the *New Era* from Louisiana as a highly respected journalist and was welcomed by Georgians, who regarded him as "a States Rights Democrat of the old school," a "conservative," and "a bold and vigorous writer," obviously acceptable until the *New Era* supported the Reconstruction Acts and then Rufus Bullock. See *Atlanta Daily New Era*, October 19, December 8, 1866; *Atlanta Constitution*, August 16, 1868; *Augusta Daily Press*, February 14, 1869. Joe Brown also worked to get the state printing for Bard (see Parks, *Brown*, 368).

60 *Atlanta Daily Press*, February 28, 1869.

61 *Augusta Daily Press*, February 28, 1869; Nathans, *Losing the Peace*, 159.

62 E. G. Cabaniss to Judge D. Invin, November 25, 1869, Elbridge G. Cabaniss Papers, Manuscript Department, Perkins Library, Duke University, Durham, N.C. Perman also quotes Cabaniss as an example of Democratic centrist strategy (*Road to Redemption*, 18); *Journal of the Senate of the State of Georgia, 1869* (Macon, Ga., 1869), 252–54 (Georgia senate and house *Journals* hereinafter cited as *Journal of Georgia Senate* and *Journal of Georgia House*).

63 Nathans, *Losing the Peace*, 154.

64 Bryant to Alex Ramsey, chairman, Senate Committee on Postal Affairs, December 11, 1869, JEB Papers.

65 Emma Bryant to John Bryant, March 12, 13, 14, April 2, 18, 1869; Stearns to Bryant, May 2, 1869, JEB Papers. There is no record that the Bryants accepted the offer; Document from Post Office Department, May 18, 1869, JEB Papers; Bryant to Bullock, May 18, 1869, Bullock Correspondence.

66 Gen. Alfred Terry to Bryant, January 9, 1869, JEB Papers; Letter from Bullock, June 10, 1869, for mass mailing, requesting petitions against Bryant. Bryant received a copy from an anonymous friend who warned him of Bullock's attack. One black friend later revealed to Bryant that he had been pressured by Bullock to sign such a petition and claimed that he did so because he was afraid for his family (Edwin Belcher to Bryant, December 31, 1869, JEB Papers).

67 Akerman to Hon. James Patterson, January 12, 1870, JEB Papers. This letter was actually written two days after Bryant had given up the fight to be confirmed.

68 Kenneth Coleman and Charles S. Gurr, eds. *Dictionary of Georgia Biography*, 2 vols. (Athens: University of Georgia Press, 1983), 1:91–93; *Griffin* [Georgia] *Semi-Weekly Star*, n.d. [August 1869?], JEB Papers.

69 *Athens Southern Banner*, July 9, 1869; Bryant to General Porter, July 22,

1869; Edmond Johnston to Bryant, August 4, 1869; Bryant to Joshua Hill, May 1871, JEB Papers. Bullock and Blodgett succeeded in having Blodgett reinstated for a time and given back pay, but Bryant replaced him in July.

70 Bryant to O. O. Howard, December 16, 1869, Howard Papers.

71 John R. Lewis to O. O. Howard, October 6, 1869, Howard Papers.

72 Drago, *Black Politicians*, 62.

73 Bryant to [William Chaflin?], October 5, 1868, Chandler Papers; Drago, *Black Politicians*, 54.

74 F. J. Robinson to Bullock, September 18, 1869; R. H. Gladding to Bullock, September 22, 1869; Daniel Lee to Bullock, October 1, 1869; Eli Barnes to Bullock, November 20, 1869; Letter, November 24, 1869, from a black man who wrote "to ask if it is in your power, in the name of God to come to our aid," Bullock Correspondence; *Senate Executive Documents*, 41st Cong., 2d sess., no. 3, 2–3; Trelease, *White Terror*, 236.

75 Isaac W. Avery, *The History of the State of Georgia from 1850–1881* (New York: Brown & Derby, 1881), 423; Gillette, *Retreat from Reconstruction*, 87–88. Gillette believes that Grant's tough action in Georgia was intended to balance his soft response in Virginia and to aid ratification of the Fifteenth Amendment.

76 Bryant to Bullock, January 10, 1870, Bullock Correspondence. In a letter to Alex Ramsey, December 11, 1869, Bryant outlined the salaries he had received: Freedmen's Bureau (five months), $800; assistant assessor of taxes (three months), $500; constitutional convention, $1,000; Georgia General Assembly, $1,500; postmaster (six months), $4,000 per year; Bryant to Horace Porter, February 7, 1870, JEB Papers; *Athens Southern Banner*, January 21, 1870. C. H. Prince was a fellow Down-easter who must have known Bryant before the war. They were about the same age, and both called Buckfield home. Prince served in the U.S. House of Representatives from July 25, 1868, until March 3, 1869. He held the postmaster position until 1882, when he left Georgia. See *Dictionary of Georgia Biography*, 2:814.

77 *Senate Reports of Committees*, 41st Cong., 2d sess., no. 58, 8; *Atlanta Constitution*, January 11, 1870.

78 *House Misc. Doc.*, no. 52, 2.

79 *Atlanta Constitution*, January 11, 1870; *Athens Southern Banner*, January 21, February 11, 1870.

80 Ulrich Bonnell Phillips, ed., *The Correspondence of Robert Toombs, Alexander Stephens, and Howell Cobb* (Washington, D.C.: American Historical Association, 1913), 707–8.

81 Bryant to Horace Porter, May 21, 1870, JEB Papers.

82 J. W. Alford, *Letters from the South Relating to the Condition of the Freedmen* (Washington, D.C.: Howard University Press, 1970), 20ff., quoted in Bloom, "The Georgia Election," 81.

83 *Atlanta New Era*, January 26, 1870.

84 Perman, *Road to Redemption*, 20. See also p. 49 for the point that some Republicans adopted a centrist posture to further their own influence in the party.

85 Nathans, *Losing the Peace*, 178; *Code of Georgia*, sec. 1, 363, p. 265;

Bryant to President Grant, March 14, 1870; Bryant to Hon. Lyman Trumbull, February 20, 1870; Volney Spalding to S. P. Chase, February 16, 1870, JEB Papers.

86   Senate Reports of Committees, 41st Cong., 2d sess., no. 58.

87   O. S. Ferry to Farrow, August 31, 1870, Farrow Papers; Senate Reports of Committees, 41st Cong., 2d sess., no. 175.

88   Col. John Bowles to Bryant, April 3, 1870; Bryant to General Porter, May 21, 1870, JEB Papers.

89   Col. John Bowles to Bryant, May 27, 1870; Amos Akerman to Hon. James Patterson, January 12, 1870, JEB Papers. McFeely says that Akerman's appointment resulted from the president's new Southern strategy as outlined by Butler and Ames. He credits Akerman with leading the Grant administration's single, short-lived effort to take seriously the Republican ideals of equality. Other motives may have played a part as well, such as Akerman's independence from Sumner's allies (Grant, 366–73, and "Amos T. Akerman," 404–9); Gillette, Retreat from Reconstruction, 175. Gillette believes that Bullock was expendable after ratification of the Fifteenth Amendment; Congressional Globe, 41st Cong., 2d sess., 42, pt. 6, 4727; pt. 3, 2740; pt. 4, 3612; Caldwell, Reminiscences, 16. Caldwell was appointed a federal judge through Bullock's influence in February 1871. See the Atlanta Methodist Advocate, February 8, 1871.

90   Nathans, Losing the Peace, 194; Journal of Georgia Senate, 1870, pt. 3, 74–75; Journal of Georgia House, 1870, 874–75.

91   House Reports, 42d Cong., 2d sess., no. 22; Trelease, White Terror, 240–41; Gillette, Retreat from Reconstruction, 88. Gillette points out the irony that voting, rather than protecting blacks, jeopardized them further.

92   Statement of N. L. Angier, state treasurer, in John E. Bryant, A Letter to Hon. Charles Sumner, of the U.S. Senate, Exposing the Bullock-Blodgett Ring in Their Attempt to Defeat the Bingham Amendment (Washington, D.C.: Gibson Brothers, 1870), 9; Dictionary of Georgia Biography, 1:93; Nathans, Losing the Peace, 203; Parks, Brown, 451–53; Foster Blodgett to H. I. Kimball, January 11, 1875, Foster Blodgett Papers, Special Collections, University of Georgia Library, Athens, Ga.

93   Brown to William T. Walters, April 4, 1877; Brown to Bullock, May 2, 1877, Brown Papers.

94   Trelease, White Terror, 389; Atlanta Daily New Era, May 25, 1871, JEB Papers; Trelease, White Terror, 391, 512; McFeely, "Amos T. Akerman," 406–9; Bryant to Akerman, May 8, 1871, JEB Papers; Gillette, Retreat from Reconstruction, 378. Gillette shows that Akerman was also concerned for Northern elections.

95   Brown to "political editor of the [Atlanta] Sun," October 11, 1871, Brown Papers; Athens Southern Banner, November 3, 1871.

96   Grant's failure to honor Akerman's request for troops to save his friend Conley signaled the administration's uneasiness with Akerman's zealous civil rights activity, according to McFeely. Akerman was replaced as attorney general soon afterward, on December 12, 1871. See McFeely, "Amos T. Akerman," 410; Grant, 373; Gillette, Retreat from Reconstruction, 89–90. It is surprising that

Akerman would request troops in this situation, knowing Grant's reluctance to use them in the South—especially to save an administration that Akerman helped demolish.

97 Richard H. Whiteley to Henry Farrow, August 15, 1870, Farrow Papers.
98 Perman also makes this point when evaluating the enthusiasm for railroads (*Road to Redemption*, 33–34).
99 *Athens Blade*, January 10, 1880; Edwin Belcher to Bryant, May 8, 1871, JEB Papers.
100 Bryant to Joshua Hill, May, 1871, JEB Papers.

FIVE. BRYANT AND THE STRATEGIC SHIFT OF REPUBLICANS IN THE 1870S

1 Vincent P. DeSantis, "Rutherford B. Hayes and the Removal of the Troops and the End of Reconstruction," in *Race, Region, and Reconstruction*, ed. Kousser and McPherson, 417–50.
2 Woodward, *Origins of the New South*, 28; Gillette, *Retreat from Reconstruction*, 334.
3 Gillette, *Retreat from Reconstruction*, 196; James M. McPherson, *The Abolitionist Legacy: From Reconstruction to the NAACP* (Princeton: Princeton University Press, 1975), 53–59, 92; Frederickson, *Black Image in the White Mind*, 182–86, 197.
4 Woodward, *Origins of the New South*, 23–50; McPherson, *Abolitionist Legacy*, 92; Gillette, *Retreat from Reconstruction*, 337–62. Joel Gray Taylor flatly calls Hayes "a prince of hypocrites." See his "Louisiana, an Impossible Task," in *Reconstruction and Redemption in the South*, ed. Otto Olsen (Baton Rouge: Louisiana State University Press, 1980), 229–30; George H. Mayer, *The Republican Party, 1854–1966* (New York: Oxford University Press, 1967), 198; Kenneth V. Davison, *The Presidency of Rutherford B. Hayes* (Westport, Conn.: Greenwood Press, 1972), 136–43.
5 Bryant to J. M. Edmunds, November 20, 1871; M. H. Hale to Bryant, January 4, 1872, JEB Papers; Carl N. Degler, *The Other South: Southern Dissenters in the Nineteenth Century* (New York: Harper & Row, 1974), 260–63. Degler notes the same problem in other states.
6 Bryant to J. M. Edmunds, April 27, 1871; Amos Akerman to Bryant, January 12, 1870; Mrs. C. W. Robbins to Bryant, September 11, 1876, JEB Papers; Powell, "Politics of Livelihood," 330–37.
7 Bryant to J. M. Edmunds, April 27, 1871; Edwin Belcher to Bryant, May 8, 11, 1871; *Atlanta Constitution*, September 10, 1868; April 23, 1880; Edwin Belcher to Bryant, December 31, 1869; C. H. Prince to Bryant, May 13, 1872, JEB Papers.
8 M. H. Hale to Bryant, January 4, 1872, JEB Papers.
9 Statement of Intent, [signed by] B. W. Frohel for the Atlantic & Great Western Canal Company, November 24, 1871, in Official Papers, JEB Papers.
10 Emma Bryant to John Bryant, October 14, 1871; John Bryant to Emma

Bryant, November 9, 1871; Alice Bryant Zeller Autobiography, JEB Papers. Although the child was called both Emma and Alice throughout her childhood, for clarity I will refer to her only as Alice.

11 John Bryant to Emma Bryant, January 24, February 13, 18, 1872, JEB Papers.

12 Mrs. C. W. Robbins to Bryant, September 11, 1876; John Bryant to Emma Bryant, January 24, 1872, JEB Papers.

13 John Bryant to Emma Bryant, February 16, 1872, JEB Papers; James Atkins, collector, to George S. Boutwell, secretary of the treasury, April 3, 1872; Oath of Office, signed by John E. Bryant, April 1, 1872, Treasury Department Records, National Archives.

14 John Bryant to Emma Bryant, May 14, 1872; Emma Bryant to John Bryant, June 22, 1872; Bryant to Sen. John Pool, May 6, 1872; Joseph F. Stears[?] to Bryant, July 2, 1877, JEB Papers.

15 Emma Bryant to John Bryant, June 26, July 25, 30, 31, August 1, 2, 3, 16, 19, 1873 (part of a letter from John to Emma Bryant glued to letter of August 19, 1873), JEB Papers.

16 W. C. Dillon to Bryant, September 3, 1870; C. H. Prince to Bryant, August 17, 1876; Broadside, "Col. Bryant on the Stump," October 19, 1877; Bryant to Sen. John Pool, May 6, 1872, JEB Papers; *Atlanta Constitution*, August 22, 1872.

17 Avery, *History of the State of Georgia*, 366; *Atlanta Constitution*, August 23, 1872; Parks, *Brown*, 476; Shadgett, *Republican Party in Georgia*, 33–34 (quoted); Perman, *Road to Redemption*, 108–31.

18 On the elitist philosophy of the Liberals, see Wilbert H. Ahern, "Laissez-faire vs. Equal Rights: Liberal Republicans and Limits to Reconstruction," *Phylon* 40 (March 1979), 52–65; Perman, *Road to Redemption*, 136.

19 Edgar Ketchum to Bryant, September 25, 1872, JEB Papers.

20 Shadgett, *Republican Party in Georgia*, 46–47; Perman, *Road to Redemption*, 59–64. Perman outlines the dilemma of the new departurists in failing to acknowledge the conflicting strategy of violence to keep blacks away from the polls on the one hand and of encouragement to make them vote Democratic on the other. Perman attributes the voter apathy to inconsistent leadership (pp. 122–23); James Harlan to Bryant, October 10, 1872, JEB Papers; *Savannah Daily Republican*, October 5, 1872.

21 Shadgett, *Republican Party in Georgia*, 47; Gillette, *Retreat from Reconstruction*, 212; handwritten copy, "A Speech Delivered in McIntier Hall, Sav[annah], August 20th, 1874, by Hon. H. M. Turner in. Reply to Charges Made Against the Hon. John E. Bryant by Hon. T. G. Campbell, Previous to His Nomination to Congress. Phonographically reported by Amey T. Adlington," JEB Papers (quoted).

22 "A Speech Delivered in McIntier Hall," JEB Papers.

23 Frank Vincent, Joseph May, John Johnson, Elmer Harper, J. R. Robeson, "To the Republicans of the First Congressional District of Georgia"; James Atkins to Bryant, August 27, 1874; W. L. Clift to Bryant, August 21, 1874, JEB Papers.

24 W. L. Clift to Bryant, August 21, 1874, JEB Papers. (Clift is not to be

confused with J. W. Clift, a native of Massachusetts representing the first district of Georgia, who was seated in the 40th Congress in July 1868.)

25 Shadgett, *Republican Party in Georgia*, 44; W. L. Clift to Bryant, August 27, 1874, JEB Papers.

26 Samuel Bard to Bryant, August 25, 31, 1874; Edwin Belcher to Bryant, August 24, 1874; Dr. Frank Hall to Bryant, August 25, 1874, JEB Papers.

27 John Bryant to Emma Bryant, August 7, 1874, JEB Papers.

28 Bryant's speech "To the Republicans of the First Congressional District," printed for distribution, 1874, JEB Papers.

29 "To the Republicans of the First Congressional District," JEB Papers.

30 "To the Republicans of the First Congressional District," JEB Papers.

31 Gillette calls the 1874 election a "referendum on Reconstruction" (*Retreat from Reconstruction*, 236–58); Document, "John E. Bryant, Contestant vs. Julian Hartridge, Contester; Contested Election for the 1st Congressional District of Georgia, December 21, 1874"; Washington Chronicle Publishing Co. to Bryant, October 21, 1874; Julian Hartridge to Bryant, January 19, 1875, JEB Papers. Later the *Atlanta Methodist Advocate* claimed Bryant had won the election fairly. See chapter 6.

32 W. L. Clift to Bryant, July 14, 1875, JEB Papers.

33 Alice Bryant Zeller Autobiography.

34 Robbins Little to Bryant, July 10, 1875, in which he quotes from Bryant's letter to the *New York Times*, JEB Papers. On the Bourbons as representatives of the New South, see C. Vann Woodward, "Bourbonism in Georgia," *North Carolina Historical Review* 16 (January 1939): 25–35; Judson C. Ward, Jr., "The New Departure Democrats of Georgia: An Interpretation," *Georgia Historical Quarterly* 41 (September 1957): 227–36; James Tice Moore, "Redeemers Reconsidered: Change and Continuity in the Democratic South, 1870–1900," *Journal of Southern History* 44 (August 1978): 368. But leadership in this "new" outlook underscores the point made in recent scholarship of the continuity between old and new. For a summary of that scholarship, see Carl N. Degler, "Rethinking Post Civil War History," *Virginia Quarterly Review* 70 (Spring 1981), 250–67. Perman, *Road to Redemption*, 59, defines the Bourbons of the Democratic party as those who resisted the political and constitutional changes of Reconstruction. They believed in home rule, decentralized power within the federal system, and free trade (p. 80); W. L. Clift to Bryant, December 28, 1875, JEB Papers; Shadgett, *Republican Party in Georgia*, 50–51; W. A. Pledger to John H. Deveaux, March 28, 1876. Alice Bryant Zeller, Bryant's daughter, paid Pledger's widow two dollars, presumably for "the letters" that she bought from her; thus the Pledger Letterbook is included in the Bryant Papers. Alice Zeller's primary purpose in the inquiry was to recover her father's library, which Pledger had purchased when Bryant left Atlanta. Unfortunately, the books had already been sold. O. C. Fuller to Mrs. J. C. Zeller, February 13, 1905, JEB Papers.

35 G. P. Goodyear to John J. Bigby, April 6, 1872, JEB Papers.

36 John E. Talmadge, *Rebecca Latimer Felton: Nine Stormy Decades* (Athens: University of Georgia Press, 1960), 36–45. Fourteen Independents were

elected to the general assembly in 1874, while Republican strength was reduced to eight. See Shadgett, *Republican Party in Georgia,* 62; Perman, *Road to Redemption,* 87.

37 *Atlanta Constitution,* January 8, 11, April 11, 1876; W. A. Pledger to J. H. Deveaux, March 28, 1876; W. A. Pledger to George Bangs, February 2, 1876; W. A. Pledger to Henry Farrow, January 12, 1876; *Athens Blade,* February 6, 1880; W. A. Pledger to Bryant, November 18, 1875, JEB Papers.

38 W. L. Clift to Bryant, February 8, 14, 16, 1876; November 27, 1875; January 6, 1876, JEB Papers. According to John Talmadge, Stephens's failure to back the fusion ticket and his refusal to be its candidate for governor killed the Independent movement in 1882 ("The Death Blow to Independentism in Georgia," *Georgia Historical Quarterly* 39 [December 1955]: 46; see also Shadgett, *Republican Party in Georgia,* 72).

39 Andrew [Clark] to Bryant, February 27, 1876; W. L. Clift to Bryant, February 14, 1876; Bryant to S. A. Darnell, July 28, 1876, JEB Papers.

40 Shadgett, *Republican Party in Georgia,* 54; Bryant to S. A. Darnell, August 14, 1876; *Atlanta Constitution,* May 4, 5, 1876; William W. Brown to Bryant, May 12, 1876; James Atkins to Bryant, March 27, 1876; Shadgett, *Republican Party in Georgia,* 62; Bryant to S. A. Darnell, August 3, 1876, JEB Papers.

41 *Atlanta Constitution,* August 17, 1876; Judson Clements Ward, Jr., "Georgia Under the Bourbon Democrats, 1872–1890" (Ph.D. diss., University of North Carolina, 1947), 89. Shadgett defends Norcross against the charge of racism in this 1876 election (*Republican Party in Georgia,* 59).

42. W. A. Pledger to E. R. Belcher, March 9, 1876, JEB Papers; *Atlanta Constitution,* May 5, 1876; see also Ruth Currie-McDaniel, "Black Power in Georgia: William A. Pledger and the Takeover of the Republican Party," *Georgia Historical Quarterly* 62 (Fall 1978): 227.

43 *Atlanta Constitution,* August 17, 1876; Edwin Belcher to Bryant, July 11, 1876, JEB Papers. Belcher did not carry out his threat.

44 Wire from J. Norcross to Bryant, August 14, 1876; W. A. Pledger to Bryant, August 14, 1876, JEB Papers.

45 Emma Bryant to John Bryant, August 5, 1876; C. H. Prince to Bryant, August 17, 1876; Bryant to Volney Spalding, November 4, 1876; Z[achariah] Chandler to Bryant, August 7, 1876, JEB Papers.

46 Emma Bryant to John Bryant, August 18, 5, December 18, 1876; April 5, 1877, JEB Papers.

47 Bryant to L. M. Morrill, secretary of the treasury, December 9, 1876; David Porter to Bryant, September 8, 1876. Atkins also turned on Bryant in the customhouse, as recounted below; W. L. Clift to Bryant, January 6, 11, 25, February 14, 16, 1876. W. A. Pledger was also an avid crusader for temperance, serving as the Grand Worthy Master of the United Order of True Reformers, a black temperance league in Georgia related to the Good Templars; see Pledger Scrapbook, JEB Papers. Reconstruction governor Bullock returned to the state in May 1876 and was tried for embezzlement of public funds. His acquittal must have

angered Bryant. Bullock had made his peace with the Redeemers and went on to become a "leading citizen" in Atlanta. C. Vann Woodward says that Redeemers lumped "idealists" and "corrupt adventurers" together but that "economic carpetbaggers were a different kettle of fish" (*Reunion and Reaction: The Compromise of 1877 and the End of Reconstruction* [Boston: Little, Brown, 1966], 64). In an interesting series of letters, Bullock tried to cash in on old promises related to the railroad lease, but Joe Brown resisted him (see letters March–May, 1877, Brown Papers). Bullock was surely behind the effort to discredit Bryant.

48 Edwin Belcher to Bryant, August 6, 1875; Bryant to S. A. Darnell, July 26, 1876, JEB Papers; John G. Clark to Joseph Brown, May 7, 1877, Brown Papers.

49 Printed copy, "Letter to the President [Hayes] of the United States related to the character and antecedents of John Emory Bryant with a letter from Gen. Davis Tillson, last USA," Atlanta, April 26, 1877. The epithet "big Skowhegan chief" was used in an unidentified newspaper account of the Republican convention in Macon on August 16, 1876; Lafeyette McLaws to Bryant, September 29, 1876, JEB Papers.

50 E. C. Wade to Bryant, September 26, 1876; George Fisher to V. Spalding, September 21, 28, 1876, JEB Papers.

51 Card from [illegible, Pleasant?] to [Bryant], September 20, 1876; "The Reply of Hon. John E. Bryant to John G. Clark, James Atkins, and Other Persons Who Have Attempted to Blast the Character of Mr. Bryant," September 1876; E. Yulee to Bryant, September 23, 1876, JEB Papers. Yulee states that Bryant paid him to continue the paper "three weeks longer."

52 Ward, "Georgia Under the Bourbon Democrats," 91; David Porter to Bryant, September 8, 1876; A. G. Gould to Bryant, November 9, 1876; *Atlanta Constitution,* October 25, 1876, clipping in scrapbook, JEB Papers.

53 John Michael Matthews, "The Negro in Georgia Politics, 1865–1880" (M.A. thesis, Duke University, 1967), 109–10. Matthews reports that, out of six thousand eligible blacks in Savannah in 1876, only six hundred were registered to vote; H. C. Swift to Bryant, November 12, 1876; H. M. Turner to Bryant, December 8, 1876, JEB Papers. Turner had advised Bryant not to run, fearing not only the realized outcome but also the possibility that the candidate would end up deeply in debt. He congratulated Bryant that the latter did not occur, surely a result of the support Bryant had from the Georgia Association in Washington

54 Gillette, *Retreat from Reconstruction,* 311, 317–20, 333.

55 Bryant to L. M. Morrill, secretary of the treasury, January 16, 1877, Records of the Treasury Department (Record Group 56), National Archives; "Proceedings of the Republican State Central Committee of Georgia, Called to Investigate the Charges Made Against the Chairman, Hon. John E. Bryant, January 10, 1877"; *Atlanta Constitution,* January 14, 1877; S. M. Griffin to Bryant, January 23, 1877, JEB Papers.

56 W. L. Clift to Bryant, January 16, 1877; Bryant to George Fisher, October 7, 1876; Bryant to President Grant, October 2, 1876; Bryant to L. M. Morrill, secretary of the treasury, December 18, 1876, JEB Papers; James Atkins to L. M. Morrill, August 19, 28, December 15, 1876; Bryant to L. M. Morrill, January 16,

1877, Records of the Treasury Department, National Archives; Bryant to L. M. Morrill, February 6, 1877; C. H. Prince to Bryant, March 22, 1876; Theodore Basch, chairman, Robert Crumly, secretary, Republican Committee of Chatham County, to Bryant, March 7, 1877; Bryant to Charles Folger, secretary of the treasury, February 24, 1882, JEB Papers. Bryant learned that the inspector had been a subordinate of Tillson's, which he thought confirmed his feeling that the inspection was biased.

57 *Journal of Georgia House,* 1868, 357; 1870, 510–25; Charles E. Evans to H. P. Farrow, December 7, 1881, JEB Papers.

58 R. H. Whiteley to Bryant, January 23, 1873; Whitney to Bryant, January 2, 1874; W. L. Clift to Bryant, April 18, 1876, JEB Papers.

59 George Fisher, Thomas Robinson, John Quarles, W. L. Clift, Virgil Hillyer, and W. P. Prince to David Porter, April 10, 1877, JEB Papers; Woodward, *Origins of the New South,* 23–50; Woodward, *Reunion and Reaction,* 117; Davison, *Presidency of Hayes,* 137. Historians continue to debate the extent of any bargain Hayes may have made in 1877. For a review of the issues involved and the context for symbolically "withdrawing" the troops, see DeSantis, "Hayes and the Removal of the Troops," 417–50; Mayer, *Republican Party,* 197–98; Vincent P. DeSantis, *Republicans Face the Southern Question: The New Departure Years, 1877–1897* (Baltimore: Johns Hopkins University Press, 1959), 111–21; Gillette, *Retreat from Reconstruction* 336–38.

60 DeSantis, *Republicans Face the Southern Question,* 73, 118; DeSantis, "Hayes and the Removal of the Troops," 437–38; James M. McPherson, "The Antislavery Legacy: From Reconstruction to the NAACP," in Barton J. Bernstein, ed., *Towards a New Past: Dissenting Essays in American History* (New York, Vintage, 1969), 142; see also McPherson, *Abolitionist Legacy,* 95; Bryant to Gen. Benjamin Harrison, president-elect, February 8, 1889, JEB Papers.

61 Stanley P. Hirshon, *Farewell to the Bloody Shirt: Northern Republicans and the Southern Negro, 1877–1893* (Bloomington: Indiana University Press, 1962), 36; quoted in DeSantis, *Republicans Face the Southern Question,* 116.

62 Fisher et al. to David Porter, April 10, 1877, Bryant's handwritten note at the bottom of the page, JEB Papers.

63 Bryant to President Hayes, October 24, 1877; Volney Spalding to Messrs. Stroughton and Kister, November 17, 1877, JEB Papers.

64 J. R. Wikle to Bryant, July 7, 1877; A. N. Wilson to S. A. Darnell, secretary of state central committee, August 6, 1877; George Gorham to Bryant, June 11, 1878, JEB Papers.

65 Bryant to George Rowell & Co., January 26, 1878; W. L. Clift to Bryant, February 25, 1876; A. E. Buck to Bryant, April 20, 1876, JEB Papers.

66 Bryant to President R. B. Hayes, July 16, 1877; John G. Clark to Stanley Matthews, October 17, 1877; clipping from the *Atlanta Independent,* October 14, 1877, Rutherford B. Hayes Papers, Rutherford B. Hayes Presidential Center, Fremont, Ohio. Bryant ruled that the rump meeting with only nine members did not constitute a quorum of the state central committee, so he retained his chairmanship.

67   Judson C. Ward, Jr., "The Republican Party in Bourbon Georgia, 1872–1890," *Journal of Southern History* 9 (May 1943): 199; Bryant "To the President," August 28, 1877, Hayes Papers; *Atlanta Constitution,* April 30, 1880; Henry Farrow to editor of *Providence Journal,* handwritten copy, January 15, 1881, Farrow Papers; V. Spalding to C. R. Knight, February 16, 1878, JEB Papers. Although the spelling of his name is usually different, Spalding perhaps was a relative of Emma's.

68   Perman, *Road to Redemption,* 184; Coleman, *History of Georgia,* 219; Avery, *History of the State of Georgia,* 528.

69   Perman, *Road to Redemption,* 184; Avery, *History of the State of Georgia,* 412–13, 530.

70   V. Spalding to Bryant, November 13, 1877, JEB Papers; Perman, *Road to Redemption,* 208. Perman sees Bourbon power at the convention as a return of the Democratic party to its Jacksonian roots, the dismantlement of the whiggish partnership between government and business.

71   Avery, *History of the State of Georgia,* 45; M. H. Hale to Bryant, January 4, 1872; Bryant to Gen. W. L. Krzyznowski, June 26, 1870; Gen. W. L. Krzyznowski to Bryant, June 27, 1870, JEB Papers.

72   The AMA quoted in James M. McPherson, "Many Abolitionists Fought On After the Civil War," *University: A Princeton Quarterly,* no. 39 (Winter 1968–1969), 31; see also McPherson, *Abolitionist Legacy,* 139, 184–202.

73   Bryant to S. A. Darnell, July 28, 1876; Speech, "The South: The Condition, the Cause, the Remedy" [1879?], JEB Papers; Bryant to W. K. Rogers, secretary [to the president], April 13, 1877, Hayes Papers.

74   Emma Bryant to John Bryant, July 26, August 8, 1878; John Bryant to Emma Bryant, June 19, July 27, 1878, JEB Papers.

75   Bryant to Eugene Hale, chairman, Republican Congressional Committee, June 3, 1878; John Bryant to Emma Bryant, August 10, 1878, JEB Papers.

76   Alice Bryant Zeller's Autobiography, JEB Papers. Some of Alice's dates seem inaccurate. She says they lived in Atlanta when she was "about nine years old," but that would have been in 1880, when they were in Illinois.

77   V. Spalding to Bryant, November 4, 1878; July 19, 1879, JEB Papers.

78   V. Spalding to Bryant, July 14, 19, 1879, JEB Papers.

79   Emma Bryant to John Bryant, December 11, 1879; August 19, 1881, JEB Papers.

80   Hirshon, *Farewell to the Bloody Shirt,* 40; Mayer, *Republican Party,* 198; Shadgett, *Republican Party in Georgia,* 143 (quoted); Gillette, *Retreat from Reconstruction,* 353–54.

81   Matthews, "The Negro in Georgia Politics," 116–19; Bryant to Henry S. Wayne, December 28[?], 1876, JEB Papers; Ward, "The Republican Party," 199; Shadgett, *Republican Party in Georgia,* 72–73; Judson C. Ward, Jr., "The Election of 1880 and Its Impact on Atlanta," *Atlanta Historical Society Journal* 25 (Spring 1981): 5–15; Lewis N. Wynne, "The Bourbon Triumvirate: A Reconsideration," *Atlanta Historical Society Journal* 24 (Summer 1980): 39–55.

82   *Athens Blade,* February 20, 6, 27, 1880.

83 *Athens Blade,* April 23, 1880; Currie-McDaniel, "Black Power in Georgia," 233–35.
84 "Old Pelicon's Letter," *Athens Blade,* April 23, 1880.
85 W. A. Pledger to J. H. Deveaux, March 28, 1876; E. Q. Fuller to Bryant, April 29, 1880, JEB Papers.
86 V. Spalding to Bryant, August 31, 1880, JEB Papers.
87 John Bryant to Emma Bryant, February 1, 1880, JEB Papers.

SIX. THE CLOSING DECADES

1 McPherson, "Antislavery Legacy," 126–57; McPherson, *Abolitionist Legacy,* 152–60.
2 Emma Bryant to Bryant, September 20, 1880, JEB Papers.
3 Albion W. Tourgée, *A Fool's Errand, by One of the Fools* (New York: Fords, Howard & Hulbert, 1879), 20, 118, 120; John Bryant to Emma Bryant, February 1, 1880, JEB Papers; on Tourgée see Ruth Currie-McDaniel, "Courtship and Marriage in the Nineteenth Century: Albion and Emma Tourgée, a Case Study," *North Carolina Historical Review* 61 (July 1984): 285–310; Otto H. Olsen, *Carpetbagger's Crusade: The Life of Albion Winegar Tourgée* (Baltimore: Johns Hopkins University Press, 1965), especially 221–41.
4 Ironically, the *Methodist Advocate* announced on September 15, 1880, that "it was now admitted that Hon. J. E. Bryant was honestly elected to Congress by 600 majority in the 1st district, in 1874." It failed to identify those who were so convinced.
5 The meeting in 1873 was actually the reorganization of the Southern Historical Society, founded in 1869 by Benjamin M. Palmer, a conservative Presbyterian minister in New Orleans. "Transactions of the Southern Historical Society, Proceedings at Richmond. Richmond, Va., October 29, 1873, Address of Gen. Wade Hampton"; Bryant's speech on the Southern Advance Association versus the Southern Historical Society, untitled, n.d., JEB Papers.
6 Bryant's speech on the Southern Advance Association versus the Southern Historical Society. Stephens's books include *A Comprehensive and Popular History of the United States . . . to the Present Time* (1882); *A Compendium of the United States from the Earliest Settlements to 1883* (1883). Derry's book was *History of the United States for Schools and Academies* (1875), which went through many editions; "The Southern Question; the Conflict Between the Two Civilizations [in which] the Southern Historical Society [is condemned]," speech by Bryant, JEB Papers.
7 Henry Farrow to S. A. Darnell, December 21, 1880; Farrow to "Editor of the Journal," handwritten copy, Farrow Papers.
8 Henry Farrow to S. A. Darnell, December 21, 1880; Farrow to "Editor of the Journal," handwritten copy, Farrow Papers. Farrow had his own critics. In 1879 he faced a blistering attack over an alleged money-making scheme as attorney general of Georgia, wherein he reportedly used his post to clog the courts

with unprecedented numbers of prosecutions and then, for a fee, dismissed the accused with suspended sentences. See G. B. Raum, commissioner in Office of Internal Revenue, Treasury Department, to Henry Farrow, December 11, 1879, Farrow Papers.

9 "The Opportunity for Christian Work: The Mission of the Methodist Episcopal Church in the Southern States," speech by Bryant, JEB Papers; Emory Stephens Bucke, ed., *The History of American Methodism*, 3 vols. (New York: Abingdon, 1964), 2:376.

10 Bryant to [Farrow?], July 1, 1880, Farrow Papers; "The South: The Condition, the Cause, the Remedy, no. 2: Report of the Second Annual Meeting [of the] Atlanta Publishing Company," December 3, 1879, JEB Papers.

11 *Atlanta Methodist Advocate*, January 3, 1877; March 18, 1874: "The Thieving Carpetbaggers," reprinted in the *Atlanta Methodist Advocate*, May 16, 1877.

12 *Atlanta Methodist Advocate*, September 19, 1872; the Reverend R. Pierce in the *Atlanta Methodist Advocate*, September 1, 1875; *The History of American Methodism*, 2:376.

13 *Atlanta Methodist Advocate*, April 7, 1880.

14 Miss M. H. Stokes to Bryant, November 30, April 2, 1883, JEB Papers.

15 Resolution of the Marietta Street Methodist Episcopal Church, Atlanta, Ga., June 18, 1883; Resolution of the Board of Directors, Educational Society of the Georgia Conference of the Methodist Episcopal Church, June 19, 1883; Resolution of the Educational Convention of the Methodist Episcopal Church, Chattanooga, Tenn., June 20, 1883; Resolution of the Educational Committee of the Methodist Episcopal Church, November 26, 1883; all handwritten copies of the resolutions, JEB Papers.

16 R. J. Cooke to Bryant, September 19, 1881; "At Missionary Meeting, M. E. Church, Mission Rooms, New York, November, 1883," typed report, JEB Papers.

17 Report of the meeting of "Lay Conference Within the Bounds of the Georgia Conference of the Methodist Episcopal Church," held in Atlanta, Ga., November 23, 1883; Bryant to "Dear Col." May 21, 1884, JEB Papers.

18 William B. Gravely, *Gilbert Haven, Methodist Abolitionist: A Study in Race, Religion, and Reform, 1850–1880* (Nashville: Abingdon, 1973), 251; *Atlanta Methodist Advocate*, June 2, 1875.

19 *Atlanta Methodist Advocate*, June 21, 1876.

20 Ralph E. Morrow, *Northern Methodism and Reconstruction* (East Lansing: Michigan State University Press, 1956), 200; Bryant to "Dear Col.," May 21, 1884, JEB Papers.

21 David S. Monroe, ed., *Journal of the General Conference of the Methodist Episcopal Church, Held in Philadelphia, Pa., May 1–28, 1884* (New York: Phillips & Hunt, 1884), 334, 365; O. H. Warren, editor of the *Northern Christian Advocate*, to Bryant, December 23, 1886, JEB Papers.

22 *Atlanta Constitution*, July 6, 1880.

23 Jonathan Norcross et al. to Henry Farrow, May 23, 1880, Farrow Papers.

24   Bryant to James G. Blaine, April 4, 1884, JEB Papers. Farrow, on the other hand, called Longstreet "our old hero." See Farrow to the president, October 16, 1881, Farrow Papers.
25   James Atkins to Henry Farrow, October 29, 1881, Farrow Papers.
26   Shyam Krishna Bhurtel, "Colonel Alfred Eliab Buck: Carpetbagger in Alabama and Georgia" (Ph.D. diss., Auburn University, 1981), 74–164; Carl Evans Stipe, "Colonel Alfred Eliab Buck" (M.A. thesis, Emory University, 1944), 22; Henry Farrow to "Friends," December 8, 1881, Farrow Papers.
27   Emory Speer to Farrow, December 8, 1881; Alexander N. Wilson to Farrow, April 25, 1881, Farrow Papers.
28   *Atlanta Constitution*, August 1–5, 1882 (quoted); Currie-McDaniel, "Black Power in Georgia," 336–37; *Atlanta Constitution*, August 2, 4, 1882; Talmadge, "The Death Blow to Independentism," 46.
29   "A. E. Buck, Chairman of the State Central Committee, Republican Party of Georgia, Introducing John E. Bryant, Secretary of the Southern Advance Association, and Secretary of the Republican State Central Committee," September 11, 1882; "The South: The Condition, the Cause, the Remedy, no. 2: Report of the Second Annual Meeting [of the] Atlanta Publishing Company," December 3, 1879; "Loyalists in Council," Report of the annual meeting of the National Council of the Union League of America, reprinted "from *The Press* of Philadelphia, of December 11, 1879," JEB Papers. This holdover from the radical Loyal League of the 1860s was, like Bryant, something of an anachronism in the 1880s. Its continued existence was characterized by social meetings and upheld by former carpetbaggers such as Tourgée, who was honored by the Loyal League Club of New York in 1881. See Currie-McDaniel, "Courtship and Marriage, Tourgée Case Study," 305; Thomas G. Baker to Bryant, April 1, 1886; C. H. Grosvenor "To the President," March 1, 1889, JEB Papers.
30   A. E. Buck to Bryant, March 6, 1882, JEB Papers; A. E. Buck to Henry P. Farrow, February 25, 1883, Farrow Papers; [author's name missing] to Bryant, August 4, 1883, JEB Papers.
31   John Bryant to Emma Bryant, April 23, 1882; copies of letters from Joseph Brown to President Arthur, February 22, 1884, and from C. H. Prince to President Arthur, May 20, 1881; Emma Bryant to John Bryant, October 13, 1881, JEB Papers.
32   Emma Bryant to John Bryant, March 28, 1883; W. N. Richardson to Bryant, May 4, 1883, JEB Papers.
33   Emma Bryant to John Bryant, March 28, 1883, JEB Papers.
34   Emma Bryant to John Bryant, March 28, 1883, JEB Papers.
35   Emma Bryant to John Bryant, letters in February and March 1883, JEB Papers.
36   Emma Bryant to John Bryant, May 30, 1883, JEB Papers.
37   Emma Bryant to John Bryant, May 30, 1883, JEB Papers. Alice Bryant Zeller's autobiography relates the tantalizing fact that Emma was a suffragist. One wishes for more information on her involvement with the movement. Alice reveals an amusing incident that occurred in Washington. Emma was "discussing woman's rights with a woman who after exhausting her arguments against it

made the sarcastic remark: 'I never knew a suffraget who didn't have a small insignificant husband.' Just then my father, who was a tall, handsome, commanding personality came up and my mother introduced him."

38   Alice Bryant Zeller's Autobiography; Emma Bryant to John Bryant, April 29, May 3, 1883, JEB Papers.

39   John Bryant to Emma Bryant, August 21, 25, 1883; Emma Bryant to John Bryant, September 9, 1883, JEB Papers.

40   *Atlanta Constitution,* May 1, 1884.

41   *Atlanta Constitution,* May 1, 8, 1884.

42   See above, chapter 5.

43   *Atlanta Constitution,* June 6, 1884.

44   Shadgett holds that Norcross has unfairly been labeled a racist, that he was merely a political realist and believed in a program of separate-but-equal politics. Supporting this interpretation is Norcross's own letter to the editors of the *Atlanta Constitution* in which he claimed that "we have one white man's and negro hating party, and that was enough for Georgia, and that any party formed upon wrong cornerstones or in hostility to a portion of the voters would continue to be wrong in principles and practice, and that I could not and would not continue to act with any such a party." Norcross explained his walkout from the Whig Republican meeting with this letter. *Atlanta Constitution,* May 3, June 7, 1884. A. E. Buck was known as "Boss Buck" in Georgia. The matter of Arthur's illness versus his desire to win is a moot point, since he did put his name in contention for the nomination.

45   *Atlanta Constitution,* August 2, 1884.

46   Alice Bryant Zeller's Autobiography, JEB Papers.

47   O. E. Mitchell to Bryant, March 24, 1888, JEB Papers.

48   Unidentified clipping found in letter from Bryant to President Harrison, March 18, 1889, JEB Papers. Ironically, Speer had claimed that the carpetbaggers were "not creditable representatives of any party." His view had perhaps changed when Bryant backed his appointment for judge. See Shadgett, *Republican Party in Georgia,* 102–4.

49   Alice Bryant to John Bryant, January 15, 1889; Alice Bryant Zeller's Autobiography; Emma Bryant's sales slips and receipts, JEB Papers.

50   Bryant to President Benjamin Harrison, February 8, 9, March 18, 1889; Bryant to William Windom, secretary of the treasury, April 25, 1889; Bryant's speech, representing Grant Memorial University (East Tennessee Wesleyan), n.d.; unidentified newspaper clipping reporting Cable's speech, JEB Papers.

51   Bryant's speech, representing Grant Memorial University, JEB Papers.

52   John Bryant to Emma Bryant, November 19, 1889, JEB Papers.

53   John Bryant to Emma Bryant, September 25, 1891, JEB Papers.

54   John Bryant to Emma Bryant, September 25, 1891, JEB Papers.

55   Alice Bryant Zeller's Autobiography; John Bryant to Emma Bryant, September 25, 1891, JEB Papers.

56   Alice Bryant Zeller's Autobiography; Bryant's correspondence in 1890s, passim, JEB Papers. In operating the mission, Bryant and O. O. Howard found another mutual concern. JEB continued to correspond frequently with Howard

and to solicit his aid for various wards of the mission. Bryant and Howard also lunched together on occasion. See Bryant to O. O. Howard; O. O. Howard to Bryant correspondence, 1891–1895, Howard Papers.

57 Alice Bryant Zeller's Autobiography, JEB Papers.

58 Last Will and Testament, and Accompanying Documents, of John Emory Bryant, Surrogates' Court, County of Westchester, State of New York.

CONCLUSION: JOHN EMORY BRYANT IN RETROSPECT

1 Alice Bryant Zeller's Autobiography, JEB Papers.

2 See Ellen Carol DuBois, *Feminism and Suffrage: The Emergence of an Independent Women's Movement in America, 1848–1869* (Ithaca, N.Y.: Cornell University Press, 1978), 53–78, for a discussion of the Radicals' willingness to sacrifice feminist issues when debating the Fourteenth Amendment. In recent research, as yet unpublished, Eugene Genovese and Elizabeth Fox-Genovese have explored this inconsistency pointed out by Southerners.

3 See Otto H. Olsen, "Southern Reconstruction and the Question of Self-Determination," in *A Nation Divided: Problems and Issues of the Civil War and Reconstruction*, ed. George M. Frederickson (Minneapolis: Burgess Publishing, 1965), 113–41, for a helpful discussion of this issue and the role of the carpetbaggers.

Selected Bibliography

MANUSCRIPT COLLECTIONS

Foster Blodgett Papers. Special Collections, University of Georgia Library, Athens, Ga.
Joseph Emerson Brown Papers. Felix Hargrett Collection, University of Georgia Library, Athens, Ga.
John Emory Bryant Correspondence. Maine State Archives, Augusta, Maine.
John Emory Bryant Correspondence and Papers. American Missionary Association Archives, Amistad Research Center, New Orleans, La.
John Emory Bryant Papers. Manuscript Department, Perkins Library, Duke University, Durham, N.C.
Governor Rufus Bullock Correspondence. Georgia Department of Archives and History, Atlanta, Ga.
Elbridge G. Cabaniss Papers. Manuscript Department, Perkins Library, Duke University, Durham, N.C.
William E. Chandler Papers. Library of Congress, Washington, D.C.
Henry Crydenwise Papers. Manuscript Department, Perkins Library, Duke University, Durham, N.C.
The DeRenne Collection. Special Collections, University of Georgia Library, Athens, Ga.
Henry P. Farrow Papers. Special Collections, University of Georgia Library, Athens, Ga.
Rutherford B. Hayes Papers. Rutherford B. Hayes Presidential Center, Fremont, Ohio.
O. O. Howard Papers. Special Collections, Bowdoin College Library, Brunswick, Maine.
Edward W. Kinsley Papers. Manuscript Department, Perkins Library, Duke University, Durham, N.C.
Reconstruction File. Georgia Department of Archives and History, Atlanta, Ga.
Ella Thomas Papers. Manuscript Department, Perkins Library, Duke University, Durham, N.C.
Albion Winegar Tourgée Papers. Chautauqua County Historical Society, Westfield, N.Y.

Selected Bibliography

MANUSCRIPT COLLECTIONS CANVASSED

James G. Blaine Papers. Library of Congress, Washington, D.C.
Benjamin F. Butler Papers. Library of Congress, Washington, D.C.
William Chaflin Papers. Rutherford B. Hayes Presidential Library, Fremont, Ohio.
William Pitt Fessenden Collection. Bowdoin College, Brunswick, Maine.
William Pitt Fessenden Collection. Library of Congress, Washington, D.C.
U.S. Grant Papers. Chicago Historical Society, Chicago.
U.S. Grant Papers. Henry H. Huntington Library, San Marino, Calif.
U.S. Grant Papers. Illinois State Historical Society, Springfield, Ill.
U.S. Grant Papers. Library of Congress, Washington, D.C.
U.S. Grant Papers. New York Historical Society, New York.
U.S. Grant Papers. Rutherford B. Hayes Presidential Library, Fremont, Ohio.
Alexander Stephens Papers. Emory University, Atlanta, Ga.
Alexander Stephens Papers. Historical Society of Pennsylvania, Philadelphia.
Alexander and Linton Stephens Papers. Manhattanville College, Purchase, N.Y.
Charles Sumner Correspondence. Houghton Library, Harvard University, Cambridge, Mass.
Charles Sumner Correspondence. Massachusetts Historical Society, Boston.

DOCUMENTS

Chandler, Allen D., comp. *The Confederate Records of the State of Georgia*. Atlanta, Ga., 1911.
Congressional Globe. 41st Cong., 2d sess., 42, pt. 6. Washington, D.C., 1870.
Custom House Nominations, Savannah, Ga. (June 1871–October, 1877). Record Group 56 (Treasury Department). National Archives, Washington, D.C.
General Court Martial, [Proceedings in the case of] Capt. John E. Bryant, Co. "C," 8th Maine Vols., Headquarters, U.S. Forces, Port Royal Island, Beaufort, S.C., January 23, 1863. National Archives, Washington, D.C.
Journal of the House of Representatives of the State of Georgia, 1868–1870. Macon, Ga., 1870
Journal of the Senate of the State of Georgia, 1868–1869. Macon, Ga., 1869.
Last Will and Testament, and Accompanying Documents, of John Emory Bryant. Surrogates' Court, County of Westchester, State of New York.
Monroe, David S., ed. *Journal of the General Conference of the Methodist Episcopal Church, Held in Philadelphia, Pa., May 1–28, 1884*. New York: Phillips & Hunt, 1884.
Registers and Letters Received by the Commissioner of the Bureau of Refugees, Freedmen, and Abandoned Lands, 1865–1872. Microcopy 752. National Archives, Washington, D.C.
U.S. Congress. House. *Miscellaneous Documents*. 40th Cong., 3d sess. Washington, D.C., 1869.
U.S. Congress. House. *Report of the Joint Committee on Reconstruction*. 39th Cong., 1st sess., pt. 3. Washington, D.C., 1866.

U.S. Congress. Senate. *Index to the Reports of the Committees of the Senate of the United States.* 41st Cong., 2d sess. Washington, D.C., 1870.
U.S. Statutes at Large, Washington, D.C., 1868.
War of the Rebellion, Official Records of the Union and Confederate Armies. Washington, D.C., 1894–1900.

NEWSPAPERS

Athens Blade. 1879–1880, scattered issues.
Athens Southern Banner. 1869–1872.
Atlanta Constitution. 1868–1900.
Atlanta Daily New Era. 1866–1868.
Atlanta Methodist Advocate. 1869–1883.
Atlanta Southern Advance. 1882–1886, scattered issues.
Atlanta Weekly Defiance. October 3, 1885.
Augusta Constitutionalist. December 1867–February 1868.
Augusta Daily Press. January–April 1869.
Augusta Loyal Georgian. 1866–1868, scattered issues.
Augusta National Republican. July–December 1868.
Macon Daily Telegraph. 1865, scattered issues.
Macon Georgia Weekly Telegraph. 1860–1863; 1865–1868.
New York Times. 1862–1863; 1880s.

PRINTED PRIMARY SOURCES

Ames, Blanche Butler, comp. *Chronicles from the Nineteenth Century: Family Letters of Blanche Butler and Adelbert Ames.* 2 vols. Clinton, Mass.: Colonial Press, 1957.
Caldwell, John H. *Reminiscences of the Reconstruction of Church and State in Georgia.* Wilmington, Del.: Thomas, 1895.
Phillips, Ulrich Bonnell, ed. *The Correspondence of Robert Toombs, Alexander Stephens, and Howell Cobb.* Washington, D.C.: American Historical Association. 1913.
Stearns, Charles. *The Black Man of the South and the Rebels.* New York: American News, 1872.

MONOGRAPHS

Abbott, Martin. *The Freedmen's Bureau in South Carolina, 1865–1872.* Chapel Hill: University of North Carolina Press, 1967.
Avery, Isaac Wheeler. *The City of Atlanta.* Louisville: Inter-state Publishing, 1892–1893.
———. *The History of the State of Georgia from 1850 to 1881.* New York: Brown & Derby, 1881.
Beale, Howard K. *The Critical Year: A Study of Andrew Johnson and Reconstruction.* New York: Ungar, 1958.

Belz, Herman. *A New Birth of Freedom: The Republican Party and Freedmen's Rights, 1861–1866*. Westport, Conn.: Greenwood Press, 1976.

———. *Reconstructing the Union: Theory and Policy During the Civil War*. Ithaca, N.Y.: Cornell University Press, 1969.

Bentley, George R. *A History of the Freedmen's Bureau*. Philadelphia: University of Pennsylvania Press, 1955.

Bernstein, Barton J., ed. *Towards a New Past: Dissenting Essays in American History*. New York: Vintage, 1969.

Berry, Mary Frances. *Military Necessity and Civil Rights Policy: Black Citizenship and the Constitution, 1861–1868*. Port Washington, N.Y.: Kennikat Press, 1977.

Berwanger, Eugene H. *The Frontier Against Slavery: Western Anti-Negro Prejudice and the Slavery Extension Controversy*. Urbana: University of Illinois Press, 1967.

Butchart, Ronald E. *Northern Schools, Southern Blacks, and Reconstruction: Freedmen's Education, 1862–1875*. Westport, Conn.: Greenwood Press, 1980.

Carse, Robert. *Department of the South: Hilton Head Island in the Civil War*. Columbia, S.C.: State Printing, 1961.

Carter, Dan T. *When the War Was Over: The Failure of Self-Reconstruction in the South, 1865–1867*. Baton Rouge: Louisiana State University Press, 1985.

Carter, Hodding. *Their Words Were Bullets: The Southern Press in War, Reconstruction, and Peace*. Athens: University of Georgia Press, 1969.

Coleman, Kenneth, ed., *A History of Georgia*. Athens: University of Georgia Press, 1977.

Coleman, Kenneth, and Charles S. Gurr, eds. *Dictionary of Georgia Biography*. 2 vols. Athens: University of Georgia Press, 1983.

Conway, Alan. *The Reconstruction of Georgia*. Minneapolis: University of Minnesota Press, 1966.

Cornish, Dudley Taylor. *The Sable Arm*. New York: Longmans, Green, 1956.

Coulter, E. Merton. *Negro Legislators in Georgia During the Reconstruction Period*. Athens: Georgia Historical Quarterly, 1968.

———. *The South During Reconstruction*. Baton Rouge: Louisiana State University Press, 1947.

Cox, Lawanda. *Lincoln and Black Freedom: A Study in Presidential Leadership*. Columbia: University of South Carolina Press, 1981.

Cox, Lawanda, and John H. Cox. *Politics, Principles, and Prejudice, 1861–1866*. London: Collier-Macmillan, 1963.

Craven, Avery. *Reconstruction: The Ending of the Civil War*. New York: Holt, Rinehart & Winston, 1969.

Cruden, Robert. *The Negro in Reconstruction*. Englewood Cliffs, N.J.: Prentice-Hall, 1969.

Current, Richard N. *Northernizing the South*. Athens: University of Georgia Press, 1983.

———, ed. *Reconstruction in Retrospect: Views from the Turn of the Century*. Baton Rouge: Louisiana State University Press, 1969.

Curry, Richard O., ed. *Radicalism, Racism, and Party Realignment: The Border States During Reconstruction.* Baltimore: Johns Hopkins University Press, 1969.
Davison, Kenneth V. *The Presidency of Rutherford B. Hayes.* Westport, Conn.: Greenwood Press, 1972.
Degler, Carl N. *The Other South: Southern Dissenters in the Nineteenth Century.* New York: Harper & Row, 1974.
_____. *Out of Our Past: The Forces That Shaped Modern America.* New York: Harper & Row, 1959.
DeSantis, Vincent P. *Republicans Face the Southern Questions: The New Departure Years, 1877–1897.* Baltimore: Johns Hopkins University Press, 1959.
Drago, Edmund L. *Black Politicians and Reconstruction in Georgia: A Splendid Failure.* Baton Rouge: Louisiana State University Press, 1982.
Duberman, Martin B., ed. *The Antislavery Vanguard: New Essays on the Abolitionists.* Princeton: Princeton University Press, 1965.
Durden, Robert F. *James Shepherd Pike: Republicanism and the American Negro, 1850–1882.* Durham, N.C.: Duke University Press, 1957.
Edelstein, Tilden G. *Strange Enthusiasm: A Life of Thomas Wentworth Higginson.* New Haven: Yale University Press, 1968.
Fielder, Herbert. *A Sketch of the Life and Times and Speeches of Joseph E. Brown.* Springfield, Mass.: Press of Springfield Printing, 1883.
Filler, Louis. *The Crusade Against Slavery, 1830–1860.* New York: Harper & Row, 1960.
Fleming, Walter Lynwood. *The Sequel of Appomattox: A Chronicle of the Reunion of the States.* New Haven: Yale University Press, 1920.
Foner, Eric. *Free Soil, Free Labor, Free Men: The Ideology of the Republican Party Before the Civil War.* New York: Oxford University Press, 1970.
_____. *Politics and Ideology in the Age of the Civil War.* New York: Oxford University Press, 1980.
Frederickson, George M. *The Black Image in the White Mind: The Debate on Afro-American Character and Destiny, 1817–1914.* New York: Harper & Row, 1971.
_____. *The Inner Civil War: Northern Intellectuals and the Crisis of the Union.* New York: Harper & Row, 1965.
_____, ed. *A Nation Divided: Problems and Issues of the Civil War and Reconstruction.* Minneapolis: Burgess Publishing, 1965.
Genovese, Eugene D. *The Political Economy of Slavery: Studies in the Economy and Society of the Slave South.* New York: Vintage, 1965.
Gillette, William. *Retreat from Reconstruction, 1865–1879.* Baton Rouge: Louisiana State University Press, 1979.
Gravely, William B. *Gilbert Haven, Methodist Abolitionist: A Study in Race, Religion, and Reform, 1850–1880.* Nashville: Abingdon, 1973.
Grizzell, Emit Duncan. *Origin and Development of the High School in New England Before 1865.* New York: Macmillan, 1923.
Higginson, Thomas Wentworth. *Army Life in a Black Regiment.* Boston: Fields,

Osgood, 1870. Reprint. East Lansing: Michigan State University Press, 1960.

Hirshon, Stanley P. *Farewell to the Bloody Shirt: Northern Republicans and the Southern Negro, 1877–1893.* Bloomington: Indiana University Press, 1962.

Hofstadter, Richard. *American Political Tradition and the Men Who Made It.* New York: Vintage, 1948.

Hudson, Winthrop S. *Religion in America.* New York: Scribner, 1965.

Jones, Jacqueline. *Soldiers of Light and Love: Northern Teachers and Georgia Blacks, 1865–1873.* Chapel Hill: University of North Carolina Press, 1980.

Kousser, J. Morgan, and James M. McPherson, eds. *Race, Region, and Reconstruction: Essays in Honor of C. Vann Woodward.* New York: Oxford University Press, 1982.

Lacy, Dan. *The White Use of Blacks in America.* New York: Atheneum, 1972.

Litwack, Leon F. *Been in the Storm So Long: The Aftermath of Slavery.* New York: Knopf, 1979.

Loye, David. *The Healing of a Nation.* New York: Norton, 1971.

McFeely, William S. *Grant: A Biography.* New York: Norton, 1981.

———. *Yankee Stepfather: General O. O. Howard and the Freedman.* New Haven: Yale University Press, 1968.

McKitrick, Eric L. *Andrew Johnson and Reconstruction.* Chicago: University of Chicago Press, 1960.

McManus, Edgar J. *Black Bondage in the North.* Syracuse, N.Y.: Syracuse University Press, 1973.

McPherson, James M. *The Abolitionist Legacy: From Reconstruction to the NAACP.* Princeton: Princeton University Press, 1975.

———. *The Negro's Civil War.* New York: Vintage, 1967.

———. *The Struggle for Equality: Abolitionists and the Negro in the Civil War and Reconstruction.* Princeton: Princeton University Press, 1964.

Mayer, George H. *The Republican Party, 1854–1966.* New York: Oxford University Press, 1967.

Mohr, James C., ed., and Richard E. Winslow III, assoc. ed. *The Cormany Diaries: A Northern Family in the Civil War.* Pittsburgh: University of Pittsburgh Press, 1982.

Montgomery, David. *Beyond Equality: Labor and Radical Republicans, 1862–1872.* New York: Knopf, 1967.

Morris, Robert. *Reading, 'Riting, and Reconstruction: The Education of Freedmen in the South, 1861–1870.* Chicago: University of Chicago Press, 1981.

Morrow, Ralph E. *Northern Methodism and Reconstruction.* East Lansing: Michigan State University Press, 1956.

Nathans, Elizabeth Studley. *Losing the Peace: Georgia Republicans and Reconstruction, 1865–1871.* Baton Rouge: Louisiana State University Press, 1968.

Oakes, James. *The Ruling Class: A History of American Slaveholders.* New York: Knopf, 1982.

Olsen, Otto H. *Carpetbagger's Crusade: The Life of Albion Winegar Tourgée.* Baltimore: Johns Hopkins University Press, 1965.

―――, ed. *Reconstruction and Redemption in the South*. Baton Rouge: Louisiana State University Press, 1980.
Oubre, Claude F. *Forty Acres and a Mule: The Freedmen's Bureau and Black Land Ownership*. Baton Rouge: Louisiana State University Press, 1978.
Painter, Nell Irvin. *The Exodusters: Black Migration to Kansas After Reconstruction*. New York: Knopf, 1977.
Parks, Joseph H. *Joseph E. Brown of Georgia*. Baton Rouge: Louisiana State University Press, 1977.
Patrick, Rembert Wallace. *The Reconstruction of the Nation*. New York: Oxford University Press, 1967.
Perman, Michael. *Reunion Without Compromise: The South and Reconstruction, 1865–1868*. Cambridge: Cambridge University Press, 1973.
―――. *The Road to Redemption: Southern Politics, 1869–1879*. Chapel Hill: University of North Carolina Press, 1984.
Phillips, Ulrich Bonnell. *The Life of Robert Toombs*. New York: Macmillan, 1913.
Potter, David M. *The Impending Crisis, 1848–1861*. New York: Harper & Row, 1976.
―――. *The South and the Sectional Conflict*. Baton Rouge: Louisiana State University Press, 1968.
Powell, Lawrence N. *New Masters: Northern Planters in the Civil War and Reconstruction*. New Haven: Yale University Press, 1980.
Quarles, Benjamin. *The Negro in the Civil War*. New York: Russell & Russell, 1968.
Rable, George C. *But There Was No Peace: The Role of Violence in the Politics of Reconstruction*. Athens: University of Georgia Press, 1984.
Randall, J. G., and David Donald. *The Civil War and Reconstruction*. 2d ed. Boston: Heath, 1961.
Ransom, Roger L., and Richard Sutch. *One Kind of Freedom: The Economic Consequences of Emancipation*. New York: Cambridge University Press, 1977.
Reagan, Alice E. *H. I. Kimball, Entrepreneur*. Atlanta: Cherokee, 1983.
Reed, Wallace Putnam. *History of Atlanta, Georgia*. Syracuse, N.Y.: Mason, 1889.
Richards, Leonard L. *Gentlemen of Property and Standing: Anti-Abolition Mobs in Jacksonian America*. New York: Oxford University Press, 1970.
Roark, James L. *Masters Without Slaves: Southern Planters in the Civil War and Reconstruction*. New York: Norton, 1977.
Rose, Willie Lee. *Rehearsal for Reconstruction: The Port Royal Experiment*. New York: Vintage, 1964.
Sefton, James E. *The United States Army and Reconstruction, 1865–1877*. Baton Rouge: Louisiana State University Press, 1967.
Shadgett, Olive Hall. *The Republican Party in Georgia from Reconstruction Through 1900*. Athens: University of Georgia Press, 1964.
Sherburne, James. *The Way to Fort Pillow*. Boston: Houghton Mifflin, 1972.

228 | Selected Bibliography

Sibley, John Langdon. *History of the Town of Union, in the County of Lincoln, Maine.* Boston: Mussey, 1851.
Simpson, Mathew, ed. *Cyclopaedia of Methodism,* 4th rev. ed. Philadelphia: Everts, 1881.
Small, Walter Herbert. *Early New England Schools.* Boston: Ginn, 1914.
Stampp, Kenneth M., ed. *Causes of the Civil War.* Englewood Cliffs, N.J.: Prentice-Hall, 1965.
Stampp, Kenneth M., and Leon F. Litwack, eds. *Reconstruction: An Anthology of Revisionist Writings.* Baton Rouge: Louisiana State University Press, 1969.
Swint, Henry Lee. *The Northern Teacher in the South, 1862–1870.* New York: Octagon Books, 1967.
Talmadge, John E. *Rebecca Latimer Felton: Nine Stormy Decades.* Athens: University of Georgia Press, 1960.
Thompson, Clara Mildred. *Reconstruction in Georgia: Economic, Social, and Political, 1865–1872.* New York: Columbia University Press, 1915.
Thornbrough, E. L., ed. *Black Reconstructionists.* Englewood Cliffs, N.J.: Prentice-Hall, 1972.
Tourgée, Albion W. *A Fool's Errand, by One of the Fools.* New York: Fords, Howard & Herbert, 1879.
Tyler, Alice Felt. *Freedom's Ferment: Phases of American Social History to 1860.* Minneapolis: University of Minnesota Press, 1944.
Walker, Margaret. *Jubilee.* Boston: Houghton Mifflin, 1966.
Whitman, William E. S., and Charles H. True. *Maine in the War for the Union.* Lewiston, Maine: Dingley, 1865.
Williamson, Joel. *After Slavery: The Negro in South Carolina During Reconstruction, 1861–1877.* Chapel Hill: University of North Carolina Press, 1965.
Wilson, Joseph Thomas. *The Black Phalanx.* 1890. Reprint. New York: Arno, 1968.
Woodward, C. Vann. *American Counterpoint: Slavery and Racism in the North-South Dialogue.* Boston: Little, Brown, 1971.
―――. *The Burden of Southern History.* Rev. ed. New York: Mentor, 1960.
―――. *Origins of the New South, 1877–1913.* Baton Rouge: Louisiana State University Press, 1967.
―――. *Reunion and Reaction: The Compromise of 1877 and the End of Reconstruction.* Boston: Little, Brown, 1951.

ARTICLES IN PERIODICAL LITERATURE

Ahern, Wilbert H. "Laissez Faire vs. Equal Rights: Liberal Republicans and Limits to Reconstruction." *Phylon* 40 (March 1979): 52–65.
Belz, Herman. "The Freedmen's Bureau Act of 1865 and the Principle of No Discrimination According to Color." *Civil War History* 21, no. 3 (September 1975): 197–217.
Brandon, William P. "Calling the Georgia Constitutional Convention of 1877." *Georgia Historical Quarterly* 17 (September 1933): 189–203.

Carter, Dan T. "The Anatomy of Fear: The Christmas Day Insurrection Scare of 1865." *Journal of Southern History* 42 (August 1976): 345–64.
Cason, Roberta F. "The Loyal League in Georgia." *Georgia Historical Quarterly* 20 (June 1936): 125–53.
Chafe, William H. "The Negro and Populism: A Kansas Case Study." *Journal of Southern History* 34 (August 1968): 402–19.
Cimbala, Paul. "The Talisman Power: Davis Tillson, the Freedmen's Bureau, and Free Labor in Reconstruction Georgia, 1865–1866." *Civil War History* 28, no. 2 (June 1982), 153–71.
Coleman, Kenneth. "The Georgia Gubernatorial Election of 1880." *Georgia Historical Quarterly* 25 (June 1941): 89–117.
Coulter, E. Merton. "Henry M. Turner, Georgia Negro Preacher-Politician During the Reconstruction Era." *Georgia Historical Quarterly* 48 (December 1964): 371–410.
Currie-McDaniel, Ruth. "Black Power in Georgia: William A. Pledger and the Takeover of the Republican Party." *Georgia Historical Quarterly* 62 (Fall 1978): 225–39.
———. "Courtship and Marriage in the Nineteenth Century: Albion and Emma Tourgée, a Case Study." *North Carolina Historical Review* 61 (July 1984): 285–310.
Curry, Richard O. "The Abolitionists and Reconstruction: A Critical Appraisal." *Journal of Southern History* 34 (November 1968): 527–45.
Daniell, Elizabeth Otto. "The Ashburn Murder Case in Georgia Reconstruction, 1868." *Georgia Historical Quarterly* 59 (Fall 1975): 296–312.
Davis, David Brion. "The Emergence of Immediatism in British and American Antislavery Thought." *Mississippi University Historical Review* 49 (September 1962): 209–30.
Degler, Carl N. "Rethinking Post Civil War History." *Virginia Quarterly Review* 70 (Spring 1981): 250–67.
Durden, Robert F. "Abraham Lincoln: Honkie or Equalitarian?" *South Atlantic Quarterly* 71, no. 3 (Summer 1972): 281–91.
Freehling, William W. "The Founding Fathers and Slavery." *American Historical Review* 77 (1972): 81–93.
Friedel, Frank. "The Loyal Publication Society." *Mississippi Valley Historical Review* 26 (December 1939): 359–76.
Gambill, Edward L. "Who Were the Senate Radicals?" *Civil War History* 11, no. 3 (September 1965): 237–38.
Harris, William C. "The Creed of the Carpetbaggers: The Case of Mississippi." *Journal of Southern History* 40 (May 1974): 199–224.
Herndon, Jane. "Henry McNeal Turner's African Dream: A Re-evaluation." *Mississippi Quarterly* 22, no. 4 (1969): 327–36.
Hoffnagle, Warren. "The Southern Homestead Act: Its Origins and Operation." *Historian*, 32, no. 4 (August 1970): 612–29.
Klingman, Peter, and David Keithman. "Negro Dissidence and the Republican Party, 1864–1872." *Phylon* 40 (June 1979): 172–82.

Kinkaid, Larry. "Victims of Circumstance: An Interpretation of Changing Attitudes Toward Republican Policy Makers and Reconstruction." *Journal of American History* 57 (June 1970): 48–66.

Kolchin, Peter. "Scalawags, Carpetbaggers, and Reconstruction: A Quantitative Look at Southern Congressional Politics, 1868–1872." *Journal of Southern History* 45 (February 1979): 63–78.

Lebsock, Suzanne D. "Radical Reconstruction and the Property Rights of Southern Women." *Journal of Southern History* 43 (May 1977): 195–216.

McPherson, James M. "Coercion or Conciliation: Abolitionists Debate President Hayes' Southern Policy." *New England Quarterly* 39 (December 1966): 474–97.

———. "Many Abolitionists Fought On After the Civil War." *University: A Princeton Quarterly*, no. 39 (Winter 1968–1969): 14–18, 30–34.

Moore, James Tice. "Redeemers Reconsidered: Change and Continuity in the Democratic South, 1870–1900." *Journal of Southern History* 44 (August 1978): 357–78.

Murphy, William F. "A Note on the Significance of Names." *Psychoanalytic Quarterly* 26 (1957): 91–106.

Nichols, Roy F. "A Hundred Years Later: Perspectives on the Civil War." *Journal of Southern History* 33 (May 1967): 153–62.

Paludan, Phillip S. "The American Civil War Considered as a Crisis in Law and Order." *American Historical Review* 77, no. 4 (October 1972): 1013–34.

Pease, William H., and Jane H. Pease. "Antislavery Ambivalence: Immediatism, Expediency, Race." *American Quarterly* 17 (1965): 682–95.

Powell, Lawrence N. "The American Land Company and Agency: John A. Andrew and the Northernization of the South." *Civil War History* 21, no. 4 (December 1975), 293–308.

Rable, George C. "Bourbonism, Reconstruction, and the Persistence of Southern Distinctiveness." *Civil War History* 26, no. 4 (December 1980), 135–53.

———. "Southern Interests and the Election of 1876: A Reappraisal." *Civil War History* 26, no. 4 (December 1980): 347–61.

Redkey, Edwin S. "Bishop Turner's African Dream." *Journal of American History* 54 (September 1967): 271–90.

Riddleburger, Patrick W. "The Radicals' Abandonment of the Negro During Reconstruction." *Journal of Negro History* 45 (April 1960): 88–102.

Russ, William Adam, Jr. "Radical Disfranchisement in Georgia, 1867–1871." *Georgia Historical Quarterly* 19 (September 1935): 175–209.

Savitt, Todd. "Politics in Medicine: The Georgia Freedmen's Bureau and the Organization of Health Care, 1865–1866" *Civil War History* 28, no. 1 (March 1982): 45–64.

Shortreed, Margaret. "The Antislavery Radicals: From Crusade to Revolution, 1840–1868." *Past and Present* 16 (November 1959): 65–87.

Sproat, John G. "Blueprint for Radical Reconstruction." *Journal of Southern History* 23 (February 1957): 25–44.

Sweet, William Warren. "The Church as Moral Courts on the Frontier." *Church History* 2 (March 1933): 3–21.
Talmadge, John E. "The Death Blow to Independentism in Georgia." *Georgia Historical Quarterly* 39 (December 1955): 37–47.
Thomas, John L. "Romantic Reform in America, 1815–1865." *American Quarterly* 17 (Winter 1965): 656–81.
Ward, Judson C., Jr. "The Election of 1880 and Its Impact on Atlanta." *Atlanta Historical Society Journal* 25 (Spring 1981): 5–15.
―――. "The New Departure Democrats of Georgia: An Interpretation." *Georgia Historical Quarterly* 41 (September 1957): 227–36.
―――. "The Republican Party in Bourbon Georgia, 1872–1890." *Journal of Southern History* 9 (May 1943): 196–209.
Weisberger, Bernard A. "The Dark and Bloody Ground of Reconstruction Historiography." *Journal of Southern History* 25 (November 1959): 427–47.
Woodward, C. Vann. "Bourbonism in Georgia." *North Carolina Historical Review* 16 (January 1939): 25–35.
Wynne, Lewis N. "The Bourbon Triumvirate: A Reconsideration." *Atlanta Historical Society Journal* 24 (Summer 1980): 39–55.

UNPUBLISHED THESES

Bhurtel, Shyam Krishna. "Colonel Alfred Eliab Buck: Carpetbagger in Alabama and Georgia." Ph.D. diss., Auburn University, 1981.
Bloom, Charles G. "The Georgia Election of April, 1868: A Reexamination of the Politics of Georgia Reconstruction." M.A. thesis, University of Chicago, 1963.
Cimbala, Paul. "The Terms of Freedom: The Freedmen's Bureau and Reconstruction in Georgia, 1865–1870." Ph.D. diss., Emory University, 1983.
Hume, Richard L. "The 'Black and Tan' Constitutional Conventions of 1867–1869 in Ten Former Confederate States: A Study of Their Membership." Ph.D. diss., University of Washington, 1969.
Matthews, John Michael. "The Negro in Georgia Politics, 1865–1880." M.A. thesis, Duke University, 1967.
Miller, Herman. "Congressional Reconstruction as a Means of Perpetuating Radical Republicanism." M.A. thesis, Emory University, 1934.
Smith, Allen Chandler. "The Republican Party in Georgia, 1867–1871." M.A. thesis, Duke University, 1937.
Smith, Wallace Calvin. "Rufus B. Bullock and the Third Reconstruction of Georgia, 1867–1871." M.A. thesis, University of North Carolina, 1964.
Stipe, Carl Evans. "Colonel Alfred Aliab Buck." M.A. thesis, Emory University, 1944.
Ward, Judson Clements, Jr. "Georgia Under the Bourbon Democrats, 1872–1890." Ph.D. diss., University of North Carolina, 1947.

Index

Abbott, Martin, 49
Abolitionism, 13, 15, 24, 32, 44, 78, 155
Adams, John, 5
African Methodist Episcopal Church, 61
Akerman, Amos T., 84, 85, 87, 95, 99, 104, 109, 112–14, 117, 125, 202 (n. 18), 208 (nn. 89, 94, 96)
American Missionary Association (AMA), 27, 47, 63–64, 105, 148
American party, 14
Ames, Adelbert, 205 (n. 50), 208 (n. 89)
Angier, Nedom L., 99
Annapolis, Maryland, 19–20
Antislavery. See Abolitionism
"Antislavery myth," 16
Appomattox, 42, 158
Arthur, Chester, 168, 174, 219 (n. 44)
Ashburn, George W., 88, 203 (n. 28)
Athens, Georgia, 108
Athens, Tennessee, 176
Atkins, James, 121, 125, 133, 135, 137–39, 141–43, 166, 168, 181
Atlanta, Georgia, 45, 105, 125, 135, 145, 149, 161–62, 167, 169, 172, 173, 176, 180
Atlanta Methodist Advocate. See *Methodist Advocate*
Atlanta Publishing Company, 145–46, 157, 160, 168
Atlanta Republican, 145–46, 157, 160, 165
Atlanta Republican Publishing Company. See Atlanta Publishing Company
Augusta, Georgia, 49–51, 54, 57, 66–67, 72, 74, 76, 80, 85, 87, 99, 103–4, 106, 124–25, 180

Augusta, Maine, 19
"Augusta ring," 80, 84–88, 90, 140, 202 (n. 14)

Bangor, Maine, 14
Bard, Samuel, 100, 102, 117, 130–31, 206 (n. 59)
Battle of the Crater, 40
Bay Point, South Carolina, 20
Beaird, Simeon, 200 (n. 76)
Beaufort, South Carolina, 30, 40
Belcher, Edwin, 122–23, 131, 136, 138, 180, 206 (n. 66)
Bingham Amendment, 112
Black codes, 42, 66
Black Republicans, 17, 187 (n. 38)
Black schools, 59, 62, 64, 160. See also Public education
Black soldiers, 13, 24, 31–37
Black teachers, 63, 198 (n. 50)
Blade (Athens), 133, 135, 151, 153
Blaine, James G., 166, 174
Blodgett, Foster, 80, 84, 86, 89–92, 98, 100–101, 103–5, 108–11, 114–16, 121, 138, 178, 204 (n. 39), 207 (n. 69)
Board of Education of the Georgia Educational Association, 64. See also Georgia Educational Association
Bourbons, 132–33, 143, 146–47, 151, 158, 167, 211 (n. 34), 215 (n. 70)
Bowles, John, 112
Bradley, Aaron A., 204 (n. 43)
Brisbane, William Henry, 35
Bristol, Maine, 5
Brown, Joseph E., 80, 83, 85–86, 92, 94, 98–99, 106, 109, 111, 113–14, 116,

234 | Index

Brown, Joseph E. *(continued)*
125, 127–28, 133, 151, 169, 203 (n. 28), 204 (n. 38), 205 (n. 47), 213 (n. 47)
Brunswick and Albany Railroad Company, 141
Bryant, Benjamin, 5–7, 10
Bryant, Benjamin, Jr., 7
Bryant, Betsey, 5
Bryant, Emma Alice (Zeller), 11, 124, 126, 131–32, 137, 149–50, 156, 170, 172, 175–76, 178, 179, 210 (n. 10), 211 (n. 34)
Bryant, Emma Spaulding, 10–11, 17, 22–23, 27–28, 34–36, 38–41, 49–50, 66–67, 72, 80–81, 91, 97, 103, 105, 124–26, 131–32, 137, 149–50, 156, 169–72, 177–79, 181–82, 203 (n. 22), 218 (n. 37)
Buck, A. E., 166–68, 174, 219 (n. 44)
Buckfield, Maine, 17, 24, 207 (n. 76)
Bullock, Rufus, 80, 84–92, 95–103, 105–17, 121–22, 127, 137–38, 141–42, 178, 206 (n. 57), 212–13 (n. 47)
Bureau of Refugees, Freedmen, and Abandoned Lands. *See* Freedmen's Bureau
Butler, Benjamin, 24–25, 208 (n. 89)

Cabaniss, Elbridge G., 102
Cable, George Washington, 176–77
Caldwell, John, 89–95, 97, 100, 115, 181, 208 (n. 89)
Calliopen Society, 12–14
Camilla (Georgia) riot, 96
Campbell, Tunis G., 129, 200 (n. 76)
Charleston, South Carolina, 20, 51
Chase, Salmon P., 16
Chatham County, Georgia, 140–42
Chicago, Illinois, 126, 174
Christmas Day riot fears, 56
Cincinnati, Ohio, 135
Civil and Political Rights Association, 95, 101, 107
Civil Rights Bill (1874), 129
Clark, John G., 138–39, 168
Clark, W. L., 145–46, 157, 165, 182
Clay, Henry, 5
Cleveland, Ohio, 126
Clift, J. W., 104, 211 (n. 24)

Clift, W. L., 130, 132, 134, 138, 142, 145, 210–11 (n. 24)
Colored American, 65
Colquitt, Alfred H., 135, 139
Combahee River, 37
Compromise of 1850, 32
Conley, Benjamin, 80, 84, 115
Conley, John L., 140–41, 166, 173
Constitution (Atlanta), 109, 165, 172, 174, 219 (n. 44)
Constitution of Georgia (1868): office-holding rights, 83–84, 94, 102, 129; franchise clause, 83–85, 129; relief clause, 84, 87; women's property rights, 202 (n. 17)
Constitutional Convention of 1868, 81–82, 129, 180
Constitutional Convention of 1877, 146–47
Contraband of war, 24–25. *See also* Black soldiers
Contracts, 52, 55, 196 (n. 34)
Cooper, Sarah Jane, 182, 201 (n. 11)
"Coosaw Island," 35
Court martial (Bryant), 30
Creswell, J. A. A., 104
Current, Richard, 43
"Custom House Ring," 133, 137

Daily Chronicle and Sentinel (Augusta), 55
Daily New Era (Atlanta), 83, 86
Daily Press (Augusta), 99
Darnell, S. A., 148
Darwin, Charles, 120
Democratic Redeemers, 118, 144, 155
"Department of the South," 19, 26, 32, 37
Derry, Joseph T., 158
Devereaux, John H., 174, 199 (n. 67)
Dudley, Jim, 151
DuPont, Samuel Francis, 20

East Tennessee Wesleyan University, 176
Earlville, Illinois, 72
Eberhart, G. L., 59, 63–64
Eberhart, Maria, 80
Eighth Maine, Company "C," 19–20, 41
Eighth Maine Infantry Regiment, 19–20, 23, 30, 32–34, 37–41
Ellijay, Georgia, 161

Emancipation Proclamation, 26, 31, 35, 61
Emory, John, 5
Exeter Academy, 4
Exposition, 14, 39, 187 (n. 30)
Expulsion of blacks, 94–96, 102, 106–7. See also Constitutional Convention of 1868

Farrow, Henry P., 62, 81, 85–86, 89, 110, 122, 125, 133–35, 141, 146, 151, 158–59, 165–68, 172–73, 180–81, 217 (nn. 8, 24)
Fayette, Maine, 5
Felton, William L., 133, 151, 166
Fifteenth Amendment, 102, 107, 111, 116, 207 (n. 75), 208 (n. 89)
Fifty-first Massachusetts Regiment, 32
First South Carolina Volunteers, 26–27, 31–33, 35–37
Foner, Eric, 15
Fool's Errand, 157
Fort Pulaski, 20
Fortress Monroe, Virginia, 24
Fort Sumter, 18
Fourteenth Amendment, 74, 111, 205 (n. 47), 220 (n. 2)
Frederickson, George, 13, 15
"Free common schools," 136. See also Public education
Freedmen's Aid Society, 160
Freedmen's Bureau, 41, 43–45, 47–49, 51–52, 54–59, 62–64, 66–73, 79, 89, 97, 104–5, 138, 181, 193 (n. 17), 194 (n. 18)
Freedmen's Bureau Bill (1866), 69, 70
Freedmen's Bureau contracts. See Contracts
"Free Soil," 15–16
Frémont, John C., 17, 25
French, Mansfield, 27, 30, 37, 44, 47, 50, 181
Fuller, Erasmus Q., 153, 159–61, 163, 169–71, 181–82
Fullerton, Joseph S., 69–70
Fulton County, Georgia, 135
Fusion politics, 109–10

Garfield, James A., 165, 168
Garrison, William Lloyd, 104

Genovese, Eugene, 49
Georgia Educational Association, 62–64, 74, 196 (n. 38)
Georgia Equal Rights and Educational Association, 74
Georgia Equal Rights Association (GERA), 57–66, 69, 71, 74, 79, 82, 92, 105, 180
Georgia Publishing Company, 74, 90. See also Loyal Georgian Publishing Company
Georgia Republican, 105, 112, 121, 124, 127, 146, 149–50. See also *Loyal Georgian*, *Southern Advance* and *Georgia Republican*
Georgia Republican Association, 132, 134, 143, 213 (n. 53)
Gillette, William, 120
Gillmore, Quincy A., 37–38
Glynn County, Georgia, 133
Gordon, John B., 87, 138
Grant, Ulysses S., 96–97, 104, 107, 109, 112, 115, 118, 125, 142, 207 (n. 75), 208 (nn. 89, 96)
Greeley, Horace, 127–28, 192 (n. 6)
Griffin, Georgia, 104

Hale, M. H., 123
Hamlin, Hannibal, 39
Hampton, Wade, 158
Harris, A. L. ("Fatty"), 108
Hartridge, Julian, 140
Haven, Gilbert, 163
Hayes, Rutherford B., 118, 120–21, 140, 143–46, 150–51, 157, 166, 214 (n. 59)
Hayes directive (1877), 145
Higginson, Thomas Wentworth, 32–35, 37–38, 47, 49
Hill, Benjamin, 87, 114, 140
Hill, Joshua, 89, 92, 110, 117, 125
Hilton Head, South Carolina, 20
Homestead Act (1862), 47. See also Southern Homestead Act
Homesteading, 193 (n. 15)
Howard, Oliver Otis, 46–49, 51, 54–55, 61, 67–68, 70, 73, 97, 104–6, 219 (n. 56)
Hume, Richard, 82
Hunter, David M., 25–26, 31

Independents of Georgia, 133, 139–40, 146, 151, 165–67, 175, 211–12 (n. 36), 212 (n. 38)

Jackson, Andrew, 5
Jacksonville, Florida, 51
Jefferson, Thomas, 5
Johnson, Andrew, 42, 47, 52, 54, 61, 69, 78, 128
Johnson, James, 71
Journal (Providence), 158, 173

Kansas-Nebraska Bill, 15–16
Kent's Hill, Maine, 6, 12, 14
Key to Uncle Tom's Cabin, 9, 13
Kimball, Hannibal I., 99, 114, 116, 206 (n. 57)
Kimball Opera House, 99
King, Thomas S., 172
Know-Nothings. *See* American party
Ku Klux Klan, 78, 87–88, 96, 107, 113–16, 136

LaGrange, Georgia, 89
Lee, Robert E., 158
Lewis, John R., 64, 105–6
Liberal Republicans, 127–28
Liberty laws, 32
Lincoln, Abraham, 17–18, 24–26, 42, 47, 61
Long, John D., 180
Long Island, New York, 20
Longstreet, James, 165–66, 174
Louisville, Kentucky, 144
Loyal Georgian, 57–58, 64–65, 69, 71–72, 74, 79, 87, 90, 100, 105, 145. *See also Georgia Republican*
Loyal Georgian Publishing Company, 73–74, 200 (n. 76). *See also* Georgia Publishing Company
Lyceum, 12, 27

McFeely, William, 46, 54
McDowell, H. T., 86
McKinley, William, 180
Macon, Georgia, 70, 74, 95, 158
McPherson, James, 155
McWhorter, R. L., 110
Maine Wesleyan Seminary, 6, 12

Marietta, Georgia, 84
Marietta Street Methodist Episcopal Church, 162
"Markam House Conference," 166. *See also* "Syndicate"
Meade, George C., 87, 94
Mechanics and Laborers Association, 105
Memphis, Tennessee, 144
Methodist Advocate (Atlanta), 153, 159–60, 211 (n. 31), 216 (n. 4)
Methodist Episcopal Church, North, 159–60; General Conference (1880), 161; General Conference (1884), 162–64
Methodist Episcopal Church, South, 159
Militia Act (1792), 26
Military, gambling and drinking, 22, 27, 30
Milledgeville, Georgia, 147
Miller, H. V. M., 92, 110
Millerites, 10, 186 (n. 17)
Missouri Compromise, 15
Moderate Republicans (Georgia), 98, 201–2 (n. 14)
Monroe, James, 5
Montgomery, James, 34
Mount Vernon, New York, 178–79
Mount Washington (New Hampshire), 9

Napoleon I, 5
National Era (Washington), 16
"National Republican Party of the Union," 80. *See also* Republican party
Nativism, 14
Negro code. *See* Black codes
Negrophobia, 16
New Era (Atlanta), 100, 102, 110, 130
New South, 49, 116, 155
New York, New York, 80, 85, 149, 162, 172, 176, 179
Norcross, Jonathan, 135–37, 139, 141, 151, 165, 175, 219 (n. 44)
North Wayne, Maine, 7–8, 17
Northern Methodist Church. *See* Methodist Episcopal Church, North

Oakes, James, 49
Ocean Grove, New Jersey, 172
Omnibus Bill (1868), 205 (n. 47)

Ostracizing of whites, 44, 66–67, 147, 192 (n. 7), 199–200 (n. 72)

Packard (teacher), 170
Palmer, Benjamin M., 216 (n. 5)
Paternalism, 49, 55, 58, 155
Perman, Michael, 110
Petersburg, Virginia, 40
Philadelphia, Pennsylvania, 72, 149, 172
Pittsfield, Massachusetts, 176
Pledger, William A., 133–37, 151–53, 164–65, 167, 174, 181, 211 (n. 34), 212 (n. 47)
Poll tax, 129–30, 205 (n. 53)
Pope, Alexander, 9
Port Royal, South Carolina, 24–26, 35, 37, 43–44, 47, 51, 63
"Port Royal Experiment," 19, 27
Port Royal Relief Committee, 27
Porter, David, 140
Porter, Horace, 104, 109, 112
Potter, David, 13
Preliminary Emancipation Proclamation. *See* Emancipation Proclamation
Prince, C. H., 166, 169, 200 (n. 76), 207 (n. 76)
Prolongation issue, 111–12
Providence, Rhode Island, 149
Public education, 92, 131, 148. *See also* Black schools

Quitman, Georgia, 141

Radical Republicans, 46, 73, 78, 82, 88, 98, 118, 155, 192 (n. 8); in Georgia, 201–2 (n. 14)
Raynolds (adjutant), 38
Readfield, Maine, 6
Reconstruction Acts (1867), 74, 77–78, 81
Redeemers. *See* Democratic Redeemers
Reorganization Act (1869), 107
Republicanism, 18, 61, 66, 77–78; platform (1868), 87; glorious cause, 149
Republican party: birth of, 14–15, 17; convention, 24, 89, 174; goals, 59–60, 73, 77–78; in Georgia, 60, 74, 79–80, 86, 101, 110, 121, 133, 139, 152; policy, 118; lily-white party, 133, 135, 153, 165–66

Richardson, C. C., 76, 85–86, 202 (n. 76), 203 (n. 22)
Rockport, Maine, 5, 30
Romantic radicalism, 13
Rose, Willie Lee, 19
Rust, John D., 30–34, 39

Savannah, Georgia, 20, 45, 48, 62, 124–27, 129–31, 133, 137–38, 141–42, 145, 213 (n. 53)
Savannah Journal, 127. *See also Loyal Georgian, Georgia Republican*
Saxton, Rufus, 26–27, 31–32, 34, 36–37, 39–41, 44–45, 47–49, 51, 53–57, 69, 71, 181, 195 (n. 32)
Saxton, Willard, 51
Sea Islands, 20, 26, 35–36, 43, 49
Second Confiscation Act, 26
Second South Carolina Volunteer Regiment, 34
Sherman (boardinghouse), 149
Sherman, Thomas W., 20, 22
Sherman, William T., 45, 51; Field order no. 15, 51
Sixth Connecticut Regiment, 33
Skowhegan, Maine, 5
"Skowhegan Chief," 138
"Skowheganite," 101, 143, 147, 213 (n. 49)
Sloan, Andrew, 128–30, 132, 138, 141
Smith, E. P., 64
Smith, James M., 115, 127–28
Social Darwinism, 120, 156
Southern Advance Association, 157–58, 161–64, 167, 169, 171–73, 176
Southern Banner (Athens), 96, 109
Southern Advance and Georgia Republican, 146, 160. *See also Loyal Georgian, Georgia Republican*
Southern Historical Society, 158–59, 216 (n. 5)
Southern Homestead Act (1866), 48. *See also* Homestead Act (1862)
Southern problem, 148, 157
Southwest Georgian (Oglethorpe), 127
Spalding, Volney, 121, 146–47, 149–50
Spaulding, Emma. *See* Bryant, Emma Spaulding
Spaulding, Greenleaf, 82, 176

Speer, Emory, 175, 219 (n. 48)
Stanton, Edwin, 26, 46
"State Council of the National Guard," 121
Stearns, Charles, 53, 67, 103, 181
Stearns, Etta, 103
Steedman, James B., 69–70
Stephens, Alexander H., 99, 134, 144, 151, 158, 167
Stephens, Linton, 99
Stokes, M. H., 161, 169
Stowe, Harriet Beecher, 13
Strictland, Augustus H. (Lee), 19
Sumner, Charles, 47, 208 (n. 89)
"Syndicate," 165–66, 168

Tappan, Lewis, 27
Taylor (school superintendent), 7
Teachers (missionary), 27–28
Temperance, 9–10, 12, 17, 22
Terry, Alfred, 103, 107–8
Terry's Purge, 107
Thomas, Ella, 52
Tilden, Samuel, 140
Tillson, Davis, 55–59, 63, 67–68, 70–73, 78, 106, 138–39, 181, 195–96 (n. 34), 199–200 (n. 72), 200 (n. 77)
Timoney, E. M., 85–86
Toombs, Robert, 109
Tourgée, Albion W., 156–57, 160, 200 (n. 81)
Tribune (Chicago), 16
Tribune (New York), 16, 33–34
Turner, Henry M., 61, 65, 71, 83, 94–95, 101, 123, 129, 135, 140, 180–81, 204 (n. 43), 213 (n. 53)
Turner, Nat, 32
Tyler, John, 128

Uncle Tom's Cabin, 9, 13
Union, Maine, 5
Union League (Loyal League), 61–62, 65, 74, 79, 81; in Georgia, 61, 81, 85, 205 (n. 51); convention (1866), 72; of America, 167–68, 172, 176, 200 (n. 74)
Union Republican Party of Georgia, 80. *See also* Republican party in Georgia

Van Buren, Martin, 5
Vesey, Denmark, 32
Viele, E. L., 22, 24
Violence, 66–67, 96, 107. *See also* Ku Klux Klan

Wade, Benjamin F., 16
Walker, Dawson A., 85, 127
Washington, Booker T., 58
Washington, George, 5, 8, 20
Washington, D.C., 124, 132, 137, 149, 167
Washington Chronicle, 112
Wayne, Maine, 5
Webster, Daniel, 4–6
Wesley, John, 10
Wesleyan Female College, 158
Western and Atlantic Railroad, 86, 92, 114–16, 124, 173
Whig (Atlanta), 127
Whipple, George R., 27
White, W. J., 152
Whiteley, Richard, 110
White vs. Clements, 106
Wilmot, David, 16
Wilson, Alexander N., 168, 174
Woodward, C. Vann, 50
Worcester, Massachusetts, 32

Young Men's Christian Association (YMCA), 105–6
Yulee, E., 139, 182, 213 (n. 51)

Zeller, Emma Alice Bryant. *See* Bryant, Emma Alice
Zeller, R. B., 185 (n. 1)

www.ingramcontent.com/pod-product-compliance
Lightning Source LLC
Chambersburg PA
CBHW051423290426
44109CB00016B/1415